Luke/Acts
FOR BEGINNERS

MIKE MAZZALONGO

THE "FOR BEGINNERS" SERIES

The "For Beginners" series of video classes and books provide a non-technical and easy to understand presentation of Bible books and topics that are rich in information and application for the beginner as well as the mature Bible student.

For more information about these books, CDs and DVDs visit: **bibletalk.tv/for-beginners**

ISBN: 978-1-945778-70-4

BibleTalk Books
14998 E. Reno
Choctaw, Oklahoma 73020

For Dr. Bailey McBride, Oklahoma Christian University

TABLE OF CONTENTS

ACTS

CHAPTER 1
INTRODUCTION

The gospel writers each had an audience and a purpose in mind when producing their records of Jesus' life and ministry. These naturally influenced the way they presented the material in each of their books. For example:

- **Matthew:** Matthew wrote his book primarily with Jews in mind. His material is well structured with a series of narrative descriptions of Jesus' movements and ministry, along with a record of the various discourses He had with different individuals and groups. Matthew's gospel is an apologetic (defense) effort to prove, according to Scripture, that Jesus was the Messiah spoken of in the Old Testament. This explains why he supports Jesus' actions, teachings, and miracles with proof texts and prophecies about the Messiah and what He would say and do. Matthew, therefore, constructs his eyewitness account using Jewish history and custom (genealogy, etc.) and presents his arguments based on the fulfillment of prophecy concerning the Jewish Messiah.

- **Mark:** Mark's gospel is the shortest and one of the earlier inspired books produced (64-67 AD) in the New Testament (Matthew, 60-65 AD). Mark's purpose was to present Jesus as the divine Son of God based on His works. He spends little time on background information or theological speculation, but gets right to the point he wants to make in his opening verse introducing Jesus as the Son of God and then describing His many miracles to prove his point. This short and direct method of presenting material appealed to the Roman mindset and thus Mark's gospel was Gentile friendly and uncluttered with Jewish genealogies and references to Old Testament prophets that would be lost on a Gentile reading his book. Although Mark's gospel is the shortest, it is the gospel record most copied from (Luke uses 350 verses taken from Mark) and describes the most miracles (18 of a possible 35) in an effort to clearly and concisely present Jesus as the Son of God.

- **John:** John's gospel was written when the difference between Jew and Gentile had largely disappeared (after the destruction of the Temple in Jerusalem by the Romans in 70 AD). He is writing from Asia Minor (Turkey) where false doctrines such as Gnosticism are challenging the claims of Christianity and so his purpose is to show that Jesus was both fully human and fully divine. This was to counter Gnostic teaching that Jesus was either not fully human or not fully divine, but only parts of each at different times. For example, the divine element of His being descended on Him at baptism and left Him at the crucifixion. John's purpose, therefore, is to show Jesus as the fully divine Son of God and that salvation was found in Him alone. This he does by presenting a series of events where Jesus is displaying His divine glory through inspired teaching or powerful miracles, and then describing the reaction of belief or disbelief by those who witnessed these things.

- **Luke:** Both Matthew and John were chosen Apostles and personally witnessed Jesus' baptism, ministry, death, resurrection and ascension to heaven, and their record reflects this. Mark served as an early co-worker with Paul and Barnabas on their first missionary effort but left to return home before the trip was completed. He was then mentored by Barnabas, his cousin, after Paul refused to have him accompany them on the next missionary trip. He was eventually restored to Paul's good graces (we will study this when we get to the book of Acts), and eventually ended up serving as Peter the Apostle's secretary, and so his gospel is largely what he wrote and organized concerning Peter's witness and experience with Jesus as an Apostle. In the same way, Luke was not one of the chosen Apostles but came by his knowledge of the gospel and details of Jesus' life and teachings by association with the Apostles, Paul, Peter and other leaders of the early church.

Luke – History

In Luke's description of an event taking place in Antioch (Acts 11:27-30) he uses grammar that suggests that he himself was present and describing a scene that he personally witnessed. This would mean that he was a Gentile convert probably coming to Christ as Christians went out from Jerusalem due to persecution by the Jews and preached the gospel throughout Judea and the northern regions. During this time, a church was established in Antioch where Luke lived (Acts 11:19). He is referred to as a physician and a Gentile (Colossians 4:10-14) and could have received his medical training in Antioch since there was a famous medical school located there at the time. This would mean that a quarter of the New Testament was written by a Gentile convert to Christianity.

Luke and Paul

Luke, therefore, was a Gentile convert who was a member of the first mixed (Jew and Gentile) congregation. He was converted before Paul was recruited by Barnabas to go there and teach in 43 AD (Acts 11:25). This means that he met Paul and received further teaching from him for an entire year while the Apostle was in Antioch, and was present when Paul and Barnabas were chosen and sent out on their first missionary journey (Acts 13:1-3).

Luke's Ministry

The first glimpse we have of Luke's ministry with Paul occurs in Acts 16:10 where he is with Paul in Troas where the Apostle receives the vision to go and preach in Macedonia while on his second missionary journey (49 AD). This is a "we" passage where Luke's name is not mentioned but, as the author, his presence is assumed since he is describing events witnessed in the first-person plural. Luke is also present and ministering to Paul during his initial imprisonment in Caesarea after returning from his third missionary journey (53 AD). It is at this time, while visiting the Temple, that the Apostle is caught up in a riot and arrested (Acts 24:23). After several years of confinement, Luke accompanies Paul on his dangerous journey to Rome and subsequent trial before Caesar in 62 AD (Acts 27:1). We learn that Luke remains with Paul during his first imprisonment in Rome (Acts 28:30-31). Paul mentions Luke one final time in II Timothy during his second imprisonment in Rome while awaiting his execution (66-67 AD). Luke is the only remaining worker left to minister to Paul's needs while in prison.

Luke's Gospel

Luke had many first-hand resources to draw from in the writing of his gospel. As an early member of the church at Antioch he was immersed in the first century preaching of the Apostles and their disciples (Barnabas, Acts 11:22). He was also taught by Paul for a year and accompanied him on several missionary journeys hearing his preaching and teaching, and witnessing his miracles. In addition to this he spent years interacting with Paul while the Apostle was in prison writing his many epistles. He also had a working relationship with John Mark (writer of the gospel). In Philemon 24 and II Timothy 4:10 we note that both these men ministered to Paul while in prison and were present at his execution. This background prepared him to write (under the direction of the Holy Spirit) a gospel account which was not based on his own witness of Jesus' life, death and burial, but on the eyewitness accounts of his contemporaries among the Apostles (Paul and Peter) as well as the disciples of the Apostles (Mark) and members of the early church in Jerusalem (Barnabas). Luke states in his opening verses that his gospel is a compilation of several sources of information about Jesus which he will carefully lay out in order to explain and reveal the truth of the gospel concerning Jesus Christ.

Date

Most scholars agree that when the codex (book) form for the New Testament was produced, it placed the four gospels in order of writing: Matthew (60-64 AD), Mark (64-68 AD), Luke (66-68 AD), and John (80 AD).

Theme

An orderly account. While the other gospels have theological goals (Matthew: Jesus is the Messiah, Mark: Jesus is the divine Son of God, John: Jesus is both God and man), Luke's main theme is not to show that Jesus is God, but that the Son of God lived among men in a historical setting. Whereas Matthew went to great lengths to support his premise that Jesus was the Jewish Messiah, providing numerous proof texts from the Old Testament prophets, Luke provides all kinds of historical markers (names of rulers, historical events, intimate interactions with disciples and friends) to situate the presence of Jesus not only in human history but human settings as well. Luke presents a well-structured narrative of Jesus' extraordinary birth, life, death, resurrection and ascension, against the very ordinary setting of first century Jewish life in and around the areas of Jerusalem and the region of Galilee.

Outline

R. C. H. Lenski, in his commentary, provides the simplest outline that matches Luke's division of material (St. Luke's Gospel - R.C.H. Lenski)

- The Beginning – 1:1-3:38
- Jesus in Galilee – 4:1-9:50
- Jesus Facing Jerusalem – 9:51-18:30
- Jesus Entering Jerusalem – 18:31-21:38
- The Consummation – 22:1-24:53

Summary

Luke writes a step-by-step account of Jesus' life that lays out the signs and events that preceded His birth. He follows with a precise historical account of His ministry leading up to His death, resurrection, several accounts of His appearances after His resurrection and finishing with a description of His ascension into heaven and a brief epilogue about the Apostles actions afterwards. All of this in a simple, straightforward style that helps the reader imagine the divine Son of God actually living among ordinary men at a particular time in human history.

Approach

Luke is the second longest gospel at 24 chapters (Matthew has 28). Maintaining a reasonable length for this book will not allow me to drill down and examine every event and teaching in Jesus' ministry contained in Luke. What I will try to do, therefore, is to address everything that Luke includes in his gospel, but pay special attention to those things that are only found in Luke and not in the other gospels. In this way we will be going through Luke's record section by section with a brief comment on each passage, but focusing our study on the things only Luke talks about or perhaps what he has borrowed from only one other gospel writer.

Hopefully, with this approach we will cover the entire book, with special emphasis on Luke's unique contribution, all completed in the 13 chapters that comprise the first part of this book. In order to get the most from this study, therefore, I recommend that you complete the reading assignment provided below before going on to the next chapter.

Discussion Questions

1. If you were writing a gospel record today, what particular audience would you target? Why?

2. From what you have learned so far what kind of man was Luke? Describe his personal qualities and character.

3. What type of person today do you think would be most receptive to:

   - Matthew's Gospel
   - Mark's Gospel
   - Luke's Gospel
   - John's Gospel

CHAPTER 2
THE BEGINNING

LUKE 1:1-3:38

In the previous chapter I listed the outline we will use to study Luke's gospel.

- **The Beginning – 1:1-3:38**
- Jesus in Galilee – 4:1-9:50
- Jesus Facing Jerusalem – 9:51-18:30
- Jesus Entering Jerusalem – 18:31-21:38
- The Consummation – 22:1-24:53

Introduction

Luke's gospel is unique in that it was originally written for an audience of one, a man named Theophilus.

> [1]Inasmuch as many have undertaken to compile an account of the things accomplished among us, [2]just as they were handed down to us by those who from the beginning were eyewitnesses and servants of the word, [3]it seemed fitting for me as well, having investigated everything carefully from the beginning, to write it out for you in consecutive order, most excellent Theophilus; [4]so that you may know the exact truth about the things you have been taught.
> - Luke 1:1-4

Luke begins by explaining why, how and to whom he has written this gospel.

Why?

Many others have taken it upon themselves to do this same thing (recount the life, death and resurrection of Jesus). Some were Apostles (Matthew and John) while others were simply writing and commenting on the times. Luke undertakes a similar mission.

How?

He is not an eyewitness as are the Apostles, but he has access to the writings of the eyewitnesses, and has been a co-worker with an Apostle (Paul) and one who was a disciple of Peter (Mark). Luke is an educated man and his training has enabled him to research, organize and select material that will lay out his gospel record in a clear and concise manner. He does not say this himself, but with time the early church acknowledged that his work was guided by the Holy Spirit and thus added to the canon (body of accepted inspired writings) of the New Testament.

Who?

Theophilus is only mentioned here and in Luke's other book, Acts. He was a Gentile who was a high official or very wealthy since he is addressed with the title "most excellent." Luke's book is an attempt to provide confirming information to what this man already knew about Christianity. Many think that Theophilus was eventually converted because Luke addresses him using only his name, no title, in the book of Acts, something which would not have been proper had he not become a Christian.

The Birth of John the Baptist – 1:5-80

Luke, as he has stated in his introduction, begins his account with John the Baptist who serves as both an embodiment and bridge of all that came before and up to the birth of Christ:

- He lived under the Law/Old Testament.

- He was in the likeness of Elijah, one of the great Old Testament prophets (Mark 9:13 - According to Jesus).

- He himself was a prophet (Matthew 11:9).

- His life and ministry was the fulfillment of an Old Testament prophecy concerning the coming of the Messiah.

> A voice is calling,
> "Clear the way for the Lord in the wilderness;
> Make smooth in the desert a highway for our God.
> - Isaiah 40:3

> [19]This is the testimony of John, when the Jews sent to him priests and Levites from Jerusalem to ask him, "Who are you?" [20]And he confessed and did not deny, but confessed, "I am not the Christ." [21]They asked him, "What then? Are you Elijah?" And he said, "I am not." "Are you the Prophet?" And he answered, "No." [22]Then they said to him, "Who are you, so that we may give an answer to those who sent us? What do you say about yourself?" [23]He said, "I am a voice of one crying in the wilderness, 'Make straight the way of the Lord,' as Isaiah the prophet said."
> - John 1:19-23

It is logical, therefore, that Luke begins his narrative with John who summarized all of what came before, and was chosen by God to introduce Christ to the world.

> [5]In the days of Herod, king of Judea, there was a priest named Zacharias, of the division of Abijah; and he had a wife from the daughters of Aaron, and her name was Elizabeth. [6]They were both righteous in the sight of God, walking blamelessly in all the commandments and requirements of the

Lord. ⁷But they had no child, because Elizabeth
was barren, and they were both advanced in years.
- Luke 1:5-7

A feature of Luke's writing is his historical precision. He does not want his account seen as some kind of fable or mystic tale. He is careful to ground his characters in historical accuracy and proper cultural context. For example, the "days of Herod King of Judea" refer to an exact time period in history. Zacharias is one who can be traced to a particular Jewish tribe, place and time. His role and function as priest is accurately described according to the law and custom of that era. That they were elderly and childless sets the stage for God's entry into their lives in a miraculous way.

In verses 8-80 the birth of John the Baptist is described, again in an ordered and detailed way:

Verses 8-25: John's father, Zacharias, is visited by an angel who announces that he and his elderly wife will have a son who would serve to prepare the people for the coming of the Messiah. A doubting Zacharias is struck dumb by the angel as a sign of his appearance to the elderly priest. A short while after his service in the temple and return home Elizabeth, his wife, announces her pregnancy.

Verses 26-56: Luke shifts the scene to Mary and the announcement she receives from the same angel, Gabriel, that she also is pregnant (with Jesus). Her condition, however, is truly miraculous because her conception is produced directly by God without human interaction. Luke then describes her trip to her cousin Elizabeth's home to help with her pregnancy. Luke's detailed description of Mary's interaction with the angel and her cousin Elizabeth suggests that his source was Mary herself. She was still alive after Jesus' death and ascension into heaven. Luke even mentions Mary's presence in the upper room with the Apostles and other disciples on the day leading up to Pentecost Sunday (Acts 1:13). And so, in a few verses Luke sets up the time, characters and God's presence leading up to the births of both John and Jesus.

Verses 57-80: Luke provides detailed information concerning John's birth. Elizabeth gave birth naturally at the appointed time. The custom was to circumcise and name the child on the eighth day after his birth. Luke mentions the circumcision (nothing special since all male Jews were circumcised) because it was the occasion when two other unusual things occurred:

1. He is named John

[59]And it happened that on the eighth day they came to circumcise the child, and they were going to call him Zacharias, after his father. [60]But his mother answered and said, "No indeed; but he shall be called John." [61]And they said to her, "There is no one among your relatives who is called by that name." [62]And they made signs to his father, as to what he wanted him called. [63]And he asked for a tablet and wrote as follows, "His name is John." And they were all astonished. [64]And at once his mouth was opened and his tongue loosed, and he began to speak in praise of God. [65]Fear came on all those living around them; and all these matters were being talked about in all the hill country of Judea. [66]All who heard them kept them in mind, saying, "What then will this child turn out to be?" For the hand of the Lord was certainly with him.
- Luke 1:59-66

It was customary to name a male child after its father. In this case the angel had instructed Zacharias to name him John (which meant "the Lord has been gracious" in Hebrew), and in some way had made this known to Elizabeth. Against the protests of family and friends she insists on the name John. Since it was the father who named the child (and Elizabeth spoke for Zacharias who was struck dumb by the angel) the family appeals to him, thinking that this was her idea. He confirms the name John and immediately receives back his voice.

2. Zacharias Prophesizes

After many months of pent-up emotion, Zacharias bursts forth in a psalm of praise and prophecy for God and the ministry He has given this child to perform in the future.

> [76]"And you, child, will be called the prophet of the Most High; For you will go on before the Lord to prepare His ways;
> [77]To give to His people the knowledge of salvation By the forgiveness of their sins,
> - Luke 1:76-77

Luke reports that the people were in fear (verse 65) seeing the hand of God working so powerfully and clearly among them. It had been 400 years since a prophet was among the Jewish people so this was a completely new and frightening experience for them. Luke closes this section by summarizing John's growth and development in a few words, saying that he was strong in the Spirit and lived in the desert awaiting his call to ministry.

The Birth of Jesus – 2:1-52

Mark and John do not provide any information about Jesus' birth. Matthew details how Mary conceived miraculously and describes Joseph's initial reaction and subsequent acceptance of this after being told in a dream that the child she bore was of God and he was to go ahead and take Mary as his wife. Luke provides additional information that clearly fixes the historical time-frame for Jesus' birth (Caesar Augustus was Emperor of Rome, Quirinias was Governor of Syria). The Emperor declared a census, something new at the time and to be repeated every 14 years for two centuries (Lenski, p.116).

Luke provides this information to explain why Jesus came to be born in Bethlehem and not in Nazareth where His parents lived. This became an issue later on when the Jewish leaders rejected Jesus because they assumed He was born in the city of Nazareth, His parents' home, and not in Bethlehem where the prophets said the Messiah would come from (John 7:50-52).

Jesus' birth, like John's, is accompanied by supernatural phenomena and religious ritual.

1. John was born of aged parents and an angel appeared to his father. Matthew mentions the star guiding the Magi for Jesus' birth. Luke describes the appearance of the angel guiding the shepherds to Jesus and the heavenly host of angels singing praises.

2. John was circumcised and named, and this was followed by a prophecy uttered by his father as his speech was returned to him. Jesus was also circumcised at the temple (Bethlehem being about four miles from Jerusalem) on the eighth day. Luke adds that not one but two prophecies were made about Jesus: first by Simeon then Anna about Jesus' future ministry. Whereas Zacharias clearly mentions John as the one who will be the forerunner of the Messiah, preparing His way; the two prophets in Jesus' case declare Him (an eight day old baby at the time) to be the Messiah sent by God to save the people.

> [26]And it had been revealed to him by the Holy Spirit that he would not see death before he had seen the Lord's Christ. [27]And he came in the Spirit into the temple; and when the parents brought in the child Jesus, to carry out for Him the custom of the Law, [28]then he took Him into his arms, and blessed God, and said,
> [29]"Now Lord, You are releasing Your bond-servant

> to depart in peace, According to Your word;
> [30]For my eyes have seen Your salvation,
> [31]Which You have prepared in the presence of all peoples,
> [32]A Light of revelation to the Gentiles, And the glory of Your people Israel." [...]
> [38]At that very moment she came up and began giving thanks to God, and continued to speak of Him to all those who were looking for the redemption of Jerusalem.
> - Luke 2:26-32;38

Luke leaves out Matthew's information about the family's time in Egypt and fast-forwards twelve or so years to describe the only incident recorded concerning Jesus' youth, His visit to the temple at the age of 12 (verses 41-52). This was a yearly trip that demonstrated the piety and faithfulness of the family making this 130 mile roundtrip on foot each year for the Passover feast. Luke explains that Jesus' parents lose track of Him on the return to Nazareth. They spend three days looking for Him and finally find Jesus in the temple area with the teachers who were amazed at His understanding and questions concerning the Law. Luke provides this story of young Jesus (three days lost and then found) as a preview of His public ministry (teaching and preaching) and His ultimate goal (death, three days buried, resurrection).

John's Ministry Begins – 3:1-20

> [1]Now in the fifteenth year of the reign of Tiberius Caesar, when Pontius Pilate was governor of Judea, and Herod was tetrarch of Galilee, and his brother Philip was tetrarch of the region of Ituraea and Trachonitis, and Lysanias was tetrarch of Abilene, [2]in the high priesthood of Annas and Caiaphas, the word of God came to John, the son of Zacharias, in the wilderness.
> - Luke 3:1-2

Again, Luke makes an exact historical time fix for the things that he will relate concerning John's ministry. John is true to his calling echoing his Zachariah's prophecy concerning his task of preparing the way for the One to come (Luke 1:76-77).

> [4]as it is written in the book of the words of Isaiah the prophet,
> "The voice of one crying in the wilderness,
> 'Make ready the way of the Lord,
> Make His paths straight. [...]
> [6]And all flesh will see the salvation of God.'"
> - Luke 3:4,6

Luke provides a good summary of John's ministry that includes most of what Matthew, Mark and John have recorded but leaves out the details of his eventual execution at the hands of Herod (only Matthew describes this).

His preaching announced that the time for the Messiah was near and the people had to prepare for it by purifying themselves through repentance and baptism. The idea of purifying oneself in preparation to come before God was familiar to Jews. Priests did it before ministering at the temple (Leviticus 8:1-6) and people continually did it if they were ceremonially unclean (i.e. touched a dead body, Numbers 19:11). John's preaching was powerful because it condemned the entire nation and called on all, high and low, to prepare.

> [7]So he began saying to the crowds who were going out to be baptized by him, "You brood of vipers, who warned you to flee from the wrath to come? [8]Therefore bear fruits in keeping with repentance, and do not begin to say to yourselves, 'We have Abraham for our father,' for I say to you that from these stones God is able to raise up children to Abraham.

> [9]Indeed the axe is already laid at the root of the trees; so every tree that does not bear good fruit is cut down and thrown into the fire."
> - Luke 3:7-9

Luke provides not only the high themes of John's preaching (the coming Messiah, all must prepare, He will baptize with the Spirit), he also provides the details of John's preaching to individuals:

> [10]And the crowds were questioning him, saying, "Then what shall we do?" [11]And he would answer and say to them, "The man who has two tunics is to share with him who has none; and he who has food is to do likewise." [12]And some tax collectors also came to be baptized, and they said to him, "Teacher, what shall we do?" [13]And he said to them, "Collect no more than what you have been ordered to." [14]Some soldiers were questioning him, saying, "And what about us, what shall we do?" And he said to them, "Do not take money from anyone by force, or accuse anyone falsely, and be content with your wages."
> - Luke 3:10-14

Luke also describes the excitement of the people and their curiosity whether John was himself the Messiah. This gave him the opportunity to further describe and contrast each of their work. John was there to prepare the way. The Messiah, however, would both bless (baptize with the Spirit) and bring judgment on the entire nation.

> [16]John answered and said to them all, "As for me, I baptize you with water; but One is coming who is mightier than I, and I am not fit to untie the thong of His sandals; He will baptize you with the Holy Spirit and fire.

> [17]His winnowing fork is in His hand to thoroughly clear His threshing floor, and to gather the wheat into His barn; but He will burn up the chaff with unquenchable fire."
> - Luke 3:16-17

Luke closes out his summary of John's ministry by briefly mentioning that Herod (because John had admonished the king for his many sins, including the stealing of his brother's wife) had him imprisoned. We only hear of John later (Luke 7:18) when, from prison, he sends some of his disciples to question Jesus. John believed that when the Messiah came, the judgment on the people would also be at hand. As Jesus' ministry grew, John saw no accompanying judgment on the nation and sent some of his own disciples to question if Jesus was truly the Messiah. We know that the judgment on the nation did eventually come, but only several years after John's death when the Roman army destroyed the city of Jerusalem, its magnificent temple and killed most of the people there (70 AD). He had correctly prophesied the judgment to come but was mistaken about the timing of this event.

After closing out the information about John's ministry, Luke provides a flashback scene to introduce a new section of his narrative, the ministry of Jesus.

Jesus' Ministry Begins - 3:21-38

> [21]Now when all the people were baptized, Jesus was also baptized, and while He was praying, heaven was opened, [2]and the Holy Spirit descended upon Him in bodily form like a dove, and a voice came out of heaven, "You are My beloved Son, in You I am well-pleased."
> - Luke 3:21-22

Luke gives a brief description of this event and focuses our attention on the fact that Jesus:

1. Is the divine Son of God.

2. His ministry is pleasing and from God.

3. Is the One John spoke of.

As he has done for the Baptist, Luke now establishes Jesus' ancestry, but in a more complete way tracing it to Adam and not only back one generation as was the case for John. He also fixes Jesus' age at about 30 years which, as is his style, gives us another historical marker to view his gospel.

Lessons

This first section of Luke's gospel does not contain specific teachings by John or Jesus for those who would be reading Luke's account. However, there are lessons that we can draw from this preliminary information:

Christianity is Based in History

Unlike most Eastern religions (i.e. Hinduism, Buddhism) and native or primitive religions (i.e. Native American, Voodoo) Christianity has a fixed historical starting point and is populated with people (for and against) that can be traced through history. This makes it easy to attack because the times, people and teachings are set targets that can be seen, studied and criticized. The advantage, however, is that we can more easily study, learn and believe information about people and historical facts that are permanently established.

Luke's Record is Clear and Exact

As far as teaching is concerned, Luke and Acts are great educational texts. There is little theological speculation or examination of philosophical ideas. Also, Luke does not use theological imagery as does John, or Jewish religious history and practice as does Matthew. Luke is interested in telling first the story of Jesus and then the story of the establishment and development of His church after His ascension.

Luke's approach provides us with two basic lessons:

1. When sharing our faith, we should begin by telling our own story in simple objective terms (i.e. I did this, went there, was baptized here...)

2. When teaching someone else we should likewise begin by sharing the simple story of the gospel (as Luke does) and not debate complicated or disputed points of doctrine.

Reading Assignment: Luke 4:1-6:16

Discussion Questions

1. How would you defend the inspiration of Luke's gospel since he was not a chosen Apostle?

2. In your opinion, why was it necessary to have a person and ministry like John the Baptist?

3. Using no more than 50 words, write out a summary of a typical sermon that John the Baptist would preach to people in today's society.

CHAPTER 3
JESUS IN GALILEE
PUBLIC MINISTRY BEGINS - PART 1

LUKE 4:1-6:16

Luke follows the pattern of the other gospel writers by documenting Jesus' ministry in chronological order beginning with the start of His public ministry. After a brief mention of His baptism by John, which took place in the Jordan River near Jerusalem (Matthew 3:13-17), and a description of His temptation by Satan while fasting in the desert for 40 days and nights (Luke 4:1-13), a scene also described by Matthew and Mark (so we will not discuss it here), Jesus returns to the northern part of Israel to the region of Galilee. This is where Jesus begins His public ministry near His home town and among the people He knew and grew up with.

Jesus Begins His Public Ministry — 4:14-44

General Summary

> [14]And Jesus returned to Galilee in the power of the Spirit, and news about Him spread through all the surrounding district. [15]And He began teaching in their synagogues and was praised by all.
> - Luke 4:14-15

As was the writing style of the times, Luke begins describing Jesus' ministry by giving an overall summary before providing details. He mentions the two basic components of His ministry: miracles (power of the Spirit) and teaching (in their synagogues). Luke also says that initially He was enthusiastically received by everyone (praised by all). However, this enthusiasm quickly changes as Jesus returns to His home town, Nazareth, in order to teach.

Jesus Teaches at Nazareth – 4:16-30

Before, Luke described Jesus' miracles and teaching in a general way, but now he provides a more detailed account of not only His teaching, but how the people reacted to His instruction.

> [16]And He came to Nazareth, where He had been brought up; and as was His custom, He entered the synagogue on the Sabbath, and stood up to read. [17]And the book of the prophet Isaiah was handed to Him. And He opened the book and found the place where it was written,
> [18]*"The Spirit of the Lord is upon Me,*
> *Because He anointed Me to preach the gospel to the poor.*
> *He has sent Me to proclaim release to the captives,*
> *And recovery of sight to the blind,*
> *To set free those who are oppressed,*
> [19]*To proclaim the favorable year of the Lord."*
> [20]And He closed the book, gave it back to the attendant and sat down; and the eyes of all in the synagogue were fixed on Him. [21]And He began to say to them, "Today this Scripture has been fulfilled in your hearing."
> - Luke 4:16-21

The substance of Jesus' preaching and teaching included three basic themes:

1. The Messiah and the things that would happen when He came were now at hand.

2. He was the divine Messiah according to Scripture.

3. Those who believed would become the people of God/chosen ones/kingdom/saints, etc. Those who did not believe would be excluded.

The passage that Jesus reads is from Isaiah 61:1-2. At the time of writing, Isaiah's words were meant to be a short range prophecy concerning the eventual release and return of the Jews from Babylonian captivity. I say "short range" prophecy because the prophets spoke (prophesied) in three time periods. They taught (prophesied) about current events and issues, encouraging and warning their hearers to obey God's directives, avoid certain behaviors or face the consequences of Divine judgment. They also taught (prophesied) and made short range prophecies concerning future events that could be one day, one year or one century into the future (i.e. Jeremiah's prophecy about the 70 year exile and captivity of the Jews in Babylon, Jeremiah 25:9-12). In addition to these types of utterances, they made long range prophecies about events that could be many centuries in the future (i.e. the coming of the Messiah or the end of the world). Sometimes the same prophecy had both a short and long-range significance. This passage in Isaiah 61:1-2 is one of these. As I previously mentioned, it spoke comforting words to the people of his time, promising the return of Jewish exiles from Babylon. In addition to this, Isaiah's prophecy also had a long-range vision in that it spoke of the wonderful things that would happen with the eventual coming of the Messiah at a time in the future that no one knew but the people hoped for (in this case nearly 700 years into the future).

At the beginning of the passage Luke talks about Jesus being in the Spirit and thus performing miracles and giving Spirit-filled teaching. When Jesus sits down He declares that this Scripture is fulfilled by Him ("in your hearing" refers to the one speaking to you). Essentially He is saying that the Spirit-filled teaching and the Spirit-powered miracles that they have seen and heard from Him are the things that this passage refers to. In other words, the time that Isaiah spoke of in this passage is now here, His teaching and miracles bear this out.

Jesus, therefore, begins His public ministry by declaring that the Messiah they have read about and waited for is here.

> And all were speaking well of Him, and wondering at the gracious words which were falling from His lips; and they were saying, "Is this not Joseph's son?"
> - Luke 4:22

At first they react positively to His words but are conflicted and begin to doubt because they know Him as someone who grew up among them and also knew His earthly father, Joseph.

> [23]And He said to them, "No doubt you will quote this proverb to Me, 'Physician, heal yourself! Whatever we heard was done at Capernaum, do here in your hometown as well.'" [24]And He said, "Truly I say to you, no prophet is welcome in his hometown. [25]But I say to you in truth, there were many widows in Israel in the days of Elijah, when the sky was shut up for three years and six months, when a great famine came over all the land; [26]and yet Elijah was sent to none of them, but only to Zarephath, in the land of Sidon, to a woman who was a widow. [27]And there were many lepers in Israel in the time of Elisha the prophet; and none of them was cleansed, but only Naaman the Syrian." [28]And all the people in the synagogue were filled with rage as they heard these things; [29]and they got up and drove Him out of the city, and led Him to the brow of the hill on which their city had been built, in order to throw Him down the cliff.

³⁰But passing through their midst, He went His
way.
- Luke 4:23-30

Jesus is aware of their doubt and understands that what they
want is a miracle performed in order to prove His claim. The
Lord refuses, citing examples of their lack of faith in the past.
This accusation enrages them and they attempt to kill Him,
but He escapes.

Jesus Performs Miracles – 4:31-44

Luke has given us a close-up view of Jesus' teaching and
how it affected many of the Jews, especially in His home
town. The gospel writer now describes the other major
component of Jesus' ministry: miracles.

³¹And He came down to Capernaum, a city of
Galilee, and He was teaching them on the
Sabbath; ³²and they were amazed at His teaching,
for His message was with authority. ³³In the
synagogue there was a man possessed by the
spirit of an unclean demon, and he cried out with a
loud voice, ³⁴"Let us alone! What business do we
have with each other, Jesus of Nazareth? Have
You come to destroy us? I know who You are—the
Holy One of God!" ³⁵But Jesus rebuked him,
saying, "Be quiet and come out of him!" And when
the demon had thrown him down in the midst of the
people, he came out of him without doing him any
harm. ³⁶And amazement came upon them all, and
they began talking with one another saying, "What
is this message? For with authority and power He
commands the unclean spirits and they come
out." ³⁷And the report about Him was spreading
into every locality in the surrounding district.
- Luke 4:31-37

In this scene Luke describes both the miracle and the people's reaction to it. It is interesting to note that the evil spirit acknowledges Jesus even before the Jews do. The Lord silences it because He refuses to receive witness from devils. The people are amazed and on account of this His fame spreads throughout the country.

In verses 38-44 Luke describes many more miracles that serve to establish Jesus' identity and growing ministry. He finishes the chapter with the statement that Jesus continued His teaching ministry in the synagogues located in the northern region of Galilee (this section began with a statement like this and Luke closes it with a similar one).

Jesus Chooses Disciples – 5:1-6:16

Luke has already mentioned that Jesus was busy teaching in the synagogues and performing amazing miracles. This naturally stirred interest but also created a need for others to help with Jesus' continually growing ministry.

> [1]Now it happened that while the crowd was pressing around Him and listening to the word of God, He was standing by the lake of Gennesaret; [2]and He saw two boats lying at the edge of the lake; but the fishermen had gotten out of them and were washing their nets. [3]And He got into one of the boats, which was Simon's, and asked him to put out a little way from the land. And He sat down and began teaching the people from the boat.
> - Luke 5:1-3

This event takes place in Jesus' adult home town of Capernaum the day after He healed Peter's mother-in-law (4:39).

> [4]When He had finished speaking, He said to Simon, "Put out into the deep water and let down your nets for a catch." [5]Simon answered and said,

"Master, we worked hard all night and caught nothing, but I will do as You say and let down the nets." [6]When they had done this, they enclosed a great quantity of fish, and their nets began to break; [7]so they signaled to their partners in the other boat for them to come and help them. And they came and filled both of the boats, so that they began to sink. [8]But when Simon Peter saw that, he fell down at Jesus' feet, saying, "Go away from me Lord, for I am a sinful man!" [9]For amazement had seized him and all his companions because of the catch of fish which they had taken; [10]and so also were James and John, sons of Zebedee, who were partners with Simon. And Jesus said to Simon, "Do not fear, from now on you will be catching men." [11]When they had brought their boats to land, they left everything and followed Him.
- Luke 5:4-11

It is evident that Peter and his fishing partners knew Jesus since they all lived in the same area, and Peter agreed to take Jesus out in his boat. After finishing His teaching, which Peter heard, Jesus tells him to let down his nets to fish. Peter is reluctant at first and with reason:

- He, an experienced and knowledgeable fisherman, had caught nothing. How could this rabbi (teacher) instruct him about fishing?

- It was the wrong time to fish (daytime). The time to fish was at night into the pre-dawn.

- It was the wrong place to fish. The deep waters were not where the fish were in this lake.

- It was inconvenient. Peter had finished cleaning and storing his nets, ready for the next day.

- It was demanding. Peter and the others had just put in a hard night of work and needed to be at home resting, not sailing about looking for fish at the direction of a religious teacher.

- It was embarrassing. The entire village was watching what was about to happen. If he caught nothing again he would be ridiculed by the other fishermen.

We know how this story ends, however. Jesus' teaching has brought Peter to faith (he took Jesus out on his boat so He could teach the crowds). Jesus now challenges him to take an additional step of faith (lower the nets) that is costlier than the first one (inconvenient, embarrassing, etc.). Peter's faith is rewarded by witnessing Jesus' power in a context that he can relate to: fishing. Peter, the fisherman, knows that this is a miracle catch.

He reacts in the same way that every person reacts when facing the Lord or an angelic being: weakness, shame, awe. The Bible describes both men and women who bow down or fall on their faces and worship or are blinded when they come into the presence of the Lord or one of His angels. In Peter's case he is instantly aware of his unworthiness, and Luke says that his two fishing partners (James and John) were amazed by what they saw. Jesus comforts Peter by telling him that He will give him a new task, now that his life has been changed by what he has just witnessed. And so, by His ministry of teaching and miracles, Jesus calls the first three of His 12 Apostles.

The story is told in a few verses but these three men probably knew Jesus from living in the same area and may have been early disciples receiving His teachings. However, with this miracle they make a full commitment to leave everything behind and follow after Him exclusively.

Luke continues to outline Jesus' ministry of miracles by describing two healing miracles.

The Leper

¹²While He was in one of the cities, behold, there was a man covered with leprosy; and when he saw Jesus, he fell on his face and implored Him,

> saying, "Lord, if You are willing, You can make me clean." [13]And He stretched out His hand and touched him, saying, "I am willing; be cleansed." And immediately the leprosy left him. [14]And He ordered him to tell no one, "But go and show yourself to the priest and make an offering for your cleansing, just as Moses commanded, as a testimony to them." [15]But the news about Him was spreading even farther, and large crowds were gathering to hear Him and to be healed of their sicknesses. [16]But Jesus Himself would often slip away to the wilderness and pray.
> - Luke 5:12-16

Note here that this is the first time Luke describes someone coming to Jesus in order to ask for a healing. Leprosy had no cure and those who had it were considered to be already dead. Note this man's boldness, faith and humility. He was relying completely on Jesus for his healing, and addressing Him with the same deference as Peter (Luke 5:8), both fell down before Jesus in respect and faith. The man's advanced leprosy was healed instantly.

The Paralytic

> [17]One day He was teaching; and there were some Pharisees and teachers of the law sitting there, who had come from every village of Galilee and Judea and from Jerusalem; and the power of the Lord was present for Him to perform healing. [18]And some men were carrying on a bed a man who was paralyzed; and they were trying to bring him in and to set him down in front of Him. [19]But not finding any way to bring him in because of the crowd, they went up on the roof and let him down through the tiles with his stretcher, into the middle of the crowd, in front of Jesus. [20]Seeing their faith, He said, "Friend, your sins are forgiven you." [21]The scribes and the Pharisees began to reason, saying, "Who is this man who speaks blasphemies? Who can

forgive sins, but God alone?" [22]But Jesus, aware of their reasonings, answered and said to them, "Why are you reasoning in your hearts? [23]Which is easier, to say, 'Your sins have been forgiven you,' or to say, 'Get up and walk'? [24]But, so that you may know that the Son of Man has authority on earth to forgive sins,"—He said to the paralytic—"I say to you, get up, and pick up your stretcher and go home." [25]Immediately he got up before them, and picked up what he had been lying on, and went home glorifying God. [26]They were all struck with astonishment and began glorifying God; and they were filled with fear, saying, "We have seen remarkable things today."
- Luke 5:17-26

Another amazing miracle takes place, but this time Luke describes the animosity building towards Jesus because He was healing on the Sabbath. The Pharisees (lawyers and religious teachers) taught that even the healing of a person on the Sabbath was considered "work" and violated the fourth commandment (Exodus 20:8). Later on this will become one of the major stumbling blocks for the Priests and Pharisees who will try to accuse and destroy Jesus because He worked on the Sabbath, and as seen in this passage, claimed that He was the Son of God.

In the next section, verses 27-32, we see Jesus continue adding Apostles with the call to Levi, a Jew, but a hated tax collector.

[33]And they said to Him, "The disciples of John often fast and offer prayers, the disciples of the Pharisees also do the same, but Yours eat and drink." [34]And Jesus said to them, "You cannot make the attendants of the bridegroom fast while the bridegroom is with them, can you? [35]But the days will come; and when the bridegroom is taken away from them, then they will fast in those days." [36]And He was also telling them a parable:

> "No one tears a piece of cloth from a new garment
> and puts it on an old garment; otherwise he will
> both tear the new, and the piece from the new will
> not match the old. [37]And no one puts new wine into
> old wineskins; otherwise the new wine will burst
> the skins and it will be spilled out, and the skins will
> be ruined. [38]But new wine must be put into fresh
> wineskins. [39]And no one, after drinking old wine
> wishes for new; for he says, 'The old is good
> enough.'"
> - Luke 5:33-39

This selection leads to more controversy because now Jesus is calling people not known for their academic or religious positions. This criticism provides the Lord with the opportunity to warn the people that great changes are coming and they are not prepared to receive them:

- Old cloth = unbelieving Jews
- New patch = gospel/Christians
- Old wineskin = Jewish religious system
- New wine = gospel/Christianity

The old cannot accommodate the new without damage. The old must change in order to blend with the new.

Again, we see a mixture of teaching and miracles by Jesus in order to reveal Himself and His kingdom to the people, and how they can become part of it.

> [1]Now it happened that He was passing through
> some grainfields on a Sabbath; and His disciples
> were picking the heads of grain, rubbing them in
> their hands, and eating the grain. [2]But some of the
> Pharisees said, "Why do you do what is not lawful
> on the Sabbath?" [3]And Jesus answering them
> said, "Have you not even read what David did
> when he was hungry, he and those who were with

him, [4]how he entered the house of God, and took and ate the consecrated bread which is not lawful for any to eat except the priests alone, and gave it to his companions?" [5]And He was saying to them, "The Son of Man is Lord of the Sabbath."

[6]On another Sabbath He entered the synagogue and was teaching; and there was a man there whose right hand was withered. [7]The scribes and the Pharisees were watching Him closely to see if He healed on the Sabbath, so that they might find reason to accuse Him. [8]But He knew what they were thinking, and He said to the man with the withered hand, "Get up and come forward!" And he got up and came forward. [9]And Jesus said to them, "I ask you, is it lawful to do good or to do harm on the Sabbath, to save a life or to destroy it?" [10]After looking around at them all, He said to him, "Stretch out your hand!" And he did so; and his hand was restored. [11]But they themselves were filled with rage, and discussed together what they might do to Jesus.

- Luke 6:1-11

Note that Luke separates the different instances where Jesus chooses Apostles with descriptions of His on-going teaching and performance of miracles, as well as the reaction that the people have to these.

[12]It was at this time that He went off to the mountain to pray, and He spent the whole night in prayer to God. [13]And when day came, He called His disciples to Him and chose twelve of them, whom He also named as apostles: [14]Simon, whom He also named Peter, and Andrew his brother; and James and John; and Philip and Bartholomew; [15]and Matthew and Thomas; James the son of Alphaeus, and Simon who was called the Zealot; [16]Judas the son of James, and Judas Iscariot, who became a traitor.

- Luke 12-16

Note that Jesus prayed before appointing the 12 Apostles (Apostle: one commissioned and sent; i.e. ambassador). He called up many disciples but chose only 12. His night of prayer was on their behalf, He was the Son of God and did not need guidance in choosing. He knew, however, the challenges they would face, and prayed for their faithfulness and success.

Lessons

Even though we are covering Luke's gospel in survey fashion, only reading and highlighting certain passages, the material we have examined still contains valuable and practical lessons for everyone. For example:

Rejection by Leaders at the Synagogue

Lesson: Beware of spiritual complacency.

The religious leaders were so invested in their traditions that they refused to believe a truth that contradicted their religious habits, even when this truth was supported by a miracle.

Let us always use God's word to establish and perpetuate a practice, not human ideas about what God would find pleasing. God is pleased when we obey His word.

Miracles do not Always Work

Lesson: The surest confirmation of God's presence or direction is His confirmed word, not miracles.

Jesus performed many miracles (37) and yet most rejected Him, including those who witnessed the miracles with their own eyes. Many believers base their faith on unusual or "miraculous" things they have read about in popular religious books or heard from others, but trading on these accounts is not the way to establish or build faith. "Faith comes by hearing the words of Christ" (Romans 10:17). The surest way to build faith, according to God, is to read, believe and obey His word.

Jesus is Still Calling People Today

Lesson: To this day Jesus continues to call people, through the preaching of the gospel (Matthew 28:18-20), to be saved by faith in Him and express that faith by repenting and being baptized in His name (Acts 2:38). Jesus also calls Christians into ministry a) through His word (which describes the type of person needed and the task or ministry to be fulfilled), b) through His Spirit (who moves believers' hearts toward service of some kind), and c) through the church that confirms and commends (trains and appoints) ministers (elders, deacons, evangelists and teachers) into His service.

Reading Assignment: Luke 6:17-8:3

Discussion Questions

1. Explain in your own words why Jesus' miracle of the fish made Peter feel unworthy.

2. Share with the class your own personal experiences of what Jesus described as "a prophet is not without honor, except in his home town."

3. Name the person who most influenced you to go into ministry and what skill or quality of character impressed you the most about that person.

4. In your opinion, what was the main reason why the:

   - Pharisees rejected Jesus
   - Priests rejected Jesus
   - Jewish people rejected Jesus

CHAPTER 4
JESUS IN GALILEE
PUBLIC MINISTRY BEGINS - PART 2

LUKE 6:17-8:3

Luke continues his narrative by describing key events in Jesus' ministry as He begins to preach and do miracles in the northern part of Israel. He lived as an adult in Capernaum in the region of the Sea of Galilee and it was normal that He not only began His ministry there but also call His Apostles from the town and villages in and around that area.

In the last section that we covered Luke described the choosing of the 12 Apostles (Luke 6:12-16). Luke follows the naming of the 12 with a summary of the teaching that Jesus gave after the selection of His Apostles.

The section 6:17-38 is basically a repetition of what Matthew provides in a longer and more complete way (Beatitude Section - Matthew 5:1-7:29). This passage demonstrates how the different gospel writers borrowed from each other in order to complete their records.

In 6:39-45 Jesus adds several parables in His teaching in order to amplify and provide concrete examples for His previous teaching. Note that Luke places the parable of "the house built on the rock" at the end of this passage as does Matthew (Matthew 7:24-27).

> When He had completed all His discourse in the
> hearing of the people, He went to Capernaum.
> - Luke 7:1

Luke naturally ends this teaching section by noting where Jesus is geographically so that his reader (Theophilus) will not only know what Jesus is saying and doing, but also where these things are taking place in order to ground them into some historical and physical context.

We noted that Jesus' ministry was a series of teachings followed by miracles that drew attention to the teachings which were then followed by more miracles until the final miracle (resurrection) was performed. Luke notes another miracle which was unusual because of its recipient.

The Centurion's Servant Healed – 7:2-10

Historically we know that the region we refer to as Israel was under Roman rule at that time. The Romans permitted a limited form of self-rule with local "Jewish" kings appointed to manage political and social affairs under the direction of a governor (Pilate) who commanded the soldiers posted in Jerusalem as well as other key locations throughout the country, in order to maintain peace. The headquarters for the Roman forces in Judea was in Caesarea, on the coast of the Mediterranean Sea.

Roman Army:

- Legionaries were the infantry soldiers that made up the bulk of the Roman army.

- Recruited from Roman citizens (free).

- 4'11" minimum height, 14-19 years old.

- A legion had 6000 soldiers and by 23 A.D. Rome commanded 23 legions.

- A cohort = 600 soldiers

- A century = 100 soldiers

- A centurion commanded a company of about 100 legionaries.

> And a centurion's slave, who was highly regarded by him, was sick and about to die.
> - Luke 7:2

According to Josephus (Jewish historian - Ant. 17, 8, 3 - Lenski p. 388: Luke's Commentary) there were no Roman troops stationed in Capernaum in times of peace. This Centurion apparently lived in Capernaum, he worked for king Herod Antipas whose troops were made up of foreign soldiers. Luke sets the scene by describing the favored status of this household servant and the fact that he was near death (Matthew says that the servant suffered from paralysis - Matthew 8:6).

> When he heard about Jesus, he sent some Jewish elders asking Him to come and save the life of his slave.
> - Luke 7:3

This verse reveals certain things about this man:

- He was influenced by the witness of others concerning Jesus, not having seen or heard Him personally.

- He had both influence and favor among the Jews, sending several Jewish elders (leaders) to ask for help on his behalf (we find out why in the next verses).

- He truly believed. He did not ask that Jesus come and pray, or drop by to see what He could do. He specifically asked Jesus to come and save the life of his dying servant.

> [4]When they came to Jesus, they earnestly
> implored Him, saying, "He is worthy for You to
> grant this to him; [5]for he loves our nation and it was
> he who built us our synagogue."
> - Luke 7:4-5

Luke records the arguments of the Jewish elders on behalf of this man:

- Note there is nothing said about the value and character of the slave, only that he was highly regarded by the Centurion.

- The way the elders state their case assumes that Jesus can do this, they assure the Lord that the Centurion is "worthy" not in the sense that he deserves a reward of some kind but that compared to others the Lord has blessed, he is worthy of consideration.

- They verify the sincerity of the man's faith by describing him as one who loves God's people (even though he is a Gentile) and proving his love for them and for God by building a house of prayer for them (synagogue).

> [6]Now Jesus started on His way with them; and
> when He was not far from the house, the centurion
> sent friends, saying to Him, "Lord, do not trouble
> Yourself further, for I am not worthy for You to
> come under my roof; [7]for this reason I did not even
> consider myself worthy to come to You, but just
> say the word, and my servant will be healed. [8]For I
> also am a man placed under authority, with
> soldiers under me; and I say to this one, 'Go!' and
> he goes, and to another, 'Come!' and he comes,
> and to my slave, 'Do this!' and he does it."
> - Luke 7:6-8

So far we have only heard about this man's situation, piety, love and faith. In this passage we hear the Centurion speak and in his speaking we learn several more things about him:

- He was pious. Piety is a respect for Godly things and people. In his case he respected the fact that Jesus, as a Jew, cold not enter his house without defiling (becoming unclean) Himself according to Jewish Law. Seeing that Jesus is about to do so, he sends friends to stop Him. He wanted his slave healed but not at the expense of putting Jesus in a compromising position by openly violating the Law.

- He was humble. Humility is having a realistic evaluation of ourselves. He recognized that Jesus' power was from God and greater than his own (that came from man) and thus placed himself in the correct position before Jesus, asking Him to exercise that power (say the word) in order to heal his servant.

> [9]Now when Jesus heard this, He marveled at him, and turned and said to the crowd that was following Him, "I say to you, not even in Israel have I found such great faith." [10]When those who had been sent returned to the house, they found the slave in good health.
> - Luke 7:9-10

Rarely does Jesus "marvel" at what men or women do, but here He does so because this Gentile fully grasped the concept that Jesus' power was embodied in his word, an idea that the Jewish nation, having had God's word for nearly 1400 years, failed to accept. Luke notes that at this moment the slave was fully healed and restored.

Widow's Son Resurrected – 7:11-17

As if to confirm that the power is in Jesus' word, Luke follows up the healing miracle of the Centurion's slave with an even greater miracle: the raising of the dead.

In verses 11-12 Luke quickly sketches out the situation. He again pinpoints the location (Nain) a city southwest of Capernaum, and the scene, a funeral procession for the only child of a widowed mother. In this instance no one asks Him to intervene since the person is already dead. It is His compassion for the mother that moves Him to miraculously raise her son from the dead.

> [13]When the Lord saw her, He felt compassion for her, and said to her, "Do not weep." [14]And He came up and touched the coffin; and the bearers came to a halt. And He said, "Young man, I say to you, arise!" [15]The dead man sat up and began to speak. And Jesus gave him back to his mother.
> - Luke 7:13-15

Note that He only speaks a word to raise the dead man, and Luke confirms the miracle by noting that the one who was formerly dead began to speak.

In verses 16-17 Luke describes the excited reaction of the crowd. Unlike the Centurion's slave (done before a few and for the slave of a Gentile soldier) this spectacular miracle is done before the crowd following Him, His disciples, and the crowd from the city in the funeral procession. This miracle made Him famous throughout the nation, not just in His hometown and surrounding area.

Luke is setting the scene for Jesus' eventual appearance in Jerusalem.

Summary of John's Ministry – 7:18-35

In verse 16 Luke writes that the people were praising God on account of Jesus' miracle and saying that a great "prophet" had been send by God. Luke uses this statement as a bridge to summarize and close out the work of John the Baptist who was the last prophet sent by God to the Jewish people. After this section Luke recounts time when John was in prison and he sent disciples to ask Jesus if He was the Messiah.

> [18]The disciples of John reported to him about all these things. [19]Summoning two of his disciples, John sent them to the Lord, saying, "Are You the Expected One, or do we look for someone else?"
> - Luke 7:18-19

Some are confused wondering why John would begin to doubt at this point. John's task was to announce the coming of the Messiah and the Judgement He would bring. (i.e. "And the axe is already laid at the root of the trees; therefore every tree that does not bear good fruit is cut down and thrown into the fire." - Matthew 3:10). It seems that John believed these two events would happen simultaneously, the coming of the Messiah and the Judgement.

When John saw that despite His presence there did not seem to be any judgement on the people, in fact, the leaders were actually pronouncing judgement on Jesus and attacking Him, John began to doubt and sent to the Lord for clarification and assurance. Of course, the Judgement did eventually come some years later, in 70 A.D. when Jerusalem was destroyed by Rome.

> [20]When the men came to Him, they said, "John the Baptist has sent us to You, to ask, 'Are You the Expected One, or do we look for someone else?'" [21]At that very time He cured many people of diseases and afflictions and evil spirits; and He gave sight to many who were blind. [22]And He answered and said to them, "Go and report to John what you have seen and heard: the blind receive sight, the lame walk, the lepers are cleansed, and the deaf hear, the dead are raised up, the poor have the gospel preached to them. [23]Blessed is he who does not take offense at Me."
> - Luke 7:20-23

Jesus, in word and deed, reassures them that He is the Messiah, doing all the things (miracles, teachings) that the prophets said that the Messiah would do. He gives John an exhortation to rejoice in his faith regardless of his circumstances.

In verses 24-35 Jesus finishes by confirming the person and ministry of John the Baptist and condemning the Jewish leaders who rejected John, his baptism and the Messiah he proclaimed. Even though John had a moment of doubt about Jesus, the Lord encourages the people not to harbor any doubt about John and Himself.

The Women - 7:36-8:3

Up until this time, aside from His earthly mother Mary and the prophetess Ana at the temple and those He healed, no women are prominently associated with Jesus. Luke changes this by introducing a woman who would anoint Him and a group of women who would support Him.

The Sinful Woman - 7:36-50

> Now one of the Pharisees was requesting Him to dine with him, and He entered the Pharisee's house and reclined at the table.
> - Luke 7:36

Again Luke situates the story but this time socially (Pharisee's) house for a meal, not geographically.

> [37]And there was a woman in the city who was a sinner; and when she learned that He was reclining at the table in the Pharisee's house, she brought an alabaster vial of perfume, [38]and standing behind Him at His feet, weeping, she began to wet His feet with her tears, and kept wiping them with the hair of her head, and kissing His feet and anointing them with the perfume.
> - Luke 7:37-38

The meal was served on a low table and the guests reclined on pillows leaning on their left elbows with legs stretched out away from the table. The woman (not named and not Mary Magdalene who was healed of demon possession by Jesus) who was a sinner (not necessarily a prostitute, could have been a thief or a woman divorced because of her adultery) enters and stands behind Jesus. She begins to weep and then kneels, breaks open (no cap to keep the remaining oil, once open it is all used up) a vial of anointing oil. Her tears fall on His feet while she is anointing them and having not been provided a basin and towel for His feet by His host, the woman proceeds to dry them with her hair, all the while kissing them. Her actions were a great sign of humility (she crashed the dinner), she exposed herself to possible rejection and shame, and she lowered herself before Jesus publicly.

> Now when the Pharisee who had invited Him saw this, he said to himself, "If this man were a prophet He would know who and what sort of person this woman is who is touching Him, that she is a sinner."
> - Luke 7:39

Luke inserts a kind of caption over the Pharisee showing his thoughts and thus exposing his intentions and attitude towards Jesus. He had invited the Lord just to see if what was said about Him was true. This episode merely confirmed what other Jewish leaders said, "He eats with sinners and tax collectors. He cannot be from God, He is not one of them (the Pharisees)."

> [40]And Jesus answered him, "Simon, I have something to say to you." And he replied, "Say it, Teacher." [41]"A moneylender had two debtors: one owed five hundred denarii, and the other fifty. [42]When they were unable to repay, he graciously forgave them both. So which of them will love him more?" [43]Simon answered and said, "I

suppose the one whom he forgave more." And He said to him, "You have judged correctly."
- Luke 40-43

This parable exposes the hearts of both the Pharisee and the woman. One, the woman, felt the weight of sin and the other, the Pharisee, did not.

[44]Turning toward the woman, He said to Simon, "Do you see this woman? I entered your house; you gave Me no water for My feet, but she has wet My feet with her tears and wiped them with her hair. [45]You gave Me no kiss; but she, since the time I came in, has not ceased to kiss My feet. [46]You did not anoint My head with oil, but she anointed My feet with perfume. [47]For this reason I say to you, her sins, which are many, have been forgiven, for she loved much; but he who is forgiven little, loves little." [48]Then He said to her, "Your sins have been forgiven."
- Luke 44-48

Interesting to note that Jesus says that what the woman did was done as a result of her sins being forgiven. This means that she did not anoint His feet in order to receive forgiveness, she did all these things as a show of her love toward Jesus for having already forgiven her at some previous time. In contrast to this, the Pharisee had neglected to show Jesus the basic courtesies of Jewish hospitality, let alone love. The parable simply lays out the very common sense idea that those who have been forgiven much are usually more grateful than those with smaller debts.

However, in reality both the woman and the Pharisee owed great debts for their personal sinfulness. The only difference was that she became aware of hers and the Pharisee did not. The result was that Jesus openly expressed before witnesses that the woman was actually forgiven and by His silence showed that the Pharisee was not. This declaration stirs up the other guests because in saying this Jesus was equating Himself with God, the very thing that will seal His fate to the cross later on.

The Ministering Woman – 8:1-3

In the first three verses of chapter 8, Luke will once again revert to his practical mode by describing how Jesus was supported. He has just described a man healing all kinds of diseases and infirmities, and reading people's minds. This would naturally lead people to wonder if Jesus was real, was actually human. That potential question or doubt is answered here where Luke explains that a group of female disciples provided the resources to eat, lodge and travel for both Jesus and His Apostles. A very practical footnote to add as Luke explains that Jesus and the Apostles were now fully engaged in ministry from place to place on a full-time basis, all having left their secular work to take on their Apostolic ministries.

Lessons

We will continue next time as Luke will record another series of parables and miracles taking place in Galilee before Jesus will venture forth to minister in Jerusalem and the nearby countryside.

1. The prayers of the righteous are effective on behalf of others (righteous or not).

The elders appealed to Jesus on behalf of a Gentile (Centurion), a person they were not even supposed to deal with let alone pray for.

Praying for an unfaithful husband, a friend in jail or an unbelieving grandmother is made acceptable and effective because of our faith and righteous life, not theirs.

2. Faith believes that God will find a way.

The Centurion could not bring his sick and dying slave to Jesus and Jesus could not enter the Centurion's house without defilement (and the problems this would cause His ministry). The Centurion called on Jesus nevertheless, and God found a way to answer His prayer.

In faith and prayer our job is to ask and believe, not figure out how.

Reading Assignment: Luke 8:4-9:50

Discussion Questions

1. What quality of character possessed by the Centurion do you admire most? Why?

2. How can today's disciples demonstrate piety?

3. In your opinion, what would Jesus marvel about in your life today? What would you like for Him to marvel at if you could achieve it?

CHAPTER 5
JESUS IN GALILEE
PUBLIC MINISTRY BEGINS - PART 3

LUKE 8:4-9:50

In the third part of the first section of Luke's account (Luke 8:4-9:50) every event, miracle and teaching is also contained in either or both Matthew and Mark, except for one passage at the very end of the section.

Parables – Luke 8:4-21

The Parable of the Sower and the Seed (8:4-18)

This parable is contained in both Matthew and Mark's gospels. It is the first parable used by Jesus in His teaching ministry (Lenski, p. 443).

> When a large crowd was coming together, and those from the various cities were journeying to Him, He spoke by way of a parable:
> - Luke 8:4

Luke notes that Jesus' popularity is on the rise as people not only from His own town, Capernaum, are coming out to hear Him, but many from other cities are coming as well.

In verses 5-8 Luke recounts Jesus' parable of the sower sowing seed on different types of soil (hard road / rocky soil / thorny soil / good soil) and the results of this (road/rocky/thorns = no growth, good soil = 30/60/100 times return).

> [9]His disciples began questioning Him as to what this parable meant. [10]And He said, "To you it has been granted to know the mysteries of the kingdom of God, but to the rest it is in parables, so that seeing they may not see, and hearing they may not understand.
> - Luke 8:9-10

Since this is the first time that Jesus teaches using the parable style, His Apostles want to know two things: the meaning of the parable, and why has He begun using this style of teaching. Jesus answers their second question first: why parables? The word "parable" comes from a Greek word which meant "to lay beside." It was a teaching device used to compare ideas or things in order to provide greater understanding. Jesus, therefore, was telling them a story about something physical that could easily be understood (a sower sowing seed) in order to teach them about something that they could not see and had trouble grasping (the growth of the kingdom of heaven).

The Apostles knew what parables were since they were commonly used by other teachers. They wanted to know why Jesus had begun using them to teach the crowds. The Lord explains that He will now use parables to both teach His disciples about the kingdom (its establishment and growth) and shield unbelievers and opponents from the true meaning of these matters.

In verses 11-15 He goes on to give the deeper meaning (what the parable teaches about the kingdom) behind the parable story.

The Parable of the Lamp

[16]"Now no one after lighting a lamp covers it over with a container, or puts it under a bed; but he puts it on a lampstand, so that those who come in may see the light. [17]For nothing is hidden that will not become evident, nor anything secret that will not be known and come to light. [18]So take care how you listen; for whoever has, to him more shall be given; and whoever does not have, even what he thinks he has shall be taken away from him." [19]And His mother and brothers came to Him, and they were unable to get to Him because of the crowd. [20]And it was reported to Him, "Your mother and Your brothers are standing outside, wishing to see You." [21]But He answered and said to them, "My mother and My brothers are these who hear the word of God and do it."
- Luke 8:16-21

Once Jesus has explained why He uses parables and how to interpret them (His identity is the key that unlocks them) He follows up with a second parable that calls on them to do two things:

1. Be ready to proclaim to the world the things they will learn from Him.

2. Be attentive to His teaching because the more they believed and learned, the more they would understand. On the other hand, the less one believed and learned, the less one would understand to the point where nothing would be believed or understood.

This last admonition to His disciples is a continuation of what He explained about His use of parables: some, because of their belief in Him, would gain more insight and knowledge from Him; those who did not believe would only understand the story of the parables but not the meaning which He provided. Eventually, the non-believers would lose interest altogether and completely miss the coming and fulfillment of the kingdom.

It is interesting to note here that Jesus uses the initial disbelief of His own family as a way of establishing the importance and necessity of faith in Him to access the things of the kingdom. Even the members of His earthly family have to believe if they want to enter in.

Miracles – 8:22-50

Luke now changes scenes and describes, in successive order, three miracles that Jesus performs during a trip across the Sea of Galilee. Luke has described several instances of Jesus' teachings and follows up with a demonstration of His power that will serve to confirm the credentials of the teacher Himself. As far as Theophilus, the recipient of this gospel is concerned, if Jesus can do these things then this Gentile proselyte to Christianity can safely believe all the teachings of Jesus.

These three miracles are recorded in both Matthew and Mark, so we will only summarize and review them here.

Jesus Stills the Sea (8:22-25)

The first miracle takes place while they are, according to Jesus' instructions, in a boat crossing the Sea of Galilee. Luke says that after Jesus went to sleep there arose a fierce storm that threatened to capsize their vessel. The storm must have been severe because Luke tells us that many of the Apostles, who were experienced sailors, feared for their lives.

Jesus is awakened and promptly calms the storm by speaking to it (commanding it to stop as opposed to various incantations and sacrifices used by pagan religions in their attempts to influence the weather). This was not the first miracle the Apostles witnessed (changing water into wine at Cana was first), but this one was done in their element, on the lake, and of a nature that other miracle workers in the past (e.g. prophet Elijah) had never done. This miracle forced them to reevaluate who Jesus really was (who controls the wind and sea by His word alone?): a teacher, a prophet, the Messiah, or more than these?

The Apostles came to Him in fear, perhaps hoping He could pray and ask God to save them somehow, but they were not ready for His reaction and demonstration of divine power. Afterwards, Jesus merely rebukes them for their lack of faith by asking them, "Where is your faith?"

The Demoniac Cured (8:26-39)

This is another miracle described by both Matthew and Mark. The healing takes place once they land on the other side of the lake where they were met by a demon-possessed man. Jesus has shown His power over the elements and in this instance He both converses with the demons and orders them out of the man and into a herd of pigs nearby. This not only establishes His power and authority over spiritual beings but also demonstrates that the man was actually possessed by evil spirits and not simply suffering from some type of mental illness.

It is interesting to note that even though Jesus' closest disciples had not yet grasped who He was, the evil spirits not only knew who He was but what their ultimate judgment and punishment would be (cast into the abyss, verse 31). Luke describes how the demon-possessed man is immediately returned to his right mind and that the villagers are alerted after their herd of pigs ran into the sea and drowned once the demons entered them. The people react to these things with fear and ask Jesus to leave, and the man formerly demon-possessed is sent back to his home region to witness about his healing.

Both Matthew and Mark tell us that later on Jesus returned to this region and this time was well received as people came to Him for healing (Matthew 14:34-36, Mark 7:31). The inference is that the groundwork for this was laid by the demon-possessed man who obeyed Jesus and returned to his home region to witness about his healing at the hands of the Lord.

The Woman with the Hemorrhage and Jairus' Daughter (8:40-56)

Luke closes out this section by describing two other miracles performed when Jesus and the disciples crossed back over the lake and returned home. This scene takes place several days after their return. We learn from Matthew 9:

- Jesus heals a paralytic
- Calls Matthew
- Dines at Matthew's house which was by the Sea of Galilee since, as a tax collector, much of his business was to gather taxes at the port

While He is teaching a crowd of people who had gathered at Matthew's house in Capernaum, the leader (elder) of the local synagogue named Jairus appeals to Him to come and heal his young daughter who is at home dying of an undisclosed illness. Luke forgoes several details because this incident is also described in Matthew and Mark, and so summarizes the two miracles.

Jairus' Daughter

Jesus accepts to go to the synagogue leader's home to heal the child. He is interrupted for a time by a woman also needing His help, and during this delay the girl dies. Jesus eventually arrives at the house and brings the child back to life.

The Woman with the Issue of Blood

It is interesting that Luke, a doctor himself, would add the detail that no one, not even doctors, could heal this woman who had suffered for 12 years. Her hemorrhaging stops when she touches Jesus' cloak. The Lord then forces her to publicly acknowledge her healing in order to confirm her changed status (ritually unclean to clean and thus able to return to normal social and religious activities) and witness her faith in Him.

Luke finishes with the description of Jesus' miracles and will then turn to the ministry He will entrust to His Apostles and disciples.

Ministry of/to the Twelve – 9:1-50

Apostles Sent Out (9:1-6)

Jesus has spent a considerable amount of time teaching, performing miracles and preaching in His home region of Galilee. Before heading to Jerusalem and the greater challenges awaiting there, He instructs and sends out the Apostles on their initial tour of ministry.

In only a few verses we see how thoroughly the Lord equips them.

> And He called the twelve together, and gave them power and authority over all the demons and to heal diseases.
> - Luke 9:1

He equips them with spiritual power which will give authority to their preaching. People can trust their message because they see the power behind the message. Today the "power" is the gospel itself (death, burial, resurrection of Christ - Romans 1:16) witnessed by our holy lives.

> And He sent them out to proclaim the kingdom of God and to perform healing.
> - Luke 9:2

He provides them with the content of their message (the kingdom is near). Today, the message is that the kingdom is here and all must enter in.

> ^{3}And He said to them, "Take nothing for your
> journey, neither a staff, nor a bag, nor bread, nor
> money; and do not even have two tunics
> apiece. ^{4}Whatever house you enter, stay there until
> you leave that city.
> - Luke 9:3-4

He will supply for their needs in His own way through the
hospitality of those they instruct. He cautions them not to
solicit help from door to door as beggars. The same can be
said for and to those who choose to leave all for ministry
today.

> ^{5}And as for those who do not receive you, as you
> go out from that city, shake the dust off your feet
> as a testimony against them." ^{6}Departing, they
> began going throughout the villages, preaching the
> gospel and healing everywhere.
> - Luke 9:5-6

Jesus also provides for their emotional needs. They will be
rejected and even persecuted, but they must not respond
with fear, revenge, guilt or disappointment. Their response to
these things will be their witness of the judgment to come. In
other words, they are a witness of judgment for those who
received the message but refused it. It works in the same
way today, our task is not to save, our task is to proclaim the
gospel and the judgment to come. If we have done this, we
have fulfilled our ministry.

Results of Their Ministry (9:7-11)

Herod

> ^{7}Now Herod the tetrarch heard of all that was
> happening; and he was greatly perplexed, because
> it was said by some that John had risen from the
> dead, ^{8}and by some that Elijah had appeared, and

by others that one of the prophets of old had risen again. [9]Herod said, "I myself had John beheaded; but who is this man about whom I hear such things?" And he kept trying to see Him.
- Luke 9:7-9

Their preaching was so effective that it reached the ears of Herod who was the ruler of the Galilean region. Luke reports that this evil king was perplexed because he thought that John the Baptist had somehow come back from the dead to haunt him (he thought this because he had unjustly executed John - Mark 6:14-29).

The People of that Region

[10]When the apostles returned, they gave an account to Him of all that they had done. Taking them with Him, He withdrew by Himself to a city called Bethsaida. [11]But the crowds were aware of this and followed Him; and welcoming them, He began speaking to them about the kingdom of God and curing those who had need of healing.
- Luke 9:10-11

As a result of their preaching even more people were eager to see and hear Jesus.

The 5000 Fed (9:12-17)

Here is another episode that is described by both Matthew and Mark. Suffice to say that this gathering is yet another sign of Jesus' growing ministry and a direct result of the Apostles' preaching in the region. The miracle of the multiplication of the bread and fish to feed 5000 people served the Apostles by once again demonstrating Jesus' ability to meet every need in any circumstance, and it showed the people that His teaching was based on power not persuasion.

The Cost of Discipleship (9:18-27)

The scene changes again and we find Jesus alone with His disciples after these incredible events.

> [18]And it happened that while He was praying alone, the disciples were with Him, and He questioned them, saying, "Who do the people say that I am?" [19]They answered and said, "John the Baptist, and others say Elijah; but others, that one of the prophets of old has risen again." [20]And He said to them, "But who do you say that I am?" And Peter answered and said, "The Christ of God." [21]But He warned them and instructed them not to tell this to anyone, [22]saying, "The Son of Man must suffer many things and be rejected by the elders and chief priests and scribes, and be killed and be raised up on the third day."
> - Luke 9:18-22

Jesus reveals the two truths that they must accept as His time with them draws to a close:

1. **His Identity:** To recognize and accept that He is the divine Son of God.

2. **His Mission:** The goal of His ministry here on earth is to die on the cross and then be gloriously resurrected.

Once these are revealed, Jesus goes ahead and describes the true cost of being His disciple: everything you have.

> [23]And He was saying to them all, "If anyone wishes to come after Me, he must deny himself, and take up his cross daily and follow Me. [24]For whoever wishes to save his life will lose it, but whoever loses his life for My sake, he is the one who will save it. [25]For what is a man profited if he gains the whole world, and loses or forfeits himself? [26]For

whoever is ashamed of Me and My words, the Son of Man will be ashamed of him when He comes in His glory, and the glory of the Father and of the holy angels. [27]But I say to you truthfully, there are some of those standing here who will not taste death until they see the kingdom of God."
- Luke 9:23-27

Part of a disciple's training is to know the true mission and calculate its cost.

The Transfiguration (9:28-45)

I include the transfiguration in the section on ministry to the Apostles because three Apostles are given an extraordinary opportunity to see Jesus in a glorified state. This experience should put beyond doubt their previous confession that Jesus was the Son of God and as such shared a divine nature with the Father. They believed that He was the Messiah but needed further proof concerning His divinity, and Jesus goes beyond the performing of miracles to provide it.

[28]Some eight days after these sayings, He took along Peter and John and James, and went up on the mountain to pray. [29]And while He was praying, the appearance of His face became different, and His clothing became white and gleaming. [30]And behold, two men were talking with Him; and they were Moses and Elijah, [31]who, appearing in glory, were speaking of His departure which He was about to accomplish at Jerusalem. [32]Now Peter and his companions had been overcome with sleep; but when they were fully awake, they saw His glory and the two men standing with Him. [33]And as these were leaving Him, Peter said to Jesus, "Master, it is good for us to be here; let us make three tabernacles: one for You, and one for Moses, and one for Elijah"—not realizing what he was saying. [34]While he was saying this, a cloud

> formed and began to overshadow them; and they
> were afraid as they entered the cloud. [35]Then a
> voice came out of the cloud, saying, "This is My
> Son, My Chosen One; listen to Him!" [36]And when
> the voice had spoken, Jesus was found alone. And
> they kept silent, and reported to no one in those
> days any of the things which they had seen.
> - Luke 9:28-36

Healing of the Demon Possessed Boy (9:37-45)

After this episode, Luke describes another miraculous
healing, this time of a demon possessed boy that the
Apostles, who had been left behind, failed to heal (unlike
Matthew, Luke does not explain why). After healing the boy,
Jesus, perhaps sensing that these events are making the
Apostles confident for the wrong reasons, reminds them
again that He will eventually be killed, and yet, they still do
not understand.

Who is the Greatest

> [46]An argument started among them as to which of
> them might be the greatest. [47]But Jesus, knowing
> what they were thinking in their heart, took a child
> and stood him by His side, [48]and said to them,
> "Whoever receives this child in My name receives
> Me, and whoever receives Me receives Him who
> sent Me; for the one who is least among all of you,
> this is the one who is great." [49]John answered and
> said, "Master, we saw someone casting out
> demons in Your name; and we tried to prevent him
> because he does not follow along with us." [50]But
> Jesus said to him, "Do not hinder him; for he who
> is not against you is for you."
> - Luke 9:46-50

Jesus' warning about His impending death, in order to keep
His Apostles focused, is confirmed here as they (perhaps
provoked by Peter and the others who witnessed the

transfiguration) begin debating who among them is the greatest. They may have argued that the greatest were those who performed miracles or witnessed visions or were favored by Jesus. The Lord reminds them that the one who simply believes (without the witness of miracles or visions) has both the blessing of the Father and the Son.

John, who was with Peter and James on the mount of transfiguration, reveals their collective sense of privilege (we are Jesus' Apostles) by stopping someone else doing works in Jesus' name (note he says that this person does not follow "us," the Apostles, and not "You," Jesus). The Lord answers John and closes this section with a mild rebuke telling John not to create enemies unnecessarily.

Summary and Lessons

Luke closes out his account of Jesus' growing ministry in and around His home town of Capernaum by the Sea of Galilee.

In the next chapter, we will begin where Jesus prepares Himself and the Apostles for the stiffer opposition they will face as they head south towards Jerusalem.

Here are only a few of the many lessons we can draw from the material discussed in this chapter:

Where is Your Faith?

Jesus posed this question to His Apostles after He calmed the storm. Faith is demonstrated during the storms of life, not the periods when the seas are calm. When things in life go wrong, ask yourself, "Where is my faith?" not, "Why is this storm happening to me or, why is this storm not over yet?"

Jesus is Never Late

They told Jesus that He was too late, the little girl died, no use in coming. Only those whose faith is weak see Jesus as being late, not fair, not caring, etc. Jesus is never late or early for the faithful who wait on Him patiently. His timing may not accommodate our desires but it is always right to accomplish His will and purpose for our lives.

Reading Assignment: Luke 9:51-12:12

Discussion Questions

1. Create your own parable that uses modern day references to teach something about Christianity. Read your parable to the group for comment and discussion as to its accuracy and teaching effectiveness.

CHAPTER 6
JESUS FACING JERUSALEM
- PART 1

LUKE 9:51-12:12

Let's take a look at the outline that we are using in our study of Luke's gospel. It is one that is based on His movements.

1. **The Beginning – 1:1-3:38:** Covers His birth to His baptism by John.

2. **Jesus in Galilee – 4:1-9:50:** Here Luke begins with Jesus' temptation after His baptism and follows Jesus as He begins His ministry and the gathering of His Apostles in the northern part of the country in and around His adult dwelling place in Capernaum, near the Sea of Galilee. Luke describes many miracles, teachings, confrontation with Jewish leaders and interaction with people and the one common factor to all was that they took place in the north.

The next section will describe events as He travels south to Jerusalem.

Jesus Facing Jerusalem – 9:51-18:30

In this section Luke will continue his description of Jesus' ministry but now the scene changes as Jesus leaves the more friendly area of His home town in the north and heads for Jerusalem and the fierce opposition that will face Him and the Apostles there.

Ministry Training (9:51-10:24)

Departure

> [51]When the days were approaching for His ascension, He was determined to go to Jerusalem; [52]and He sent messengers on ahead of Him, and they went and entered a village of the Samaritans to make arrangements for Him. [53]But they did not receive Him, because He was traveling toward Jerusalem. [54]When His disciples James and John saw this, they said, "Lord, do You want us to command fire to come down from heaven and consume them?" [55]But He turned and rebuked them, and said, "You do not know what kind of spirit you are of; [56]for the Son of Man did not come to destroy men's lives, but to save them." And they went on to another village.
> - Luke 9:51-56

Note that Luke shifts gears in verse 51 by simply alluding to Jesus' ascension (not crucifixion or resurrection). He refers to the final scene of His ministry in order to change the current setting from Galilee to Jerusalem. Seeing that the end (ascension) was in sight, Jesus sets His mind to travel to Jerusalem where first His death and resurrection must occur.

He encounters immediate resistance from Samaritans who will not host Him because He is a Jew (not because He claimed that He was the Messiah), and a Jewish prophet specifically bypassing their place of worship in order to preach in Jerusalem, their hated religious rival. Jesus does not demand revenge for this rejection as do James and John, but reminds them of His mission and theirs (to save not destroy) and humbly goes elsewhere.

Exacting Discipleship (9:57-62)

The move to Jerusalem will be quite challenging so Jesus clarifies how demanding becoming His disciple can be as different followers, seeing that He is about to depart, offer various excuses for not leaving with Him right away.

> But Jesus said to him, "No one, after putting his hand to the plow and looking back, is fit for the kingdom of God."
> - Luke 9:62

Jesus reminds them that becoming a disciple of His requires no looking back, you need to be ready to move when He moves, not when you feel like moving.

70 Sent Out to Minister (10:1-24)

> [1]Now after this the Lord appointed seventy others, and sent them in pairs ahead of Him to every city and place where He Himself was going to come. [2]And He was saying to them, "The harvest is plentiful, but the laborers are few; therefore beseech the Lord of the harvest to send out laborers into His harvest.
> - Luke 10:1-2

These are sent to prepare His way for the places He will visit on His journey south. He states that there is a lot of ministry to perform and not many to carry it out, then sends out 70 (35 pairs) to preach and prepare the people for His own arrival.

> [3]Go; behold, I send you out as lambs in the midst of wolves. [4]Carry no money belt, no bag, no shoes; and greet no one on the way. [5]Whatever house you enter, first say, 'Peace be to this house.' [6]If a man of peace is there, your peace will rest on him;

> but if not, it will return to you. [7]Stay in that house,
> eating and drinking what they give you; for the
> laborer is worthy of his wages. Do not keep moving
> from house to house. [8]Whatever city you enter and
> they receive you, eat what is set before you;
> - Luke 10:3-8

Guidelines for their ministry:

1. Be careful. The world is dangerous.

2. Do not bring extras, all will be provided.

3. Do not waste time with chit chat (greetings).

4. No door to door begging. Stay in the place that
   welcomes you, no moving around or trading up. The
   peace they offer is the peace of Christ and if the host
   rejects it you have done your duty as a minister and
   can receive the hospitality without guilt or offense.

5. Eat and drink what they offer, without judging either
   way.

> and heal those in it who are sick, and say to them,
> 'The kingdom of God has come near to you.'
> - Luke 10:9

Here Jesus summarizes their ministry: heal the sick
(establish divine credibility) and preach the Word (share the
good news).

> [10]But whatever city you enter and they do not
> receive you, go out into its streets and say, [11]'Even
> the dust of your city which clings to our feet we
> wipe off in protest against you; yet be sure of this,
> that the kingdom of God has come near.' [12]I say to
> you, it will be more tolerable in that day for Sodom
> than for that city.
> [13]"Woe to you, Chorazin! Woe to you, Bethsaida!
> For if the miracles had been performed in Tyre and

> Sidon which occurred in you, they would have
> repented long ago, sitting in sackcloth and
> ashes. [14]But it will be more tolerable for Tyre and
> Sidon in the judgment than for you. [15]And you,
> Capernaum, will not be exalted to heaven, will
> you? You will be brought down to Hades!
> [16]"The one who listens to you listens to Me, and
> the one who rejects you rejects Me; and he who
> rejects Me rejects the One who sent Me."
> - Luke 10:10-16

God's judgement should motivate both the hearers and the
speakers. The hearers are lost if they do not believe that
Jesus is the Son of God. The speakers need to remind the
hearers that there is a definite consequence for those who
disbelieve. The author mentions several cities and nations
destroyed by God for their disbelief, a warning to all creation
that God still cares about souls.

Results of Ministry

> [17]The seventy returned with joy, saying, "Lord,
> even the demons are subject to us in Your
> name." [18]And He said to them, "I was watching
> Satan fall from heaven like lightning. [19]Behold, I
> have given you authority to tread on serpents and
> scorpions, and over all the power of the enemy,
> and nothing will injure you. [20]Nevertheless do not
> rejoice in this, that the spirits are subject to you,
> but rejoice that your names are recorded in
> heaven."
> - Luke 10:17-20

The disciples return especially happy that they were able to
cast out evil spirits in Jesus' name (since Jesus sent them
out to heal, this extra power was a bonus). Jesus mentions
Satan "falling" as a comment on their success over the
demons. If they could do this to Satan's followers it thus
meant that Satan who empowered them was also beaten.

This power meant that they (and we as modern day disciples) have the power to also defeat the plans and schemes (serpents and scorpions are symbols for these things, creatures that injure) of the devil as well.

The Lord finishes by helping these men get some perspective on their great spiritual victory over evil spirits. The true victory, won for them by Jesus, and cause for everlasting joy is that they are guaranteed eternal life in heaven (e.g. their names are already recorded there).

Jesus' Prayer

> [21]At that very time He rejoiced greatly in the Holy Spirit, and said, "I praise You, O Father, Lord of heaven and earth, that You have hidden these things from the wise and intelligent and have revealed them to infants. Yes, Father, for this way was well-pleasing in Your sight. [22]All things have been handed over to Me by My Father, and no one knows who the Son is except the Father, and who the Father is except the Son, and anyone to whom the Son wills to reveal Him." [23]Turning to the disciples, He said privately, "Blessed are the eyes which see the things you see, [24]for I say to you, that many prophets and kings wished to see the things which you see, and did not see them, and to hear the things which you hear, and did not hear them."
> - Luke 10:21-24

Jesus's prayer develops the idea concerning the true reason they should rejoice. They experienced a measure of spiritual power and were excited and joyful concerning their experience. Others in the past had also felt and used God's power to perform miracles and healings, even raise the dead (i.e. Elijah - II Kings 4:18-37). However, they were privileged to know and serve the Messiah, the Son of God, something only hoped for by those faithful men and women who came before them.

Jesus not only rejoices on their behalf but praises the Father for the way He has finally fully revealed Himself to mankind by giving this precious knowledge to simple men and women of low status in the world. Interesting to note that Luke mentions all three persons in the Godhead in the same moment in time (verse 21).

Parable of the Good Samaritan – 10:25-37

This parable only appears in Luke's gospel and is given in response to a question posed to Him by a lawyer.

> [25]And a lawyer stood up and put Him to the test, saying, "Teacher, what shall I do to inherit eternal life?" [26]And He said to him, "What is written in the Law? How does it read to you?" [27]And he answered, "You shall love the Lord your God with all your heart, and with all your soul, and with all your strength, and with all your mind; and your neighbor as yourself." [28]And He said to him, "You have answered correctly; do this and you will live." [29]But wishing to justify himself, he said to Jesus, "And who is my neighbor?"
> - Luke 10:25-29

This question follows Jesus' comment in His prayer about the disciples names recorded in heaven. This lawyer tests Jesus by asking Him a question that he already knows the answer to and hopes to argue against and discredit what Jesus will say. Some scholars say that this lawyer was offended by Jesus' previous comments about His disciples being in heaven because of their faith in Him, and asks this question in order to draw Jesus into a debate.

Note that Jesus asks the lawyer to first answer the question himself which he does accurately quoting the correct passage on this topic, and Jesus confirms that his response is accurate according to the letter of the Law (i.e. love God and neighbor = eternal life).

The Jews and specifically the lawyers were good at watering down or circumventing God's Law in order to do what they wanted but still claim they were righteous under the Law. For example, they would divorce their wives on any small pretext (did not like her cooking) and claim they were righteous because they followed the Law by giving her a certificate of divorce. They had obeyed the letter of the Law but not the spirit of the Law.

This lawyer tried to justify himself in the same way. The Jews made a distinction when it came to neighbors. For some Jews only other Jews could be neighbors, for others it was only those in your tribe or family that qualified as neighbors. So the real question was not, "How do I obtain eternal life?" but, "Who is my neighbor?" Unlike the first question where He knew that the lawyer had the correct answer and text, He answers this one because in doing so He will correct this man's mistaken notion about who is our neighbor.

> Jesus replied and said, "A man was going down
> from Jerusalem to Jericho, and fell among robbers,
> and they stripped him and beat him, and went
> away leaving him half dead.
> - Luke 10:30

Jesus sets up the story about a Samaritan (a person from a group of people and place shunned by Jews since they considered these people half-breeds because they had a mixture of Jewish and Gentile ancestry). A man traveling is robbed, beaten, left naked and near death on a lonely backroad between Jerusalem and Jericho. Both a priest and a Levite (who serve in the temple at Jerusalem) pass by him but do not stop to help. Some say that they did so because they did not want to become ceremonially unclean by touching him and consequently not be able to serve in the temple. This is incorrect for three reasons:

1. They were coming down (meaning from and not to Jerusalem) so their temple service was done.

2. Unless they examined to see if he was circumcised, they had no way of knowing if he was a Gentile or a Jew. He could have been a priest.

3. You became ceremonially unclean of you touched a leper or a dead body, but this injured man was neither.

Jesus now introduces the main character in the parable, the Samaritan traveler. This man not only stops but attends to the wounded man and brings him to an inn to recover from his wounds. The two denarii that he leaves would have paid for two months worth of care in advance (Lenski p. 607).

Now it is Jesus' turn to question the lawyer. Actually there were three questions here, one open and two understood:

1. Which of the three acted like a good neighbor? (Open)

2. Have you been this kind of neighbor? (implied)

   ○ The implied question circles back to the lawyers original question about what one must do to receive eternal life, love God and neighbor, and challenges him with a third question:

3. Have you loved your neighbor in this way?

The lawyer haltingly answers the open question by acknowledging that the one "who had mercy" (note he could not even bring himself to utter the words "Samaritan was the neighbor"). Jesus, having revealed the hole not only in his argument (my neighbor is who I choose) but in his spiritual life as well (he was not loving others as he should) tells him to repent and act in the spirit that this command required (my neighbor is my neighbor in need).

Mary and Martha

> [38]Now as they were traveling along, He entered a village; and a woman named Martha welcomed Him into her home. [39]She had a sister called Mary, who was seated at the Lord's feet, listening to His word. [40]But Martha was distracted with all her preparations; and she came up to Him and said, "Lord, do You not care that my sister has left me to do all the serving alone? Then tell her to help me." [41]But the Lord answered and said to her, "Martha, Martha, you are worried and bothered about so many things; [42]but only one thing is necessary, for Mary has chosen the good part, which shall not be taken away from her."
> - Luke 10:38-42

Jesus and His Apostles are close to Jerusalem now since we know that these women lived in Bethany, just a few miles away from Jerusalem (John 11:1). Luke gives us a glimpse of two female disciples who were disputing over the work in hosting Jesus and the 12. In this scene, we see that two things are being offered, two important things:

1. Food for the body which Martha is preparing and trying to get her sister to help with.

2. Food for the soul which Jesus is providing with His teaching.

Both are important but one is of greater importance: feeding on God's word. In answering Martha in the way that He does, Jesus is merely pointing out this reality and truth. Mary has chosen the more important of the two. What is unspoken here is that both Martha and Mary could have chosen to sit and listen and the food could have been served later.

Instruction on Prayer – 11:1-13

> [1]It happened that while Jesus was praying in a certain place, after He had finished, one of His disciples said to Him, "Lord, teach us to pray just as John also taught his disciples." [2]And He said to them, "When you pray, say:
> 'Father, hallowed be Your name.
> Your kingdom come.
> [3]'Give us each day our daily bread.
> [4]'And forgive us our sins,
> For we ourselves also forgive everyone who is indebted to us.
> And lead us not into temptation.'"
> - Luke 11:1-4

A disciple (one of the 70) asks Jesus to instruct him on prayer in general (like John did for his disciples). Jesus responds with both a model prayer and the attitude one must have in prayer. The model prayer Jesus gives is an abbreviated version of the one He gave in the sermon on the Mount. What is unique is an illustration he makes which is only found in Luke's gospel.

> [5]Then He said to them, "Suppose one of you has a friend, and goes to him at midnight and says to him, 'Friend, lend me three loaves; [6]for a friend of mine has come to me from a journey, and I have nothing to set before him'; [7]and from inside he answers and says, 'Do not bother me; the door has already been shut and my children and I are in bed; I cannot get up and give you anything.' [8]I tell you, even though he will not get up and give him anything because he is his friend, yet because of his persistence he will get up and give him as much as he needs.
> - Luke 11:5-8

The story highlights the virtue of persistence because Jesus concludes that the man received what he asked for, not because of need or friendship but because he would not quit asking.

> [9]"So I say to you, ask, and it will be given to you; seek, and you will find; knock, and it will be opened to you. [10]For everyone who asks, receives; and he who seeks, finds; and to him who knocks, it will be opened. [11]Now suppose one of you fathers is asked by his son for a fish; he will not give him a snake instead of a fish, will he? [12]Or if he is asked for an egg, he will not give him a scorpion, will he? [13]If you then, being evil, know how to give good gifts to your children, how much more will your heavenly Father give the Holy Spirit to those who ask Him?"
> - Luke 11:9-13

In the following verses, Jesus makes two practical applications from the story to the practice of prayer:

1. Keep asking, searching, trying. Prayers are acts of faith and our continued prayers build faith and develop patience. They are the most basic form of spiritual exercise. They are always answered in some way at some time according to God's will and timetable, not ours.

2. God knows what to give us. Human fathers usually give their children good gifts and they know what those are for each child. In the same way but at a much higher level, our heavenly Father knows this as well. Jesus mentions the greatest gift of all, the Holy Spirit, who will eventually raise us from the dead (Romans 8:11).

Attack and Warning of the Pharisees – 11:14-54

The next long section highlights an ongoing conflict between Jesus and the Pharisees. Now that He and the Apostles are near Jerusalem the attacks of the Pharisees, who are concentrated in this area, are going to step up.

> [14]And He was casting out a demon, and it was mute; when the demon had gone out, the mute man spoke; and the crowds were amazed. [15]But some of them said, "He casts out demons by Beelzebul, the ruler of the demons."
> - Luke 11:14-15

Luke explains that the source of this attack centers around their efforts to discredit His miracles as works of the devil.

In verses 16-28 Jesus responds that if the devil is working against himself by casting out demons in Jesus' name, it means he is divided and thus defeated. If, on the other hand, He was casting out demons by the power of God and they, the Pharisees, were against Him then it meant that they sided with the devil.

> He who is not with Me is against Me; and he who does not gather with Me, scatters.
> - Luke 11:23

In verses 29-36, some in the crowd challenge Him by asking for a sign (a nature miracle as in Moses' day, water from a rock). He prophesizes that He will give them a spectacular miracle, His resurrection, but they neither understand His reference (sign of Jonah) and because of their disbelief will not be privileged to see this miracle when it comes. He charges them with blindness and darkness because they reject Him. The idea that their light is darkness is a way of saying that what they think is true (light) (that He is not the

Messiah) is really darkness (untrue), and will not safely guide their steps. He finished His response to them by telling them that if they accept the truth about Him (He is the Messiah) they will have a light "to guide them".

Woes Upon the Pharisees – 11:37-54

Jesus finishes by pronouncing a series of six woes on the Pharisees after He has been criticized by them for not performing the ceremonial cleansing rites required by their rules. These woes are accusation for their past sins of greed, pride, hypocrisy, impurity, oppression, violence, and obstruction of the truth (that He was the Messiah). Luke records that after this confrontation the scribes and Pharisees joined in a plot to kill Him.

Lesson

We have covered quite a number of events in this section and other than the observation that these things all took place as Jesus headed for Jerusalem, there is not general theme. But there are many possible lessons. Here is one.

We are the 70

There were only 12 chosen Apostles but the model for us are the 70 sent out. It is our job to proclaim the gospel to our neighbors and nation and confirm it with the witness of our pure lives and good works.

Discussion Questions

1. Describe what you believe is the greatest obstacle to the gospel in the place where you plan to minister and how you plan to overcome it in your ministry.

2. If you were presenting the parable of the Good Samaritan today, who would be your modern-day characters? (Robbers, Priests, Levites, Samaritan, Inn Keeper, Victim)

3. What would you say to someone who had prayed fervently for a long time but had no response and as a consequence, was discouraged and angry at God?

CHAPTER 7
JESUS FACING JERUSALEM
- PART 2

LUKE 12:1-14:6

We are looking at the part of Luke's gospel where he describes the events that occurred as Jesus was transitioning His ministry from the northern part of the country near Galilee to the south where the city of Jerusalem was located. We noted that as He drew near the holy city which housed the temple and the religious leaders (priests, scribes, Pharisees), the opposition to Him and His teachings grew. We left off at the end of chapter 11 where Luke records that these leaders were actively plotting to trap Him in what He might say (11:53-54). This was taking place because Jesus had denounced them for having rejected Him and telling the people that He was demon-possessed.

In chapter 12 Jesus responds to the opposition He is facing by warning His Apostles about the schemes of these men, and adds the admonition that being His disciple would be difficult and dangerous. He reassures them, however, with several promises:

- Their message would eventually be heard despite the opposition they faced (verses 1-3).

- The power they spoke from and witnessed about was greater than the power opposing them (verses 4-5).

- God considered them valuable even if the world did not (verses 6-7).

- Faith in Christ would be the determining factor in judgment before God, not earthly power or position (verses 8-9).

- Those who rejected God's word (Jesus is the Messiah) by saying that He and His word were of Satan would not be forgiven because they had rejected and blasphemed the only One who could save them (verse 10).

- God would provide the wisdom they needed to proclaim and defend their faith when persecuted (verses 11-12).

At this point someone in the crowd asks Jesus a question and this shifts His attention from warning His Apostles concerning the Pharisees to warning them about the dangers that were present in the world, dangers that threatened not only their ministry but their souls as well.

Parable About Bigger Barns – 12:13-21

> [13]Someone in the crowd said to Him, "Teacher, tell my brother to divide the family inheritance with me." [14]But He said to him, "Man, who appointed Me a judge or arbitrator over you?" [15]Then He said to them, "Beware, and be on your guard against every form of greed; for not even when one has an abundance does his life consist of his possessions."
> - Luke 12:13-15

The question implies that there is a dispute over money in this family and the person who asked the question wanted Jesus to mediate. The Lord refuses to get involved because He is not one of the judges normally appointed to handle these types of legal matters. He does, however, use the incident to teach the crowd about greed (never having enough), the problem that was probably causing the trouble between these family members in the first place.

His lesson is embedded in a parable.

> [16]And He told them a parable, saying, "The land of a rich man was very productive. [17]And he began reasoning to himself, saying, 'What shall I do, since I have no place to store my crops?' [18]Then he said, 'This is what I will do: I will tear down my barns and build larger ones, and there I will store all my grain and my goods. [19]And I will say to my soul, "Soul, you have many goods laid up for many years to come; take your ease, eat, drink and be merry."' [20]But God said to him, 'You fool! This very night your soul is required of you; and now who will own what you have prepared?' [21]So is the man who stores up treasure for himself, and is not rich toward God."
> - Luke 12:16-21

The story is a simple one: a rich man is blessed with an abundant harvest which makes him richer still. This sudden increase presents a dilemma: how to maintain this wealth? The man solves this problem by increasing his storage capacity - bigger barns! While he is contemplating how he will enjoy his increased wealth, he dies and his estate is given to others.

Notice that the word greed does not appear in the story. The rich man is not condemned because he was wealthy or because his fields produced a bountiful harvest, these were blessings. The sin comes when deciding about his increase, the things he did and didn't do that were motivated by greed and a lack of faith.

Things He Didn't Do:

- Did not give thanks to God.

- Did not ask God for direction in the use of his increase.

- Did not consider giving a portion to God as thanksgiving.

- Did not consider sharing with others in need.

Things He Did Do:

- He kept it all for himself.

- He only made an effort to store it so he could benefit from it later.

- He only considered how to bless himself with this new wealth.

- He assumed that he would live long enough to carry out his plans.

The greed here is seen in a person already rich welcoming an increase in wealth only as an opportunity to maintain his lifestyle here in the world. The real danger of greed is that it moves us to act in ways that only consider the physical (i.e. more stuff equals more safety, happiness, success) with little or no regard for the spiritual aspect of life.

In verse 21 Jesus makes a comparison:

1. The one that only stores physical wealth is not prepared for death and judgment.

2. The "rich toward God," meaning the one rich and becoming wealthier in the things of God (forgiveness, righteousness, fruit of the Spirit, ministry, etc.), this person is more than ready for death and judgment.

Beatitudes – 12:22-34

This parable naturally leads to a more in-depth discussion of the life led by someone rich towards God. Jesus turns His attention from the question concerning the dispute between the brothers and their inheritance, answered by the parable of the rich fool, and now addresses the crowd in general. Luke records Jesus repeating the lesson on the beatitudes originally found in Matthew's gospel (chapters 5-7), as the way one is to live if he is to be rich towards God.

> For where your treasure is, there your heart will be also.
> - Luke 12:34

Be Ready – 12:35-13:9

Once He has completed the parable and teaching, Jesus follows up with a warning to all present and future disciples that they should always be in a state of readiness.

> [35]"Be dressed in readiness, and keep your lamps lit. [36]Be like men who are waiting for their master when he returns from the wedding feast, so that they may immediately open the door to him when he comes and knocks. [37]Blessed are those slaves whom the master will find on the alert when he comes; truly I say to you, that he will gird himself to serve, and have them recline at the table, and will come up and wait on them. [38]Whether he comes in the second watch, or even in the third, and finds them so, blessed are those slaves.
> - Luke 12:35-38

The following passages describe the reason for and nature of this readiness:

Ready for What and When?

> [39]"But be sure of this, that if the head of the house had known at what hour the thief was coming, he would not have allowed his house to be broken into. [40]You too, be ready; for the Son of Man is coming at an hour that you do not expect."
> - Luke 12:39-40

The coming of Christ will take place at an unknown time. He either comes for us in death, like the rich farmer, or at the end of the world to judge. This is why we need to be in a constant state of readiness.

Ready for Who and Why?

> [41]Peter said, "Lord, are You addressing this parable to us, or to everyone else as well?" [42]And the Lord said, "Who then is the faithful and sensible steward, whom his master will put in charge of his servants, to give them their rations at the proper time? [43]Blessed is that slave whom his master finds so doing when he comes. [44]Truly I say to you that he will put him in charge of all his possessions. [45]But if that slave says in his heart, 'My master will be a long time in coming,' and begins to beat the slaves, both men and women, and to eat and drink and get drunk; [46]the master of that slave will come on a day when he does not expect him and at an hour he does not know, and will cut him in pieces, and assign him a place with the unbelievers. [47]And that slave who knew his master's will and did not get ready or act in accord with his will, will receive many lashes, [48]but the one who did not know it, and committed deeds worthy of a flogging, will receive but few.

> From everyone who has been given much, much
> will be required; and to whom they entrusted much,
> of him they will ask all the more.
> - Luke 12:41-48

Everyone should be ready, but especially those who know that He can come at any time. Non-believers go about their business unaware, but disciples know that Jesus will return at any time for the purpose of judgment, and thus have no excuse. Readiness is important because the judgment brings both reward and punishment. I believe Jesus is referring to disciples here and particularly teachers, elders, preachers and deacons. They are the slaves who have received instruction and have been left as stewards of God's word and His church. They have been given much (spiritual gifts, a calling, a ministry, opportunities for spiritual growth and blessings) and because of this, much will be required of them. This idea is also supported by James:

> Let not many of you become teachers, my
> brethren, knowing that as such we will incur a
> stricter judgment.
> - James 3:1

As to the greater and lesser punishment and rewards, Jesus Himself states that there will be degrees of difference (as does Paul in I Corinthians 3:13-15).

> [13]each man's work will become evident; for the day
> will show it because it is to be revealed with fire,
> and the fire itself will test the quality of each man's
> work. [14]If any man's work which he has built on it
> remains, he will receive a reward. [15]If any man's
> work is burned up, he will suffer loss; but he
> himself will be saved, yet so as through fire.
> - I Corinthians 3:13-15

We do not, however, have any descriptions of what these differences are or will be.

> ⁴⁹"I have come to cast fire upon the earth; and how I wish it were already kindled! ⁵⁰But I have a baptism to undergo, and how distressed I am until it is accomplished! ⁵¹Do you suppose that I came to grant peace on earth? I tell you, no, but rather division; ⁵²for from now on five members in one household will be divided, three against two and two against three. ⁵³They will be divided, father against son and son against father, mother against daughter and daughter against mother, mother-in-law against daughter-in-law and daughter-in-law against mother-in-law."
> - Luke 12:49-53

Here Jesus reveals that the battle will become extremely personal and, as a result, very painful. Your ministry, faith and readiness will be challenged by those of your own household and those you love most here on earth.

> ⁵⁴And He was also saying to the crowds, "When you see a cloud rising in the west, immediately you say, 'A shower is coming,' and so it turns out. ⁵⁵And when you see a south wind blowing, you say, 'It will be a hot day,' and it turns out that way. ⁵⁶You hypocrites! You know how to analyze the appearance of the earth and the sky, but why do you not analyze this present time? ⁵⁷"And why do you not even on your own initiative judge what is right? ⁵⁸For while you are going with your opponent to appear before the magistrate, on your way there make an effort to settle with him, so that he may not drag you before the judge, and the judge turn you over to the officer, and the officer throw you into prison.

> [59]I say to you, you will not get out of there until you
> have paid the very last cent."
> - Luke 12:54-59

The Lord confirms His warning by reminding them to simply read the signs that He has cautioned them about as they appear in the future (opposition, persecution, family division, etc.) and act accordingly by being ready at all times!

Ready How?

The Lord mentions two ways that a disciple can cultivate this state of readiness at all times.

1. Repent

> [1]Now on the same occasion there were some
> present who reported to Him about the Galileans
> whose blood Pilate had mixed with their
> sacrifices. [2]And Jesus said to them, "Do you
> suppose that these Galileans were greater sinners
> than all other Galileans because they suffered this
> fate? [3]I tell you, no, but unless you repent, you will
> all likewise perish. [4]Or do you suppose that those
> eighteen on whom the tower in Siloam fell and
> killed them were worse culprits than all the men
> who live in Jerusalem? [5]I tell you, no, but unless
> you repent, you will all likewise perish."
> - Luke 13:1-4

Repentance is the first step to discipleship and a recurring exercise to produce spiritual growth leading to maturity. Jesus, speaking mainly to the crowd, emphasizes the first and most productive spiritual exercise without which there can be no salvation or subsequent spiritual growth. All need to repent, even Pharisees.

2. Be Productive

> [6]And He began telling this parable: "A man had a fig tree which had been planted in his vineyard; and he came looking for fruit on it and did not find any. [7]And he said to the vineyard-keeper, 'Behold, for three years I have come looking for fruit on this fig tree without finding any. Cut it down! Why does it even use up the ground?' [8]And he answered and said to him, 'Let it alone, sir, for this year too, until I dig around it and put in fertilizer; [9]and if it bears fruit next year, fine; but if not, cut it down.'"
> - Luke 13:6-9

In this parable, the vineyard and tree are the Jewish nation, the vinedresser is Jesus, and the master is the Father bringing judgment. The nation has been receiving care for three years through the steady preaching of John the Baptist followed by Jesus so that it will bear the fruit of repentance because the kingdom is at hand.

The Jews (especially the religious leaders) have rejected both John and Jesus (killing one and planning to kill the other). The judgment on the nation is imminent but Jesus calls for more time (He has not died, resurrected or empowered His Apostles to go preach yet). These events constitute the "extra" year given to see if there will be a harvest of repentance and faith as a result of these efforts. We know from history that the nation, for the most part, did not respond and in 70 AD the judgment of God fell on the city of Jerusalem as the Roman army laid siege to it, killed the inhabitants, burned the city and tore the temple down to ruins (this was represented in the parable by the cutting down of the fig tree).

And so, Jesus completes a section of teaching to His disciples through the use of parables encouraging them to always be ready (by bearing the good fruit of repentance and faith) because He will return to judge when least expected. Within this warning is included an additional prophecy of judgment and punishment on the Jewish Nation (70 AD) for their lack of faith.

Healing on the Sabbath - 13:10-14:6

The next section is built by placing two instances of Jesus healing on the Sabbath on opposite ends with several of His teachings in the middle. It is interesting to note that Luke is the only gospel writer to add these healings to his record.

Healing on the Sabbath (13:10-17)

> [10]And He was teaching in one of the synagogues on the Sabbath. [11]And there was a woman who for eighteen years had had a sickness caused by a spirit; and she was bent double, and could not straighten up at all. [12]When Jesus saw her, He called her over and said to her, "Woman, you are freed from your sickness." [13]And He laid His hands on her; and immediately she was made erect again and began glorifying God.
> - Luke 13:10-13

This woman's main problem was that she was possessed by a demon. The bent over condition she suffered for 18 years was the manifestation of this demon's attack on her body. Jesus releases her from the demon-possession which in turn removes the physical symptom of its presence. She, as a woman of faith (attended synagogue despite her embarrassing symptom), breaks forth in praise to God (He gets the credit as He should).

> But the synagogue official, indignant because Jesus had healed on the Sabbath, began saying to the crowd in response, "There are six days in which work should be done; so come during them and get healed, and not on the Sabbath day."
> - Luke 13:14

The synagogue official could not deny the miracle (he may have even been witness to this woman's suffering for 18 years with no cure), but Jesus' miracle might stir up the crowd and thus jeopardize his position. The word "indignant" refers to an anger caused by some insult or challenge. This woman had suffered for nearly two decades and may have had many prayers offered on her behalf. Jesus now comes and, in an instant, she is healed to the joy and amazement of the congregation.

The official tries to cover his anger and possible envy by citing the rules about medical work. Doctors could attend to emergencies on the Sabbath but not treat various chronic conditions on that day (i.e. no doctor's office hours on the Sabbath).

> [15]But the Lord answered him and said, "You hypocrites, does not each of you on the Sabbath untie his ox or his donkey from the stall and lead him away to water him? [16]And this woman, a daughter of Abraham as she is, whom Satan has bound for eighteen long years, should she not have been released from this bond on the Sabbath day?"
> - Luke 13:15-16

Jesus denounces the hypocrisy of their attitude. It was custom to feed animals on the Sabbath (they had to be untied or released from their pens to do so). Jesus simply equates the two in order to reveal the double standard (free an animal to drink - ok; free a faithful woman from painful bondage - not ok).

> As He said this, all His opponents were being humiliated; and the entire crowd was rejoicing over all the glorious things being done by Him.
> - Luke 13:17

The ordinary people who saw through the hypocritical rules and regulations of the Pharisees, but were afraid to challenge them, rejoiced because someone was finally standing up to these people not just with words but with power! Luke mentions the humiliation of the religious leaders, and as we will see, this incident will fuel their hatred and eventually move them to plot Jesus' death.

Teaching – 13:18-35

Parable of the Mustard Seed and the Leaven (13:18-21)

Previously Jesus had issued warnings about being ready because the kingdom was at hand. Here He provides two brief parables showing what the kingdom is like:

- **Mustard seed and plant:** has dynamic growth and provides room for many to take shelter.
- **Leaven:** its growth is unseen but sure. Its presence affects all of its surroundings.

The Narrow Gate (13:22-30)

Luke adds another teaching portion that is also included in both Matthew and Mark's gospels: the call to enter by the narrow door (gate or way) which is Jesus Himself. This continues to be Jesus' invitation to the people (believe in Him is the way to enter the narrow door/gate/way). This repeated call accomplishes two things:

1. It offers a clear choice to those who see His miracles and hear His teachings.
2. It condemns those who reject Him, especially the religious leaders.

The Lament Over Jerusalem (13:31-35)

Tensions mount as Jesus approaches Jerusalem and the religious leaders try to turn the Lord away by warning Him that Herod means to capture and kill Him. The Lord merely sends a message to the wicked King, telling him that God's plan for Jesus to minister must be fulfilled. In addition to this He tells Herod that He is not worried about being killed here in the outskirts of Jerusalem (Perea) because Jerusalem is where the prophets go to die (this was an observation about the number of past prophets put to death there).

> [34]O Jerusalem, Jerusalem, the city that kills the prophets and stones those sent to her! How often I wanted to gather your children together, just as a hen gathers her brood under her wings, and you would not have it! [35]Behold, your house is left to you desolate; and I say to you, you will not see Me until the time comes when you say, 'Blessed is He who comes in the name of the Lord!'"
> - Luke 13:34-35

Jesus finishes with a sad lament over the suffering that the city and nation will experience because of their rejection of their Messiah (and history bears this out: 70 AD, etc.).

Healing on the Sabbath

> [1]It happened that when He went into the house of one of the leaders of the Pharisees on the Sabbath to eat bread, they were watching Him closely. [2]And there in front of Him was a man suffering from dropsy. [3]And Jesus answered and spoke to the lawyers and Pharisees, saying, "Is it lawful to heal on the Sabbath, or not?" [4]But they kept silent. And He took hold of him and healed him, and sent him away. [5]And He said to them, "Which one of you will have a son or an ox fall into a well, and will not immediately pull him out on a Sabbath day?" [6]And they could make no reply to this.
> - Luke 14:1-6

This is the only instance where the term "dropsy" appears in the entire New Testament. It was a disease we now refer to as edema, which is a swelling of the legs, feet or hands due to excessive fluid in the tissues (also, the only time we see Jesus heal this illness). The scenario is the same as the first healing on the Sabbath, except this one is done in a private home, and no one challenges Him this time.

The fact that it was a Pharisee's house and everyone was watching what Jesus would do with the sick man who was (conveniently) present suggests that this was a set-up to gather eyewitness evidence against the Lord for future use. Note also that the man with dropsy offered no praise or thanksgiving after he was miraculously healed.

Lessons

Jesus is becoming more pointed in His denunciations of the religious leaders, and more adamant in His demand for faithfulness and fruitfulness from His disciples.

Two lessons stand out in this section:

1. No Fruit - No Life

Being alive and remaining alive in Christ requires that we be fruitful in faith, good works, pure living, ministry, etc. There is no neutral gear in Christianity. We are either moving away from something or moving towards something as disciples.

2. The Truth Hurts

The Pharisees were standing right in front of Jesus but their envy and anger stirred up by His teaching and miracles blinded them to the truth that could save them. This same truth that God's word reveals about our lives today is also often painful and embarrassing, however, if we can allow it to lead, heal and inform us, we will grow stronger and more pleasing to God in the process. Spiritual growth can be uncomfortable at times, but it is always worth it.

Discussion Questions

1. In your opinion, what would be the lessons drawn from the parable of the rich fool (bigger barns) for an audience of people who are poor.

2. Explain how repentance and bearing fruit prepares a Christian for the return of Jesus.

3. Describe, in your own words, the work of a minister who would receive many stripes at judgement, and the work of a minister who would receive only a few stripes. What would be the main difference between the two?

CHAPTER 8
JESUS FACING JERUSALEM
- PART 3

LUKE 14:7-17:10

We are in the third of four sections examining the events taking place as Jesus is making His way to Jerusalem. His ministry up unto this point has mainly been in Galilee, close to His home in Capernaum; but the time of the Lord's ultimate rejection and crucifixion is at hand and so He makes His way to Jerusalem to face the mounting hostility of the religious leaders located there. This is seen in their attempts to denounce Him for healing people on the Sabbath.

In this section, Luke records a string of episodes where Jesus uses both parables and conventional teaching to instruct the people about the kingdom and other topics. Several of these are only found in Luke.

Parables About Dinners and Dinner Guests – 14:7-24

Since much of the socializing at that time was done over food, Jesus gives three parables: one concerning the guests, another about the host and one about the dinner itself.

Parable of the Dinner Guests

All three of these parables are about various aspects of the kingdom of God. In other parables (i.e. talents, Matthew 25:14-30) the main message was that the kingdom was at hand or the return of the king of the kingdom was unknown so one needed to be ready (faithful, productive, pure, etc.). In these parables, Jesus focuses on the attitude of the host and the guests.

> [7]And He began speaking a parable to the invited guests when He noticed how they had been picking out the places of honor at the table, saying to them, [8]"When you are invited by someone to a wedding feast, do not take the place of honor, for someone more distinguished than you may have been invited by him, [9]and he who invited you both will come and say to you, 'Give your place to this man,' and then in disgrace you proceed to occupy the last place. [10]But when you are invited, go and recline at the last place, so that when the one who has invited you comes, he may say to you, 'Friend, move up higher'; then you will have honor in the sight of all who are at the table with you. [11]For everyone who exalts himself will be humbled, and he who humbles himself will be exalted."
> - Luke 14:7-11

This parable springs from what Jesus was actually witnessing as people scrambled for honored positions at the feast He was attending. The story explains itself and its message is a familiar one: that in the kingdom, the humble are exalted and the proud brought low (i.e. Matthew 23:12). This is also an indirect denunciation of the religious leaders who, unlike the ordinary people, were too proud to receive Jesus, even with the testimony of His miracles.

This is one of the parables unique to Luke's gospel.

Parable/Instruction to the Host (14:12-15)

As a follow-up, Jesus addresses not only His host, but all those who practice hospitality.

> [12]And He also went on to say to the one who had invited Him, "When you give a luncheon or a dinner, do not invite your friends or your brothers or your relatives or rich neighbors, otherwise they may also invite you in return and that will be your repayment. [13]But when you give a reception, invite the poor, the crippled, the lame, the blind, [14]and you will be blessed, since they do not have the means to repay you; for you will be repaid at the resurrection of the righteous."
> - Luke 14:12-14

The way that the guests jostled for position suggests that they were not among the poor and disadvantaged. Hospitality is a mark of one who is part of the kingdom, however, kingdom-type hospitality is different in that it aims to serve others, not self. The difference in attitudes reflects the different objectives.

1. A self-serving attitude uses hospitality as a way to advance one's position socially or tactically.

2. Those who serve others through hospitality do so to advance the growth of God's kingdom here on earth and receive a blessing for their efforts.

> When one of those who were reclining at the table with Him heard this, he said to Him, "Blessed is everyone who will eat bread in the kingdom of God!"
> - Luke 14:15

This comment serves as an "Amen" statement to what Jesus has just said, and a bridge to the third parable about the kingdom using the story of a dinner. It implicitly asks the question, "Who will be worthy to participate in the kingdom's feast?"

Parable of the Dinner (14:16-24)

This parable summarizes the situation taking place as Jesus approaches Jerusalem and what awaits Him there. In the parable:

- The host is God.
- The dinner is the gospel message leading one into the kingdom.
- The lone slave sent to invite is Jesus.
- The original guests are the Jews, especially the religious leaders.
- The poor, lame and blind in the city are the ordinary Jews among the common people.
- The ones out on the highways (roads and hedges) are the Gentiles.

In this parable, Jesus summarizes His ministry to date, the initial response to it and its eventual outcome.

1. Ministry to Date and Response

Jesus preached and performed miracles to prove that He was the Messiah and the kingdom of God had arrived. The religious leaders, who should have been the first to realize and accept this, did not. Their response was similar to the guests who found all sorts of excuses to avoid the dinner. In the same way these men found all manner of ways to discredit, attack and finally have Jesus arrested and executed.

2. Outcome

The majority of Jesus' followers were ordinary people (then and now) and eventually the meal (message) intended first for the Jews was spread successfully among the Gentiles.

In His final injunction, Jesus warns the people who refuse to believe (like those who were first invited) that they will not enjoy the rewards of the kingdom. Faith will always be required to experience (taste) the kingdom of God.

Test of Discipleship – Luke 14:25-35

These parables lead to a discussion about discipleship and its demands (mentioned in both Matthew and Mark). Jesus leaves no doubt that disciples must renounce everything they own, not in order to practice humility or asceticism, but to learn the lesson of trusting in Him. In his commentary, R.C.H. Lenski says that what Jesus requires is that His disciples abandon their reliance on what they possess to either save them or do God's work in establishing the kingdom.

This passage is often used to make the point that would-be disciples need to "count the cost" before deciding to follow Jesus. This is a natural lesson stemming from Jesus' words here, however, making the point that we must give up all we have in order to be true disciples is not what Jesus is getting at. What we must consider before becoming disciples is that no matter what we possess, it isn't enough to pay for our sins; we have to completely rely on Jesus for this. In addition, we cannot become faithful and fruitful disciples based solely on what we possess (skill, experience, etc.). Again, we need the spiritual gifts and help that only Jesus can provide in order to succeed and be fruitful in ministry.

> So then, none of you can be My disciple who does not give up all his own possessions.
> - Luke 14:33

You don't have to become poor to be a disciple, you have to give up self-reliance to become a disciple.

> [34]"Therefore, salt is good; but if even salt has become tasteless, with what will it be

> seasoned? [35]It is useless either for the soil or for
> the manure pile; it is thrown out. He who has ears
> to hear, let him hear."
> - Luke 14:34-35

Jesus concludes by comparing disciples to salt. He points out that salt is useless if it loses its saltiness. In the same way disciples become useless if they stop acting like disciples. The Lord cautions us to first consider the cost of discipleship (one must abandon self-reliance) and then establishes the length of our service as disciples (for life). The one purpose of salt is its saltiness, and the one purpose of disciples is faithfulness. If salt loses its saltiness it loses its value and in the same way, a disciple who becomes unfaithful loses his essential value in Christ.

Lost and Found Parables – 15:1-32

The Lost Sheep, The Lost Coin (15:1-10)

> [1]Now all the tax collectors and the sinners were
> coming near Him to listen to Him. [2]Both the
> Pharisees and the scribes began to grumble,
> saying, "This man receives sinners and eats with
> them." [3]So He told them this parable, saying,
> - Luke 15:1-3

Luke changes the scene at this point and sets up the occasion for the presentation of three parables concerning things lost and found. These three are given as a response to the criticism He was receiving from the religious leaders because He not only ministered to sinners and tax collectors (outcasts) with His teaching (which they eagerly sought), but He also ate with them, as He did with the Pharisees, from time to time. The religious leaders considered these people a lost cause. Jesus, on the other hand, preached the gospel to these outcasts and mixed with them socially.

The first two parables (lost sheep and coin) are examples of the natural human desire to diligently seek for a precious thing that has been lost, and the joy one experiences when it is found. Each parable has a happy ending as both sheep and coin are located. Both parables explain why Jesus bothers making an effort to reach these "outcasts" (that are written off as not worth the effort by the religious leaders). In God's eyes the lost are still precious and the effort made to find them is worthwhile.

Jesus speaks as one who is witness to what takes place in heaven (what He says here is not a quote from an Old Testament prophet, it is a revelation from a heavenly witness).

> [7]I tell you that in the same way, there will be more joy in heaven over one sinner who repents than over ninety-nine righteous persons who need no repentance.
> [10]In the same way, I tell you, there is joy in the presence of the angels of God over one sinner who repents."
> - Luke 15:7-10

Jesus is teaching them the reason why He ministers to all (including the outcasts). Every soul is precious to God and worthy of being sought after and saved! The religious leaders placed a different value on each person based on such earthly criteria as family, education, position, wealth and culture (i.e. Jews = greatest / Gentiles = least). Jesus' parable taught that each soul had equal value (because each soul was created in the image of God, not man - Genesis 1:26).

The Lost Son (15:11-32)

After two parables about lost objects, Jesus steps up His imagery about lost and found and tells the story of the lost son. In this parable, He will include characters that represent each person present at the telling of the story: Himself, the outcasts, the religious leaders and how each plays a part in the lost/found scenario.

> [11]And He said, "A man had two sons. [12]The younger of them said to his father, 'Father, give me the share of the estate that falls to me.' So he divided his wealth between them. [13]And not many days later, the younger son gathered everything together and went on a journey into a distant country, and there he squandered his estate with loose living. [14]Now when he had spent everything, a severe famine occurred in that country, and he began to be impoverished. [15]So he went and hired himself out to one of the citizens of that country, and he sent him into his fields to feed swine. [16]And he would have gladly filled his stomach with the pods that the swine were eating, and no one was giving anything to him. [17]But when he came to his senses, he said, 'How many of my father's hired men have more than enough bread, but I am dying here with hunger! [18]I will get up and go to my father, and will say to him, "Father, I have sinned against heaven, and in your sight; [19]I am no longer worthy to be called your son; make me as one of your hired men."' [20]So he got up and came to his father. But while he was still a long way off, his father saw him and felt compassion for him, and ran and embraced him and kissed him. [21]And the son said to him, 'Father, I have sinned against heaven and in your sight; I am no longer worthy to be called your son.' [22]But the father said to his slaves, 'Quickly bring out the best robe and put it on him, and put a ring on his hand and sandals on his feet; [23]and bring the fattened calf, kill it, and let us eat and celebrate; [24]for this son of mine was dead and has come to life again; he was lost and has been found.' And they began to celebrate.
> - Luke 15:11-24

The parable of the Prodigal Son only appears in Luke's gospel and is probably one of the best known of all the parables. In this story what is "lost" is this young man's soul. He goes from being acceptable and safe in his father's house to becoming an outcast through his own sinfulness and foolishness. There is no searching here because unlike objects (sheep and coins), he has free will. His choices led to his lostness and his own choices will be what bring him back.

The father represents the heavenly Father who is present in the form of Jesus. Just as Jesus ministered to and associated with the outcasts, the father waits for his son and receives him back into the family when he returns. What he lost (his younger son) has returned to him and he rejoices.

> [25]"Now his older son was in the field, and when he came and approached the house, he heard music and dancing. [26]And he summoned one of the servants and began inquiring what these things could be. [27]And he said to him, 'Your brother has come, and your father has killed the fattened calf because he has received him back safe and sound.' [28]But he became angry and was not willing to go in; and his father came out and began pleading with him. [29]But he answered and said to his father, 'Look! For so many years I have been serving you and I have never neglected a command of yours; and yet you have never given me a young goat, so that I might celebrate with my friends; [30]but when this son of yours came, who has devoured your wealth with prostitutes, you killed the fattened calf for him.' [31]And he said to him, 'Son, you have always been with me, and all that is mine is yours. [32]But we had to celebrate and rejoice, for this brother of yours was dead and has begun to live, and was lost and has been found.'"
> - Luke 15:15-32

The older son personifies the Jewish leaders. True to the tradition, legalistic in following the rules, working for a reward, but no inward faith and love for God which would produce a kind and merciful attitude towards others.

The parable accurately describes the two sons (groups) Jesus dealt with: the outcasts who sought reconciliation and the religious leaders who refused to see their need. Both sons were "lost" but for different reasons:

- One for dissipation and immorality.
- One for self-righteous pride.

The sad reality was that only one of the sons was eventually found.

Parable of the Unjust Steward (16:1-18)

Although the parables have different characters and storylines, they all have a common thread: a condemnation of the attitudes and actions of the Pharisees and other Jewish religious leaders. The parable of the unjust steward is no exception to this pattern. It describes a steward (manager) who is audited and about to lose his job because of waste and mismanagement. Before he leaves he reduces the amount owed by his employer's customers in order to gain favor with them after he is fired. Jesus doesn't condone his conduct, but remarks that the steward's actions to save his own skin was shrewd in a worldly way. The Lord provides a parallel for disciples.

> And I say to you, make friends for yourselves by means of the wealth of unrighteousness, so that when it fails, they will receive you into the eternal dwellings.
> - Luke 16:9

In the same way, disciples should use earthly wealth to make "friends" or converts among the poor and outcast. This is so that when earthly wealth is no longer useful (at death) they will be welcomed in heaven because of the way they used their earthly riches to win souls. The idea being that the converts made here on earth through the wise use of physical resources will be in heaven to welcome and thank the faithful disciples who won them over for Christ.

This parable naturally leads to an admonition about the actual use of worldly wealth. The parable showed an unrighteous person using wealth in a shrewd, self-serving way. In the admonition Jesus instructs His disciples about the proper attitude towards earthly wealth. He also adds a warning about the impossibility of trying to pursue both wealth and discipleship as equal priorities because they demand opposite things.

> No servant can serve two masters; for either he will hate the one and love the other, or else he will be devoted to one and despise the other. You cannot serve God and wealth."
> - Luke 16:13

The Pharisees, hearing this teaching, dismiss Jesus and what He has said concerning worldly riches. This they do because the Lord has perfectly described their own greedy attitude about money. In response to their mocking, Jesus rebukes them:

> [15]And He said to them, "You are those who justify yourselves in the sight of men, but God knows your hearts; for that which is highly esteemed among men is detestable in the sight of God. [16]"The Law and the Prophets were proclaimed until John; since that time the gospel of the kingdom of God has been preached, and everyone is forcing his way into it. [17]But it is easier for heaven and earth to pass away than for one stroke of a letter of the Law to fail. [18]"Everyone who divorces his wife and marries another commits adultery,

and he who marries one who is divorced from a
husband commits adultery.
- Luke 16:15-18

1. He condemns them as religious hypocrites who hide
    their greed behind the cloak of religious self-
    righteousness.

2. He reminds them that now is the time of salvation and
    even though they are not entering the kingdom, others
    are (the outcasts).

3. They skirted the Law and watered down many of its
    provisions in order to claim personal righteousness
    based on obedience to the Law. For example, they
    would divorce their wives for no proper reason and claim
    that they were innocent of any wrong doing because
    they fulfilled the requirement established by Moses of
    giving their wives a legal "bill of divorcement." In other
    words they claimed innocence because they had
    provided the proper paperwork for the divorce!

Jesus reminds them that they had no power or authority to
change or water down the Law because the Law, unlike the
material world, never fails or changes. He then applies the
Law to their illegitimate divorces thus condemning them and
demonstrating the power of God's word. In this instance, He
is not providing in depth teaching about marriage and
divorce (as He does in Matthew 5:31-32; 19:3-9; Mark 10:1-
12). He is, however, making a simple and quick rebuke of
these religious leaders for their disregard of the permanence
of marriage (i.e. they divorced for no reason, and at times
remarried each other's wives - Lenski, p. 843-845).

Parable of the Rich Man and Lazarus (16:19-17:10)

After a pause, during which Jesus addresses the Pharisees
directly (verses 14-18), the Lord recounts a second parable
dealing with wealth and the dangers attached to it. This time
it is not about the dishonest use of wealth for personal gain
(unjust steward) but the love of and reliance on wealth that
leads to greed and selfishness.

A rich man ignores a poor and sick man who is laid at his door. Both die and the poor man goes to heaven while the rich one goes to hell. These two have a dialogue where the rich man begs for relief for his suffering and asks that a message be sent to warn his brothers about the suffering he is experiencing. These are refused. The parable has several lessons:

- The rich man was not condemned for his wealth, he was condemned for his selfishness and lack of faith.

- There is both life and joy, or suffering after death. Some think this is a lesson on the afterlife, others only see it as a parable; either way it teaches the same lessons.

- Faith expressed in love is what saves us. The rich man wanted an angel to warn his family and is told that if they didn't believe Moses (the witness sent by God to preach, lead and warn the Jews) then they will not believe an additional witness, even if He is raised from the dead. This was to be true of most Jews when the Apostles began preaching about Jesus and His resurrection.

The Lord wraps up His teaching through parables with a final warning and instruction to His disciples.

> [1]He said to His disciples, "It is inevitable that stumbling blocks come, but woe to him through whom they come! [2]It would be better for him if a millstone were hung around his neck and he were thrown into the sea, than that he would cause one of these little ones to stumble.
> - Luke 17:1-2

The Warning
The only thing worse than not having faith yourself is blocking others from coming to faith. This was something that the religious leaders were becoming guilty of.

The Instructions

Jesus closes out His teaching with admonitions to His followers about their life as disciples and what this life consisted of:

1. **Love**: Their love would be proven in the way they treated one another (with grace and mercy).

2. **Faith**: A strong faith believed and lived with the understanding that with God, all things were possible.

3. **Humility**: A recognition that one's true and most blessed position in life was as a servant of God.

These attitudes were in stark contrast to the character and practice of the religious leaders who had scoffed at and rejected Jesus, and had earned His condemnation as a result.

Lesson

If there is any one lesson we can draw from this varied mix of parables and teachings it is this: The key to the meaning of the text is usually contained in the text itself. In this section there are only four main characters: Jesus, outcasts, disciples and the religious leaders. All the conclusions, object lessons and applications must first be tied to one of these before any other lesson can be drawn accurately and contextually.

Discussion Questions

1. In today's society, who do you think are they equivalents of the following Bible characters? Why do you believe that these people fit the description?

   o Jesus

   o Religious Leaders

   o Outcasts / Sinners

   o Disciples

2. In the parable of the prodigal son, do you believe that the anger of the older brother was justified? Why? Why Not?

   o If you were the father what would you say to the older brother to make him come in to the feast?

CHAPTER 9
JESUS FACING JERUSALEM
- PART 4

LUKE 17:11-18:30

It would be good at this point to review our outline for Luke's gospel so we can situate this chapter's material in the context of the entire book of Luke. In other words, where are we so far?

1. The Beginning – 1:1-3:38
2. Jesus in Galilee – 4:1-9:50
3. **Jesus Facing Jerusalem – 9:51-18:30**
4. Jesus Entering Jerusalem – 18:31-21:38
5. The Consummation – 22:1-24:53

In the previous section, Jesus was giving instructions to His disciples concerning a variety of topics pursuant to the life of discipleship. In the section following, the author finishes with the events taking place as Jesus slowly makes His way towards the outskirts and eventually into the city of Jerusalem itself. Luke notes this fact as he prefaces the encounters with various people along the way with a reminder of where Jesus and the Apostles are geographically.

> While He was on the way to Jerusalem, He was
> passing between Samaria and Galilee.
> - Luke 17:11

The Ten Lepers Cleansed – 17:12-19

> [12]As He entered a village, ten leprous men who
> stood at a distance met Him; [13]and they raised
> their voices, saying, "Jesus, Master, have mercy
> on us!"
> - Luke 17:12-13

Leprosy is an ancient disease mentioned in both the Old and New Testaments (from a Greek word meaning a fish scale or to peel). It was what we refer to today as Hansen's disease, a term given to it in 1873 in honor of the doctor who discovered that this illness was caused by a bacterium that attacked the nervous system. People with leprosy experience disfigurement of the skin and bones as well as the twisting of their limbs and the curling of their fingers which in many cases forms a claw-like hand. The largest number of deformities that these people suffer are the result of accidents that occur because lepers eventually lose the ability to feel pain due to extensive nerve damage (e.g. inattentive sufferers can cut themselves or grasp a cup of boiling water without any sensation of pain). Leprosy, like tuberculosis to which it is related, is contagious and spreads by contact with infected skin or secretions from one suffering from this disease.

Even though all of this was not known in New Testament times, lepers were nevertheless separated from the general population and were considered as already dead from a religious perspective. Contact with them rendered one ceremonially unclean (just as contact with a dead person or animal would), and that person had to undergo a purification process before he could return to normal social interaction and worship at the temple. Lepers had to live outside the towns and villages in make-shift shelters. This explains why these men cried out to Jesus on His way into the village. Notice that their request is not for money but for mercy. They were forced to live outside of society but they knew what was going on in the society they were forbidden to interact with.

Unlike those who had access to Jesus (priests, lawyers, normal Jews) who debated His claims and refused to believe His words, these sad and desperate men, knowing what He had done for others, appealed to Him for mercy and healing.

> When He saw them, He said to them, "Go and show yourselves to the priests." And as they were going, they were cleansed.
> - Luke 17:14

The instruction to go see the priest was the proper procedure for one who had been healed or experienced a remission of the disease they were suffering from.

> And He ordered him to tell no one, "But go and show yourself to the priest and make an offering for your cleansing, just as Moses commanded, as a testimony to them."
> - Luke 5:14

Jesus describes the procedure that they needed to undergo (examination by a priest) in order to confirm that their healing was legitimate. Once done, they could then reenter normal society and participate in public worship in the synagogue and at the temple.

The important point to note here is that they were healed only after they made a move to see the priests, not before. The lepers cried out in faith and Jesus answered by giving them a test of faith. Jesus can heal or save without a test of faith (He knows if we truly believe or not). This test of faith, however, served two purposes:

1. It confirmed in the minds of the lepers that their faith in Jesus had been rewarded with this miracle.

2. The test also demonstrated that living faith (to heal, to save, to serve, etc.) is seen in action, not simply assent. A person believes and expresses that belief with action.

> You have faith and I have works; show me your faith without the works and I will show you my faith by my works.
> - James 2:18

> [15]Now one of them, when he saw that he had been healed, turned back, glorifying God with a loud voice, [16]and he fell on his face at His feet, giving thanks to Him. And he was a Samaritan. [17]Then Jesus answered and said, "Were there not ten cleansed? But the nine—where are they? [18]Was no one found who returned to give glory to God, except this foreigner?" [19]And He said to him, "Stand up and go; your faith has made you well."
> - Luke 17:15-19

There were ten lepers and one of these was a Samaritan (apparently, the division between Jew and Samaritan was forgotten as they shared a common disease). Of the ten, only the Samaritan returns to first give thanks to Jesus before going to the priests for confirmation and reestablishment. The way he does so indicates not only his gratitude, but also his reverence and devotion towards Jesus. We see this poor suffering soul put off his social redemption in order to thank and pay homage to the One that healed him.

Jesus states the obvious, *"Where are the others, has only this Samaritan come to give thanks?"* In responding to the Samaritan leper's demonstration of gratitude and honor, the Lord comments on the different results each would experience:

1. The nine asked for and received the healing, and were on the road to social acceptance and a normal life.

2. The Samaritan asked for and received the healing, however, because of his response to Christ, he was not only on the road to physical normalcy but to eternal life as well.

This scene also serves as a living prophecy concerning how the gospel will be accepted by both Jews and Gentiles. The healing of the nine Jews represents the blessings and opportunities the Jewish nation had in receiving Jesus as their Messiah. And yet, despite the Law, prophets, temple, miracles and that Jesus was one of them - the Jews rejected Him. Out of nine healed lepers, not one came back to thank or acknowledge the Lord. The lone Samaritan represents the Gentiles who, despite the odds (believing in a foreign Savior from a people who despised them), nevertheless embraced Christianity in great numbers.

This living parable, therefore, points not only to the rejection that Jesus will soon face in Jerusalem, but the eventual rejection of the gospel by the Jews and its acceptance by the Gentiles in the decades and centuries to follow.

Second Coming Foretold – 17:20-37

Both Matthew and Mark record Jesus' teaching on the coming of the kingdom, an issue brought up by the questions of the Pharisees:

> [20]Now having been questioned by the Pharisees as to when the kingdom of God was coming, He answered them and said, "The kingdom of God is not coming with signs to be observed; [21]nor will they say, 'Look, here it is!' or, 'There it is!' For behold, the kingdom of God is in your midst."
> - Luke 17:20-21

They had witnessed Jesus' works and knew that the Messiah would be revealed by great power and miracles, but they did not see the signs of the kingdom that they thought would appear when the Messiah came:

- Renewed political power
- Freedom from Roman domination
- Prosperity

'If you are the Messiah," they said, "where and when is your kingdom supposed to arrive?"

Jesus tells them that the kingdom cannot be seen according to their physical criteria and it was already among them, embodied in Himself and His disciples.

In verses 22-37 Jesus provides another proof of His divinity and legitimacy as the Messiah. He does this by prophesying concerning the manner of His death and the subsequent destruction of the nation some 40 years into the future. He also answers their question about the arrival of the kingdom. They were asking for recognizable signs of the kingdom (thinking that the kingdom would be a local, cultural and political event). Jesus responds that when the kingdom (meaning the fulfillment of the kingdom occurring at the end of the world when He would return; not the arrival of the kingdom, which had already taken place with His first appearance), when the fulfillment would come, no one would miss it. He compares it to a lightning strike, a natural phenomenon clearly and easily seen by everyone.

> But first He must suffer many things and be
> rejected by this generation.
> - Luke 17:25

In verse 25 He not only prophesizes about His own death but provides the reason these Jews missed the initial coming of the kingdom in their own time... they rejected its king!

In the rest of the passage (verses 26-37), He contrasts believers and non-believers, and what happens when the kingdom is fulfilled at the judgment (one is taken to heaven with Jesus; one is left to face judgment). There is no mysterious event that sees people disappearing leaving pots boiling on stoves or empty cars on highways because the faithful have been miraculously whisked away while others are left to continue here on earth (images popularized by books and movies based on the "Rapture"). These verses are simply a warning that along with the kingdom comes a judgment that will separate those who will be in that kingdom from those who will not.

The Apostles, still not clear about this topic, ask the Lord where this will happen and Jesus answers,

> And answering they said to Him, "Where, Lord?"
> And He said to them, "Where the body is, there also the vultures will be gathered.
> - Luke 17:37

The judgment, He says, is not a matter of "where" but of what: the dead (unbelievers) are destroyed (vultures=hell).

Parables on Prayer - 18:1-17

> Now He was telling them a parable to show that at all times they ought to pray and not to lose heart,
> - Luke 18:1

After the teaching on the kingdom and dire warnings using language they couldn't quite understand, not to mention Jesus predicting His own imminent death, the disciples are in need of encouragement and the Lord provides it in the form of teaching on prayer. These parables did not provide instructions on the words to use or topics to pray for but rather the attitudes one should have to succeed in prayer.

Success in prayer is that you receive an answer of some kind.

These two parables describe three attitudes necessary to succeed in prayer:

1. Perseverance

> [2]saying, "In a certain city there was a judge who did not fear God and did not respect man. [3]There was a widow in that city, and she kept coming to him, saying, 'Give me legal protection from my opponent.' [4]For a while he was unwilling; but afterward he said to himself, 'Even though I do not fear God nor respect man, [5]yet because this widow bothers me, I will give her legal protection, otherwise by continually coming she will wear me out.'" [6]And the Lord said, "Hear what the unrighteous judge said; [7]now, will not God bring about justice for His elect who cry to Him day and night, and will He delay long over them? [8]I tell you that He will bring about justice for them quickly. However, when the Son of Man comes, will He find faith on the earth?"
> - Luke 18:2-8

This parable is not about the qualifications of judges and how they should help those in need, etc. There is only one point to the parable: persistence pays off. Jesus' question at the end is an admonition to those in the future. Will believers continue to pray, even to the end when I return? He leaves the answer to that question up to every generation that reads this parable.

2. Humility

> [9]And He also told this parable to some people who trusted in themselves that they were righteous, and viewed others with contempt: [10]"Two men went up

> into the temple to pray, one a Pharisee and the other a tax collector. [11]The Pharisee stood and was praying this to himself: 'God, I thank You that I am not like other people: swindlers, unjust, adulterers, or even like this tax collector. [12]I fast twice a week; I pay tithes of all that I get.' [13]But the tax collector, standing some distance away, was even unwilling to lift up his eyes to heaven, but was beating his breast, saying, 'God, be merciful to me, the sinner!' [14]I tell you, this man went to his house justified rather than the other; for everyone who exalts himself will be humbled, but he who humbles himself will be exalted."
> - Luke 18:9-14

This parable is unique to Luke's gospel. The story is easy enough to understand because the characters are boldly drawn. One is proud, self-sufficient and arrogant. The other penitent, sincere and humble.

The humble man (like the poor widow in the previous parable) receives a reward as a result of his attitude in prayer, not the length or style of prayer offered. Those who persist in humble prayer (the action and the attitude) will succeed.

3. Innocence

The third lesson on prayer is not given as a parable but as the detail information about Jesus' busy public ministry.

> [15]And they were bringing even their babies to Him so that He would touch them, but when the disciples saw it, they began rebuking them. [16]But Jesus called for them, saying, "Permit the children to come to Me, and do not hinder them, for the kingdom of God belongs to such as these. [17]Truly I say to you, whoever does not receive the kingdom of God like a child will not enter it at all."
> - Luke 18:15-17

This scene supplies one other attitude for successful prayer: innocence. Not innocence because we have no sin, innocence in that our hearts and minds are free from self-justification, blame, pretentious words or arguments. Prayers like this are heard, Jesus said, because these are the people and prayers that populate the kingdom.

Parable of the Rich Young Ruler – 18:18-30

[18]A ruler questioned Him, saying, "Good Teacher, what shall I do to inherit eternal life?" [19]And Jesus said to him, "Why do you call Me good? No one is good except God alone. [20]You know the commandments, 'Do not commit adultery, Do not murder, Do not steal, Do not bear false witness, Honor your father and mother.'" [21]And he said, "All these things I have kept from my youth." [22]When Jesus heard this, He said to him, "One thing you still lack; sell all that you possess and distribute it to the poor, and you shall have treasure in heaven; and come, follow Me." [23]But when he had heard these things, he became very sad, for he was extremely rich. [24]And Jesus looked at him and said, "How hard it is for those who are wealthy to enter the kingdom of God! [25]For it is easier for a camel to go through the eye of a needle than for a rich man to enter the kingdom of God." [26]They who heard it said, "Then who can be saved?" [27]But He said, "The things that are impossible with people are possible with God."
- Luke 18:18-27

Both Mark and Matthew include this parable about not only the importance of becoming a disciple but the high cost of doing so. Note that Jesus is not adding a requirement to becoming His disciple (i.e. give away all personal goods and wealth). We know that this is so because in every other instance where people are obeying the gospel, this requirement is never mentioned (i.e. 3000 baptized on Pentecost Sunday, Acts 2:38). However, for this particular man, giving away his wealth was necessary because it was getting in the way of what he wanted: assurance that he was "perfect" and acceptable before God.

> Jesus said to him, "If you wish to be complete (perfect)...
> - Matthew 19:21

He had relied on his wealth and position as security that he was acceptable before God (because many Jews believed that personal wealth was a definite sign that God favored you over others). And yet, despite having it all, he didn't "feel" acceptable, perfect or secure in his spirit; so he comes to Jesus to find out what he needed to "add" (a rule, an insight, a practice or ritual) in order to be sure. Jesus surprises him by telling him that if he wanted completeness, wholeness and assurance, he needed to remove something, not add something. He needed to remove the wealth that was blocking him from depending completely on Jesus for his salvation, righteousness and assurance. The fact that he refused shows how trapped he was in his wealth. It owned him, he did not own it.

Jesus uses this scene to warn His disciples about the limiting of spiritual vision and life caused by worldliness and the pursuit of wealth. It is hard for a rich person to go to heaven because amassing wealth:

1. Takes up most of our time and attention.

2. Often tempts us to compromise what is good and right for what is profitable.

3. Draws us towards people who also love and seek wealth.

Needless to say, none of these things promote spiritual vision or practice because we are continually focused on shiny new and expensive things here below, not the things of light that are above. Unfortunately a moment comes when (like the young man who came to Jesus), we have to choose: God or wealth; and for those who love money, the choice will always be money.

> [28]Peter said, "Behold, we have left our own homes and followed You." [29]And He said to them, "Truly I say to you, there is no one who has left house or wife or brothers or parents or children, for the sake of the kingdom of God, [30]who will not receive many times as much at this time and in the age to come, eternal life."
> - Luke 18:28-30

Peter's question permits Jesus to reassure His disciples that whatever they have given up in order to follow Him will be returned to them in abundance, along with the eternal life sought after by the rich young ruler.

He does not give any details here, but I think that all those who have come to Christ as adults or from another faith can vouch for this. My family, to this day, won't have much to do with my wife, Lise, or myself since we became Christians, however, I can't even number the homes of brothers and sisters in Christ in this and other countries where we would be warmly welcomed as Christian family.

The wealthy have much to enjoy and look forward to (in this world) as they watch their riches grow and contemplate the things these will buy and enable them to do. Jesus, on the other hand, offers to all the reward of Christian fellowship and ministry in this world and eternal life in the next (something money can't buy).

Discussion Questions

1. If the lepers in this story had AIDS instead of leprosy, how would Jesus have dealt with them? Why?

2. If God knows that our faith is sincere (because He sees our hearts) why should He require an outward expression of faith?

3. We see in the parable of the Rich Young Ruler how wealth can be an obstacle to faith, can this be true of poverty also? Explain how and ways to overcome these obstacles to faith.

CHAPTER 10
JESUS ENTERS JERUSALEM
- PART 1

LUKE 18:31-19:48

We now begin the fourth part in our outline of Luke's gospel record:

1. The Beginning – 1:1-3:38
2. Jesus in Galilee – 4:1-9:50
3. Jesus Facing Jerusalem – 9:51-18-30
4. **Jesus Entering Jerusalem – 18:31-21:38**
5. The Consummation – 22:1-24:53

Until this point Jesus' teachings, miracles and confrontations have occurred at places outside of Jerusalem. In the next section of Luke's account, he will describe events taking place as Jesus and the Apostles are in the vicinity of Jerusalem and preparing to enter in.

Jesus Enters Jerusalem – 18:31-19:48

Jesus and the Apostles are now close to the city and the Lord prepares His Apostles for what will take place there.

Jesus Prophesizes His Death and Resurrection

[31]Then He took the twelve aside and said to them, "Behold, we are going up to Jerusalem, and all things which are written through the prophets about the Son of Man will be accomplished. [32]For He will be handed over to the Gentiles, and will be mocked and mistreated and spit upon, [33]and after they have scourged Him, they will kill Him; and the third day He will rise again." [34]But the disciples understood none of these things, and the meaning of this statement was hidden from them, and they did not comprehend the things that were said.
- Luke 18:31-35

Jesus gives the Apostles more details concerning what will take place once they enter the city as all the prophesies concerning His treatment by the Jews will be fulfilled.

Jesus' triumphal entry

Rejoice greatly, O daughter of Zion!
Shout in triumph, O daughter of Jerusalem!
Behold, your king is coming to you;
He is just and endowed with salvation,
Humble, and mounted on a donkey,
Even on a colt, the foal of a donkey.
- Zechariah 9:9

Rejection by leaders

[22]The stone which the builders rejected
Has become the chief corner stone.
[23]This is the Lord's doing;
It is marvelous in our eyes.
- Psalms 118:22-23

Betrayal by Judas

> Even my close friend in whom I trusted,
> Who ate my bread,
> Has lifted up his heel against me.
> - Psalms 41:9

Suffering and humiliation

> [7]All who see me sneer at me;
> They separate with the lip, they wag the head, saying,
> [8]"Commit yourself to the Lord; let Him deliver him;
> Let Him rescue him, because He delights in him."
> - Psalms 22:7-8

Resurrection

> [9]Therefore my heart is glad and my glory rejoices;
> My flesh also will dwell securely.
> [10]For You will not abandon my soul to Sheol;
> Nor will You allow Your Holy One to undergo decay.
> - Psalms 16:9-10

Reason for the cross

> But He was pierced through for our transgressions,
> He was crushed for our iniquities;
> The chastening for our well-being fell upon Him,
> And by His scourging we are healed.
> - Isaiah 53:5

There are many more, but these demonstrate the point Jesus was making to the Apostles: that everything He is telling them about His treatment at the hands of the Jews will happen to Him, and all prophesies concerning His death and resurrection will be fulfilled.

In verse 34, Luke states that the Apostles did not understand what Jesus was saying since the meaning was hidden from them. It could be that as in the case of John the Baptist, they assumed that when Jesus entered Jerusalem He would be hailed by everyone great and small; or, if rejected, a judgment would immediately come upon His enemies. Jesus was preparing them for a time when neither of these things would happen. The end result would be what the psalmists and prophets spoke of long ago: the Messiah would be rejected, tortured and executed, but would "rise again" on the third day.

Jesus Heals Blind Bartimaeus

> [35]As Jesus was approaching Jericho, a blind man was sitting by the road begging. [36]Now hearing a crowd going by, he began to inquire what this was. [37]They told him that Jesus of Nazareth was passing by. [38]And he called out, saying, "Jesus, Son of David, have mercy on me!" [39]Those who led the way were sternly telling him to be quiet; but he kept crying out all the more, "Son of David, have mercy on me!" [40]And Jesus stopped and commanded that he be brought to Him; and when he came near, He questioned him, [41]"What do you want Me to do for you?" And he said, "Lord, I want to regain my sight!" [42]And Jesus said to him, "Receive your sight; your faith has made you well." [43]Immediately he regained his sight and began following Him, glorifying God; and when all the people saw it, they gave praise to God.
> - Luke 18:35-43

Luke again situates the action by describing the location (Jericho, 18 miles north of Jerusalem) where Jesus and the Apostles are as they make their final approach to the great city.

This miracle is described in both Matthew and Mark's accounts. Matthew says that two blind men were healed, but Mark and Luke focus only on Bartimaeus' reaction. They describe a man who could not see Jesus or His works, but nevertheless called out to Him in faith and as a result, regained his sight.

Bartimaeus' faith will later be contrasted to that of the religious leaders in Jerusalem who actually witnessed many of Jesus' miracles but refused to believe and, consequently, remained spiritually blind.

Zaccheus Converted (19:1-10)

Once in Jericho, Jesus spots Zaccheus (a tax collector like Matthew) who because of his short stature had climbed into a tree in order to get a better view of the Lord as He passed by.

Jesus calls out to him by name and tells the diminutive tax collector that He will visit his home. The religious leaders grumble because Jesus would associate, even visit the home of a sinner/tax collector. Zaccheus is so grateful for Jesus' kindness that he confesses and repents of his past improper conduct as a tax collector, and commits to giving to the poor and returning money to those he may have defrauded (overcharged in taxes for his own profit). Jesus confirms that Zaccheus is saved but points out that these are the people He has been sent to save: sinners who believe and repent.

This event provides another contrast between those who believed and those who did not (blind Bartimaeus vs. religious leaders) and those who repented and those who did not (Zaccheus vs. self-righteous Jewish religious leaders).

Parable of the 10 Minas

Luke records another of Jesus' parables that is contained in both Matthew and Mark. This parable is yet another reference to the religious leadership in Jerusalem, however, it deals with the quality of their stewardship and not their faith or repentance.

> ¹¹While they were listening to these things, Jesus went on to tell a parable, because He was near Jerusalem, and they supposed that the kingdom of God was going to appear immediately. ¹²So He said, "A nobleman went to a distant country to receive a kingdom for himself, and then return. ¹³And he called ten of his slaves, and gave them ten minas and said to them, 'Do business with this until I come back.' ¹⁴But his citizens hated him and sent a delegation after him, saying, 'We do not want this man to reign over us.' ¹⁵When he returned, after receiving the kingdom, he ordered that these slaves, to whom he had given the money, be called to him so that he might know what business they had done. ¹⁶The first appeared, saying, 'Master, your mina has made ten minas more.' ¹⁷And he said to him, 'Well done, good slave, because you have been faithful in a very little thing, you are to be in authority over ten cities.' ¹⁸The second came, saying, 'Your mina, master, has made five minas.' ¹⁹And he said to him also, 'And you are to be over five cities.' ²⁰Another came, saying, 'Master, here is your mina, which I kept put away in a handkerchief; ²¹for I was afraid of you, because you are an exacting man; you take up what you did not lay down and reap what you did not sow.' ²²He said to him, 'By your own words I will judge you, you worthless slave. Did you know that I am an exacting man, taking up what I did not lay down and reaping what I did not sow? ²³Then why did you not put my money in the bank, and having come, I would have collected it with interest?' ²⁴Then he said to the bystanders, 'Take the mina away from him and give it to the one who has the ten minas.' ²⁵And they said to him, 'Master, he has ten minas already.' ²⁶I tell you that to everyone who has, more shall be given, but from

> the one who does not have, even what he does have shall be taken away. [27]But these enemies of mine, who did not want me to reign over them, bring them here and slay them in my presence."
> - Luke 19:11-27

Note the additional parallels that Jesus adds in this parable in order to reflect His present and coming situation: the time frame for the action is over a long period, clarifying the teaching on this matter for those like John the Baptist who thought that the coming of the kingdom and the judgment would appear at exactly the same time. Jesus, however, describes four periods of time:

1. The point when the nobleman assigns the responsibility.

2. The undisclosed amount of time he is gone during which the true attitudes of the servants are seen.

3. The time when the nobleman returns to punish and reward.

4. The destruction of the nobleman's enemies.

The order of events in the parable parallels the order of Jesus' ministry and its eventual outcome:

1. Jesus will assign the great commission to His disciples (Matthew 28:18-20, Mark 16:16).

2. The church will continue in its ministry until Jesus returns (Acts 2:37-47).

3. Jesus will return to reward and punish (I Thessalonians 4:13-18, II Thessalonians 1:6-10).

4. The end of the age and the appearing of the new heavens and earth will accompany His return (II Peter 3:11-13).

This parable may not have meant much more to the Apostles than its primary lesson on good stewardship, but once Jesus' ministry was completed they would then be able to recall and fully understand this teaching in the light of fulfilled prophecy.

The Triumphal Entry (19:28-44)

We have here another event described by both Matthew and Mark. Luke, however, adds the passage describing Jesus' personal reaction upon reaching the city. He writes that Jesus sent disciples ahead to secure a donkey to ride on: Matthew writes that they brought back two donkeys, a colt that had never been ridden and its mother (probably to stabilize the young animal as it carried its first mount through a noisy crowd, Matthew 21:1-3).

Jesus arrived at Jerusalem from Bethany where Mary, Martha and Lazarus lived, and where He often stayed when traveling back and forth from His home in Capernaum to the capital in Jerusalem. Bethany was about 1.5 miles from Jerusalem with the Mount of Olives and the Garden of Gethsemane as the last stop before going down into the valley from the garden and up again to enter the city of Jerusalem on the opposite side.

From the Garden of Gethsemane on the crest of the valley, a person could see the entire city of Jerusalem located on the opposite side. Today, from this vantage point, one can see a graveyard in front of the Eastern Gate which was the way Jesus entered the city at that time. The planting of the graveyard and the bricking over of the gate in 1530 AD was an attempt by Muslims to prevent the return of the Messiah.

> [36]As He was going, they were spreading their coats on the road. [37]As soon as He was approaching, near the descent of the Mount of Olives, the whole crowd of the disciples began to praise God joyfully with a loud voice for all the miracles which they had seen, [38]shouting: "Blessed is the King who comes in the name of the Lord; Peace in heaven and glory in the highest!" [39]Some of the Pharisees in the crowd said to Him, "Teacher, rebuke Your disciples."

> [40]But Jesus answered, "I tell you, if these become
> silent, the stones will cry out!"
> - Luke 19:36-40

Matthew quotes the Old Testament prophecy that described
the manner in which the Messiah would enter the city,
humbly riding a donkey, as opposed to being mounted on a
horse or chariot as earthly kings would enter (Matthew 21:5).

Luke continues to contrast the attitude of ordinary people
who believed, and thus rejoiced, to that of the religious
leaders who did not believe and were offended by the
demonstration of faith and praise coming from the crowd.

> [41]When He approached Jerusalem, He saw the city
> and wept over it, [42]saying, "If you had known in this
> day, even you, the things which make for peace!
> But now they have been hidden from your
> eyes. [43]For the days will come upon you when your
> enemies will throw up a barricade against you, and
> surround you and hem you in on every side, [44]and
> they will level you to the ground and your children
> within you, and they will not leave in you one stone
> upon another, because you did not recognize the
> time of your visitation."
> - Luke 19:41-44

This section is particular to Luke and in it he describes
Jesus' great sorrow for two things:

1. **What the Jews would miss** seeing because of their
   spiritual blindness caused by their disbelief. He weeps
   because the joy and gladness expressed by His
   disciples could have been shared by everyone in the
   city if they had known (accepted) what God required of
   them in order to have peace with Him (belief in the
   Son). As it was, they would be denied the blessings and
   joy that faith could have brought them.

2. **What the Jews would suffer** as a consequence of their disbelief. Jesus makes very clear the reason for the punishment that was to come, *"...because you did not recognize the time of your visitation."* (verse 44c).

Up until this time in His teaching and preaching, Jesus used parables to describe the attitude of disbelief and hostility expressed by the Jewish religious leadership. In this passage, however, he states in no uncertain terms or hidden meaning the sin of the Jews (their rejection of Him as their Messiah) and their punishment (destruction of their city and death to its people).

Traders Driven from the Temple

> [45]Jesus entered the temple and began to drive out those who were selling, [46]saying to them, "It is written, 'And My house shall be a house of prayer,' but you have made it a robbers' den." [47]And He was teaching daily in the temple; but the chief priests and the scribes and the leading men among the people were trying to destroy Him, [48]and they could not find anything that they might do, for all the people were hanging on to every word He said.
> - Luke 19:45-48

Matthew and Mark make this action the high point of the section on Jesus' entry into Jerusalem. Luke's high point, however, is Jesus' pronouncement on the Jewish nation which, for Luke's audience of one (Theophilus), will go a long way in explaining the hostility of the Jews towards Christianity and the subsequent offer of the gospel to Gentiles from Jewish Apostles and teachers. He devotes only two lines summarizing Jesus' reason for clearing out the traders from the temple courts (an action that would have had little interest to a Gentile reader).

Luke finishes the section by describing the battle lines as far as Jesus was concerned: The chief priest, scribes

(Pharisees) and leading men (elders, wealthy, political class, teachers) vs. The people.

Summary / Lessons

Luke describes the final interactions, miracles and teachings by Jesus as He approaches and enters Jerusalem. These events and teachings are such that they describe the situation and divide among the people with the disbelief and rejection of the religious and political elite contrasted by the faith, enthusiasm and joy of ordinary people and social outcasts. At this point the only thing restraining the Jewish leadership from arresting Jesus is the fear of a backlash from the common people.

In the next section, however, we will see closer infighting as Jesus is confronted by various leaders who now have easy access to Him as He ministers to people in the temple area of Jerusalem. Here are a couple of lessons we can draw from the material we have covered in this chapter.

1. Believe the Book

The great sin of the Jews was that they refused to believe their own prophets. The problem was not that Jesus didn't perfectly fulfill all that was said about the Messiah in the writing of the prophets, their issue with Him was that He didn't look or sound like the image of the Messiah they had created in their own minds (a powerful military/political miracle worker). They failed because they didn't believe their own book! We risk the same error if our Jesus is the Jesus of popular movies, ideas or movements. Our Lord, His will, His word and His church are all clearly presented and explained in His book: the Bible. Let's make sure that our lives and religious practices are based on His book and not our opinions or feelings.

2. We Will All Be "Visited"

Luke writes that the Jews didn't recognize the time of their visitation, and were lost because of it. We are all visited by Christ at one time or another. The visit comes in many forms, but it always comes. Sometimes it appears as an invitation to study the Bible or attend a service, other times the visit is a temptation allowed into our lives in order to measure our obedience. For many it materializes as an illness, accident, offense or challenge that examines our faith or love. In the end, for everyone, it comes as death signaling that there is no longer any time left to choose to believe or not because death frames how we will remain in eternity for good or bad.

Not all visitations are the same in nature or length of time, but the common denominator is that everyone gets a visit and the visit is always about whether we believe in Christ or not.

Discussion Questions

1. What are some of the popular misunderstandings of who Jesus is today? Why do you think people believe these false ideas about Jesus?

2. Describe one of your under-used talents. Explain why this talent is not developed and how it could be used in the service of the church.

3. Select one of the religious groups listed below and explain how you would proceed in trying to convert a follower of these to Christianity. Provide three scripture references.

   o   Jew, Hindu, Voodoo, Muslim, Buddhist, Atheist

CHAPTER 11
JESUS ENTERS JERUSALEM
- PART 2

LUKE 20:1-21:38

In the previous chapter we left off at the scene where Jesus chases off the money lenders from inside the temple area. In the following section, Luke describes several encounters with various Jewish leaders who try to discredit and undermine Him with their questions and traps.

Encounters – 20:1-47

Confrontation

> [1]On one of the days while He was teaching the people in the temple and preaching the gospel, the chief priests and the scribes with the elders confronted Him, [2]and they spoke, saying to Him, "Tell us by what authority You are doing these things, or who is the one who gave You this authority?" [3]Jesus answered and said to them, "I will also ask you a question, and you tell Me: [4]Was the baptism of John from heaven or from men?" [5]They reasoned among themselves, saying, "If we say, 'From heaven,' He will say, 'Why did you not believe him?' [6]But if we say, 'From men,' all the people will stone us to death, for they are

> convinced that John was a prophet." [7]So they
> answered that they did not know where it came
> from. [8]And Jesus said to them, "Nor will I tell you
> by what authority I do these things."
> - Luke 20:1-8

The chief priests, scribes and elders represented the highest levels of society. Many were members of the Sanhedrin, the ruling body charged by the Roman government to oversee the affairs of the Jewish people. They came together to make a show of force and say to Jesus, "How dare you!"

Jesus had taken it upon Himself to make a judgment call on the propriety of commercial activity in the temple area (which profited these men) and carry out a swift and rough justice on these traders. The religious leaders' response should have been: Amen, it's about time, or thank you for righting a wrong that we have ignored. Instead, they were annoyed and insulted that someone with no social standing, and from a town (Nazareth) far from the seat of power would presume to do such a thing in an area that they controlled.

He obviously had courage, but who gave Him the right to defy their authority? Of course, as the Son of God (and Lord of the temple) He had God-given authority, but to say this now would have provoked them to action before the proper time.

Jesus, therefore, finds another way to disarm them. By asking them to name the authority behind John the Baptist's ministry He does two things:

1. He maintains the important discussion about spiritual authority, but deflects attention and the point of the question from Himself to John the Baptist.

2. He forces them to acknowledge their lack of faith. If they said John's baptism was from God, they would then have to also acknowledge that He (Jesus) was also from God since this is what John testified. By

saying they didn't know they confessed to uncertainty, but they said this to avoid the displeasure of the crowd that did believe. In their hearts they did not believe and Jesus exposes this to themselves and the many who followed and watched His ministry.

Jesus' own position about John and his mission had been stated previously (Luke 7), so by not answering Him the leaders lost the authority to demand an answer concerning Jesus' conduct in the temple. The Lord follows this exchange with a parable that described the attitude and end of those who rejected Him.

Parable of the Vine-Growers (20:9-18)

This parable is a thinly veiled rebuke of the disbelief and violence that He would ultimately suffer at the hands of these religious leaders.

In the parable, vine-growers are entrusted with a vineyard by its owner who then leaves. People sent by him to check on its progress are harassed and killed, even the owner's son is murdered by the vine-growers in an attempt to seize possession of the vineyard. The owner eventually returns to execute these men and gives their position to others.

It was easy to spot the parallel between the conduct of the vinedressers and the religious leaders.

One interesting feature of this parable is that Jesus quotes several Old Testament passages (Psalms 118:22, Isaiah 8:14) to support His teaching that rejection and violence against the Messiah was spoken of by the psalmist and prophets long ago.

> The stone which the builders rejected
> Has become the chief corner stone.
> - Psalms 118:22

In the parable the builders are the religious leaders who were referred to at times as the "builders of Israel." The stone was the Messiah, who should have been laid as the foundation of the kingdom by these builders but was rejected (because they wanted to rule the kingdom themselves). The stone will cause many to stumble (direct opposition to the stone will fail), but those on whom the stone falls (judgment) will be destroyed.

It was unusual for Jesus to mix a Scripture reference with a parable which normally stood alone as a teaching unit.

Tribute to Caesar (20:19-26)

> [19]The scribes and the chief priests tried to lay hands on Him that very hour, and they feared the people; for they understood that He spoke this parable against them. [20]So they watched Him, and sent spies who pretended to be righteous, in order that they might catch Him in some statement, so that they could deliver Him to the rule and the authority of the governor.
> - Luke 20:19-20

This passage is a description of the reaction of these religious leaders to Jesus' parable and serves as a bridge to the next scene of confrontation/entrapment.

> [21]They questioned Him, saying, "Teacher, we know that You speak and teach correctly, and You are not partial to any, but teach the way of God in truth. [22]Is it lawful for us to pay taxes to Caesar, or not?" [23]But He detected their trickery and said to them, [24]"Show Me a denarius. Whose likeness and inscription does it have?" They said,
> "Caesar's." [25]And He said to them, "Then render to Caesar the things that are Caesar's, and to God the things that are God's." [26]And they were unable to catch Him in a saying in the presence of the

people; and being amazed at His answer, they
became silent.
- Luke 20:21-26

If confrontation didn't work perhaps trickery would succeed.
Note in verse 23, Jesus detects the trap and the attitude
behind the question.

If He answered that they should pay the tax, they would
brand Him as a Roman sympathizer to discredit Him before
the people. If He supported the non-payment of the tax, they
would report Him to the Roman authorities as an agitator and
have Him arrested. Instead, Jesus solves a dilemma faced
by many sincere Jews who were conflicted because they
were being forced to pay taxes to a foreign ruler using
coinage that was blasphemous to them (the coins had the
image of a pagan king). Jesus goes to the heart of the matter
by making a distinction between the material and the
spiritual.

Some things (like taxes) belong strictly to the material world
and while here we must deal with these accordingly. Other
matters are spiritual and we must follow God's commands
regarding these (worship, morals, etc.). The problem occurs
when we mix the two, we make money our god, or we
worship God and conduct ourselves according to man-made
rules and ideas.

God has created both the spiritual and material worlds and
has instructed us in how we are to function in each.

Question Concerning the Resurrection (20:27-44)

The leaders have tried confrontation and trickery and have
failed at both, so they attempt to discredit Jesus through
ridicule.

The Sadducees bring Jesus a hypothetical situation with a
view to mock and ridicule His teaching on the matter. These
priests considered only the Pentateuch (Genesis-
Deuteronomy) as inspired and thus authoritative texts. They

were a small group of conservative, wealthy religious leaders. Their political support came from the wealthy class whereas the Pharisees (teachers and experts in the Law) held sway over the common people.

The Sadducees believed that there was a great distance between God and man (much like Deists do today). They believed that man's task was to maintain his daily life here because there was no after-life. They taught that wealth and position were blessings from God given to show His approval. This is why many thought poverty was a curse and a sign of God's displeasure.

> [27]Now there came to Him some of the Sadducees (who say that there is no resurrection), [28]and they questioned Him, saying, "Teacher, Moses wrote for us that if a man's brother dies, having a wife, and he is childless, his brother should marry the wife and raise up children to his brother. [29]Now there were seven brothers; and the first took a wife and died childless; [30]and the second [31]and the third married her; and in the same way all seven died, leaving no children. [32]Finally the woman died also. [33]In the resurrection therefore, which one's wife will she be? For all seven had married her."
> - Luke 20:27-33

Their question was impertinent and mocking. They saw themselves as wise and were ready to trip up this country rabbi with a trick question.

> [34]Jesus said to them, "The sons of this age marry and are given in marriage, [35]but those who are considered worthy to attain to that age and the resurrection from the dead, neither marry nor are given in marriage; [36]for they cannot even die anymore, because they are like angels, and are sons of God, being sons of the resurrection. [37]But that the dead are raised, even Moses showed, in

> the passage about the burning bush, where he
> calls the Lord the God of Abraham, and the God of
> Isaac, and the God of Jacob. [38]Now He is not the
> God of the dead but of the living; for all live to
> Him."
> - Luke 20:34-38

Jesus responds to impertinence with knowledge, a knowledge that reveals immediately His superior, divine understanding and their ignorance about matters they thought they knew well. The Lord uses the very skill they prided themselves in (scholarly examination and commentary of the Scripture) to prove that their teaching about the resurrection was mistaken.

1. Jesus correctly interprets the meaning of a key passage to prove that bodily resurrection takes place after death. He does so by drawing the logical conclusion based on the proper grammatical usage of the verb in the sentence in question.

> [5]Then He said, "Do not come near here; remove
> your sandals from your feet, for the place on which
> you are standing is holy ground." [6]He said also, "I
> am the God of your father, the God of Abraham,
> the God of Isaac, and the God of Jacob." Then
> Moses hid his face, for he was afraid to look at
> God.
> - Exodus 3:5-6

The use of the verb, "Am" in the present tense (I am the God of your father...) grammatically supports the conclusion that Abraham, Isaac and Jacob are also present and alive before God. The proper understanding of the use of the verb and how it leads to a correct interpretation of the passage defeats the "no resurrection" position of the Sadducees. They only accepted the teachings of the Law as authoritative, so Jesus proves His point using their method as well as their text to demonstrate that they were mistaken.

2. He also demonstrates His divine knowledge (and by doing so His divine nature as well) by revealing things concerning resurrection that only someone from heaven could know. He reveals to them that resurrected beings are like angels (pure spirits with similar powers). They do not marry or reproduce because they are eternal (no need for reproduction when there is no death).

> [39]Some of the scribes answered and said, "Teacher, You have spoken well." [40]For they did not have courage to question Him any longer about anything.
> - Luke 20:39-40

Some scribes, who were serious students and teachers of the Scriptures (Sadducees served as priests) agree with Jesus but the rest were silent not wishing further humiliation.

3. Jesus, at this point, poses the religious leaders a question.

> [41]Then He said to them, "How is it that they say the Christ is David's son? [42]For David himself says in the book of Psalms, 'The Lord said to my Lord, "Sit at My right hand, [43]Until I make Your enemies a footstool for Your feet."' [44]Therefore David calls Him 'Lord,' and how is He his son?"
> - Luke 20:41-44

Jesus dealt with intimidation, trickery and mocking. He has answered the questions and corrected their mistaken understanding about the resurrection. He now goes one step further by asking them a question about the Scriptures. His previous question about John the Baptist was tactical in nature. He boxed them in so that no matter what they answered, they would lose the argument.

This question asks them to interpret a passage of Scripture concerning the dual nature of the Messiah. The answer to His question (verse 44) is the following:

- The Lord (God the Father) said to my Lord (Jesus the Son) sit at my right hand until I make your enemies a footstool for your feet (complete victory including victory over death) (Psalms 110:1).

- David spoke this prophecy (through the power of the Holy Spirit).

- Question: If David calls Him Lord, how then is He his (David's) Son?

- Answer: David calls the Son of God Lord before He comes into the world as a man named Jesus (Matthew 1:6-16).

- At the time David spoke these words, Jesus had not yet come. Approximately 1000 years later Jesus became man by the power of the Holy Spirit and entered the world through a family whose head (Joseph) was a descendant of David.

The Scribes and priests knew this Scripture and acknowledged that the Messiah would be a descendant of David but did not realize or refused to admit that (as Jesus had just demonstrated) the Messiah would also be divine. What really bothered them was that this Jesus who stood before them claimed that He was that divine Messiah!

Warning Against the Scribes

[45]And while all the people were listening, He said to the disciples, [46]"Beware of the scribes, who like to walk around in long robes, and love respectful greetings in the market places, and chief seats in the synagogues and places of honor at banquets,

[47]who devour widows' houses, and for appearance's sake offer long prayers. These will receive greater condemnation."
- Luke 20:45-47

The epilogue to this section is Jesus' warning concerning the hypocrisy of the scribes (this included the Pharisees). The warning is twofold:

1. Be careful that you not be victims of their schemes, unduly impressed by their pretense at holiness and importance.
2. Be careful not to be like them in their attitude and deeds.

Jesus reveals yet another hidden fact that only God would know concerning the judgment: there will be degrees of guilt and condemnation.

Signs of the End – 21:1-38

Jesus has just condemned the scribes for their hypocrisy and continues this line of teaching as He describes the events leading to and including the final judgment.

> [1]And He looked up and saw the rich putting their gifts into the treasury. [2] And He saw a poor widow putting in two small copper coins. [3] And He said, "Truly I say to you, this poor widow put in more than all of them; [4] for they all out of their surplus put into the offering; but she out of her poverty put in all that she had to live on."
> - Luke 21:1-4

As a way of balancing His warnings about the hypocrisy of the scribes, Jesus comments on the sincere faith and generous spirit of the widow's sacrificial offering when compared to the perfunctionary giving of others with more physical resources. These may have given a greater amount, but not a sacrificial amount as was the case with the poor widow.

This event takes place in the temple area and naturally sets up a question about the temple itself which Jesus uses to elaborate on the issue of judgment, something the Jews will soon face because of their rejection of Jesus as the Messiah.

> [5]And while some were talking about the temple, that it was adorned with beautiful stones and votive gifts, He said, [6]"As for these things which you are looking at, the days will come in which there will not be left one stone upon another which will not be torn down." [7]They questioned Him, saying, "Teacher, when therefore will these things happen? And what will be the sign when these things are about to take place?"
> - Luke 21:5-7

Their questions lead Jesus into a long teaching concerning the end times. Both Matthew (Matthew 24) and Mark (Mark 13) include this section in their gospels. When taken together these passages contain three questions by the Apostles:

1. When will this happen (destruction of the temple) and what are the signs for this?

2. What will be the sign of your coming (return)?

3. What about the end times?

Luke only records the first question asked by the Apostles but includes the answers to both the first and second questions.

In verses 8-24 He answers the first question by describing the political and social situation in the world as well as the persecution of the church that will precede the end of the city of Jerusalem (70 AD). He also describes the suffering and destruction that will take place.

In verses 25-36 Jesus gives them information concerning His return which will coincide with the end of the world. The Lord finishes with an encouragement to be alert for both the destruction of Jerusalem and His return at the end.

In verses 37-38 Luke adds a comment that Jesus' devoted followers were listening to Him teach daily in the temple and Jesus would spend evenings in prayer. This call to prepare for judgment sets up the final events in Jesus' ministry: His crucifixion, death and resurrection.

Lessons

1. We should all strive to give sacrificially, not just regularly

We can easily become complacent in our giving (and thus receive no blessing from it) if there is no element of sacrifice in our offering to the Lord.

2. The judgment is sure

The Jews ignored Jesus' warning of judgment to come (and we know historically that it did come in 70 AD when the Roman army destroyed the city of Jerusalem and its temple along with the majority of its citizens). Let's not make the same mistake.

Discussion Questions

1. What type of attack or confrontation on your own personal faith do you find most challenging?

   o   Why is this so?

   o   How can you improve your response?

2. Summarize, in your own words, the answer to the question, "What will happen at the end of the world when Jesus returns?"

   o   Can you provide Scriptures for your answer?

CHAPTER 12
THE CONSUMMATION
- PART 1

LUKE 22:1-23:25

This chapter begins the last main section in our outline of Luke's gospel.

1. The Beginning – 1:1-3:38
2. Jesus in Galilee – 4:1-9:50
3. Jesus Facing Jerusalem – 9:51-18:30
4. Jesus Entering Jerusalem – 18:31-21:38
5. **The Consummation – 22:1-24:53**

We will now examine Luke's description of events from the preparation of the Passover to Jesus' second appearance before Pilate.

Jesus' Final Hours with the Apostles – 22:1-62

The first thing to notice about the entire "Consummation" section is that Luke's gospel has very little original information exclusive to his record. Only Jesus' brief appearance before Herod is found only in Luke's gospel.

Everything else from Luke 22:1-24:53 is also found in Matthew, Mark and in some instances in John as well (since John was an eye-witness of these events). John could be writing from his memory of events or sampling key events from Matthew, Mark or even Luke's record since John wrote his gospel last.

Preparing the Passover (22:1-13)

> [1]Now the Feast of Unleavened Bread, which is called the Passover, was approaching. [2]The chief priests and the scribes were seeking how they might put Him to death; for they were afraid of the people.
> - Luke 22:1-2

In two simple verses Luke establishes both the time of the year and time in Jesus' ministry arc.

1. Time of year: Feast of Unleavened Bread - Passover

It was the time in the year and festival calendar for Passover and the Feast of Unleavened Bread which are mentioned together but are separate things. The Passover observance was limited to one 24-hour period and it commemorated the night when the angel of death struck down every first born human and animal in Egypt but spared the Jews who were living in slavery there at that time (Exodus 12:1-14). God had warned the Jews of this event and promised that every family that sprinkled the blood of a sacrificial lamb on the doorposts of their dwellings, and ate the sacrificial meal in the safety of their homes, would be spared. When the angel of death came and saw the blood of the lamb, he would "pass over" that house and not exact judgment.

When the Jews were freed from slavery, God commanded Moses to instruct the people to commemorate this incident by sharing a Passover meal consisting of the same elements that they had eaten on the original night: the sacrificial lamb, the unleavened bread (unleavened because in their haste to

162

leave Egypt there was no time for the bread to rise as in the normal baking process), bitter herbs were herbs that had a harsh or bitter taste (chicory, wild lettuce, coriander, dandelion), these were eaten as a reminder of the harsh treatment the Jews experienced in Egyptian captivity.

Later on, when the Jews arrived and settled in the Promised Land, several cups of wine were added to the meal symbolizing the happiness and prosperity of the Promised Land.

The meal was conducted as a ceremony with the father or chief person leading the people around the table (he would first eat of the meat and they would follow; he would dip the unleavened bread into the bitter herbs and they would do likewise; he would take his cup of wine and offer a blessing and the others would Amen and drink). In a family situation at some point a younger person would ask the father to explain the meaning of the meal and this would permit the leader an opportunity to teach the family about the history and significance of this commemorative event.

The Feast of Unleavened Bread was part of the Passover commanded by God and fell on the day after Passover. The day before Passover was known as the day of Preparation where the Jews prepared for both the Passover and Feast of Unleavened Bread by cleaning their homes, preparing the lamb and meal, and removing all forms of leaven in the house. Leaven signified decay and sin, and this exercise reflected a person's desire to root out and eliminate sin in their lives.

> [14]'Now this day will be a memorial to you, and you shall celebrate it as a feast to the Lord; throughout your generations you are to celebrate it as a permanent ordinance. [15]Seven days you shall eat unleavened bread, but on the first day you shall remove leaven from your houses; for whoever eats

> anything leavened from the first day until the
> seventh day, that person shall be cut off from
> Israel.
> - Exodus 12:14-15

For seven days after the Passover the people celebrated the Feast of Unleavened Bread with convocations at the temple and refraining from eating bread with leaven. These were the first feasts given to the Jews to celebrate in the first month of their religious calendar (Nissan=March/April).

Luke situates the time of year (spring) and religious significance against which the following events would take place: Jewish Passover and Feast of Unleavened Bread (a time when Jews recalled their rescue by God and their devotion to purity and obedience to the will of God).

2. The Arc of Jesus' Ministry

Luke describes the intent of the Jewish religious leaders and their motivation. They planned to have Jesus killed since they had failed in trying to debate Him, humiliate Him or trap Him in some inconsistency. They feared that continued unrest among the people would lead to their rejection in favor of Jesus, or a military solution imposed upon them by their Roman superiors. Either way, Jesus and those who followed Him jeopardized their positions. Their firm intent to have Him killed meant that His teaching and performance of miracles were about to end and the final stage of His ministry that included His death, burial and resurrection was about to begin.

In verses 3-6, Luke shows that the plot to kill Him was gaining momentum as Judas, succumbing to his doubts and greed, joined forces with the Jewish leaders in the plan to arrest Jesus.

> They were glad and agreed to give him money.
> - Luke 22:5

Note that in verse 5, Luke reports two things:

1. The plotters were glad. They rejoiced in the plan.

2. The leaders agreed to give Judas money. This was his idea and Matthew tells us that he was paid right then and there.

Judas then attended the Passover meal with the money in his bag, seeking at this point how he would betray the Lord.

In verses 7-13, Jesus sends only two to prepare the lamb because Temple rules limited the number of those who presented Passover lambs to two persons. Peter and John's sense of self-importance may have been heightened because of their selection to carry out this task, and set up the room and seating arrangements for the meal. We get a hint of this later on when a dispute arises among the Apostles about rank and position.

The Lord's Supper (22:14-23)

> [14]When the hour had come, He reclined at the table, and the apostles with Him. [15]And He said to them, "I have earnestly desired to eat this Passover with you before I suffer; [16]for I say to you, I shall never again eat it until it is fulfilled in the kingdom of God." [17]And when He had taken a cup and given thanks, He said, "Take this and share it among yourselves; [18]for I say to you, I will not drink of the fruit of the vine from now on until the kingdom of God comes."
> - Luke 22:14-18

Once again Jesus reminds them of His imminent death linked so closely to the symbolism of the Passover meal. He was the true sacrificial lamb whose blood would shield all believers from final and eternal death. He was eager to eat this particular Passover meal because it was to be the last symbolic meal preparing the people for the true lamb sacrificed for sin.

Note that the Lord takes a cup of wine and gives thanks. This was one of the four or five cups shared where the father or host would offer a blessing which Jesus does.

> [19]And when He had taken some bread and given thanks, He broke it and gave it to them, saying, "This is My body which is given for you; do this in remembrance of Me." [20]And in the same way He took the cup after they had eaten, saying, "This cup which is poured out for you is the new covenant in My blood.
> - Luke 22:19-20

There are three main teachings about the meaning of Jesus' words regarding the Lord's Supper (Communion) here:

A. Transubstantiation
A Catholic teaching says that the bread and wine are miraculously transformed into the actual body and blood of Christ, only the appearance of bread and wine remain. This teaching stems from the words in verse 19 where Jesus says, "This is my body" and in Matthew 26:28, "This is my blood." Roman Catholics interpret these expressions literally.

B. Consubstantiation
A primarily Lutheran teaching which says that the bread and wine at communion remain physical elements but the body and blood of Jesus co-exist with the bread and wine at communion. Based on the same premise (this is my body, blood) with a different conclusion (originally developed by Martin Luther).

C. Commemoration
A simple ritual with bread representing Jesus' body, and wine His blood, taken to remember His sacrifice for

believers. This teaching based on verse 19, "Do this in remembrance of Me." In this verse we have both the command (do this) and the reason (in remembrance). We reject the other two reasons because they are based on faulty understanding of Jesus' use of metaphors in His teaching method. He said, "I am the door" in John 10:7 and "I am the vine" in John 15:5. Did He literally mean that He was a wooden door or a plant? In the same way, the Lord uses the bread and wine as metaphors for His body and blood offered on the cross, a sacrifice we as Christians remember each Lord's day (Sunday) by partaking of unleavened bread and fruit of the vine.

In verses 21-23, Luke summarizes the reaction of the Apostles when Jesus declares that there is a traitor among them. He spends little time reviewing the response of the Apostles and departure of Judas preferring instead to devote a long passage to a dispute among the 11 (Judas having left before the Lord's supper was given, John 13:30).

Who is the Greatest (22:24-38)

This section begins with a dispute about who is the greatest among the Apostles, an argument that could have been caused by Peter and John's seating arrangements (since they set the table and places). They may have taken the most honored positions for themselves: to the right and left of Jesus.

Again, Luke summarizes Jesus' repeated teaching on this topic: that in the kingdom the greatest are the least and those who serve others. In verses 28-38, He reassures them that they are destined for greatness in the kingdom of heaven but before that happens, Peter will be tested by Satan and ultimately deny Jesus. He also tells them that they will be without His protection and He will be killed.

The Passion, Part I - 22:39-23:25

Once Jesus and the remaining 11 Apostles leave the upper room and head for the Garden of Gethsemane, the Lord's "Passion" begins.

The term Passion comes from the Latin word Passionem (suffering/enduring) and is used to refer to His suffering and death on the cross. There are 10 major events that occur during Jesus' Passion:

1. Jesus prays in Gethsemane
2. Jesus' betrayal and arrest
3. Peter's denial of Jesus
4. Jesus before Annas, before the High Priest Caiaphas and other Jewish leaders
5. Jesus before the Governor, Pilate – 1
6. Jesus before King Herod
7. Jesus before the Governor, Pilate – 2
8. Jesus tortured and bears the cross
9. Jesus' death on the cross
10. Jesus is laid in the tomb

We will briefly review the events from the Garden to Jesus' final appearance before Pilate which ultimately led to His condemnation and death. We will then conclude our study of Luke's gospel in the next and final chapter.

1. Gethsemane (22:39-46)

Luke provides an abbreviated version of this event which mentions only one rebuke to the Apostles for sleeping and not the three described by Matthew (Matthew 26:36-46). Luke is the only gospel to record that His sweat turned into drops of blood (hematidrosis) and that an angel appeared to comfort Him in this hour of trial. The point to note here is that this was a test of faith and obedience for Jesus' human nature, not His divine one. The human part of Jesus had to accept the will of the Father.

2. Jesus' Betrayal and Arrest (22:47-53)

Judas, accompanied by a great number of soldiers along with a crowd of onlookers, makes his way to the spot in the garden where Jesus and His Apostles are located. The traitorous Apostle steps forward to kiss Jesus (a pre-arranged sign to point out the one to be arrested). Lenski, the Greek commentator, writes that the verbs which Matthew and Mark use to describe the kiss suggests that Judas was repeatedly kissing Jesus. Luke notes that Jesus offers Himself to His captors (to protect the Apostles with Him) even as they make an attempt at defending Him. John says that Peter struck Malchus, the High Priest's servant and cut off his ear. Luke reports that Jesus then healed this slave of his injury (verse 51).

Jesus' only response to Judas is to question the method and seriousness of his treachery; you betray the Son of Man (divine Messiah) using a false act of love and friendship: a kiss? This was both a comment and judgment on Judas.

3. Peter's Denial (22:54-62)

Peter, along with another disciple (unknown) follow the soldiers and the crowd to Caiaphas' courtyard to witness the interrogation of Jesus by the High Priest and other leaders. Peter is in danger because he is a known Apostle and because he injured the High Priest's slave. He is also vulnerable because his Galilean accent gives him away as one from the same region as Jesus. As the Lord predicted, Peter denies his knowledge of and association with Jesus when pressured by different people in the courtyard. That night two of Jesus' Apostles actually denied Him and the other 10 ran away in fear. However, only one of the deniers would eventually be restored and I'll explain why at the end of this chapter.

4. Jesus Before Caiaphas and the Council

> [63]Now the men who were holding Jesus in custody were mocking Him and beating Him, [64]and they

blindfolded Him and were asking Him, saying, "Prophesy, who is the one who hit You?" [65]And they were saying many other things against Him, blaspheming. [66]When it was day, the Council of elders of the people assembled, both chief priests and scribes, and they led Him away to their council chamber, saying, [67]"If You are the Christ, tell us." But He said to them, "If I tell you, you will not believe; [68]and if I ask a question, you will not answer. [69]But from now on the Son of Man will be seated at the right hand of the power of God." [70]And they all said, "Are You the Son of God, then?" And He said to them, "Yes, I am." [71]Then they said, "What further need do we have of testimony? For we have heard it ourselves from His own mouth."
- Luke 22:63-71

There were two sessions of the Sanhedrin/Council (71 elders, judges and priests) required when deciding capital cases (involving the death penalty) and these sessions were to be separated by a one day recess.

John 18:13 says that Jesus was first questioned by Annas, the father-in-law of Caiaphas the High Priest, who had previously served as high priest. Luke only records the two illegal meetings where Jesus was not only charged but was also mocked and tortured by actual members of the Sanhedrin. It's as if the judge in a trial permitted the jury to make fun of and torture the accused in open court.

Both meetings were illegal for many reasons, here are two:

1. They were held in the middle of the night. This was not permitted according to law.

2. They did not allow a 24-hour recess between the first and second meeting where the death penalty was pronounced.

Both Matthew and Mark record that many false witnesses and accusers were brought forward, but Jesus remained silent throughout the trials and abuse. Only when directly asked if He was indeed the Messiah did Jesus reply in the affirmative because even though His opponents and Apostles denied Him, He could not deny this truth about Himself, even if it meant His sure death.

5. Jesus Before Pilate – 1

Having obtained the evidence necessary for an execution according to Jewish Law (Jesus claiming that He was the divine Messiah), the Jewish leaders bring Jesus to Pilate (since only the Romans could carry out an execution).

> [1]Then the whole body of them got up and brought Him before Pilate. [2]And they began to accuse Him, saying, "We found this man misleading our nation and forbidding to pay taxes to Caesar, and saying that He Himself is Christ, a King." [3]So Pilate asked Him, saying, "Are You the King of the Jews?" And He answered him and said, "It is as you say." [4]Then Pilate said to the chief priests and the crowds, "I find no guilt in this man." [5]But they kept on insisting, saying, "He stirs up the people, teaching all over Judea, starting from Galilee even as far as this place." [6]When Pilate heard it, he asked whether the man was a Galilean. [7]And when he learned that He belonged to Herod's jurisdiction, he sent Him to Herod, who himself also was in Jerusalem at that time.
> - Luke 23:1-7

The accusations and lies rehearsed at the trials before the Sanhedrin are now repeated before the Roman Prefect or Governor of the province of Judea, Pontius Pilate.

- **Pontius** – His family name from a tribe in south-central Italy.

- **Pilate** – His title, procurator - someone employed by the Roman Emperor to manage finances and taxes.

Pilate finds no grounds for execution but recognizes that a decision for or against Jesus will cause trouble either way, so he hands the matter off to Herod, a subordinate ruler (tetrarch=ruler of a quarter) who was responsible for the northern region of Galilee where Jesus was from.

6. Jesus Before Herod (23:8-12)

Herod was not interested in judging or executing Jesus for similar reasons that Pilate had. After all, Jesus came from the north and His base of support was there as well. Herod was curious to see a miracle but when Jesus refused even to answer any of his questions, Herod had him mocked and abused, and sent back to Pilate.

7. Jesus Before Pilate – 2

[13]Pilate summoned the chief priests and the rulers and the people, [14]and said to them, "You brought this man to me as one who incites the people to rebellion, and behold, having examined Him before you, I have found no guilt in this man regarding the charges which you make against Him. [15]No, nor has Herod, for he sent Him back to us; and behold, nothing deserving death has been done by Him. [16]Therefore I will punish Him and release Him." [17][Now he was obliged to release to them at the feast one prisoner.] [18]But they cried out all together, saying, "Away with this man, and release for us Barabbas!" [19](He was one who had been thrown into prison for an insurrection made in the city, and for murder.) [20]Pilate, wanting to release Jesus, addressed them again, [21]but they kept on calling out, saying, "Crucify, crucify Him!" [22]And he said to them the third time, "Why, what evil has this man done? I have found in Him no guilt demanding death; therefore I will punish Him and release Him." [23]But they were insistent, with loud voices

> asking that He be crucified. And their voices began
> to prevail. [24]And Pilate pronounced sentence that
> their demand be granted.
> - Luke 23:13-24

Luke is fairly dispassionate in his record describing, as a journalist might report, the three attempts by Pilate to set Jesus free and each time being overruled by the Jewish leaders and the rabble they had assembled. Luke presents the events of the trial but makes no mention of motives other than the fact that by Law, Jesus was not a candidate for execution. He leaves to Matthew the observation that Pilate knew that the Jews were trying to have Jesus executed out of envy. He describes a Roman official who gives in to the mob's demands out of a desire to curry favor with the people (Mark 15:14) and fear that the Jewish leaders would cause trouble for him with his superiors in Rome (John 19:12).

In keeping with his factual style, Luke summarizes the outcome of this momentous event with a few simple words.

> And he released the man they were asking for who
> had been thrown into prison for insurrection and
> murder, but he delivered Jesus to their will.
> - Luke 23:35

We will review the last three events in the Passion narrative in the next chapter.

Coda: the difference between Judas and Peter.

1. Judas - This Apostle's denial and betrayal of Jesus was motivated by disbelief (he did not believe Jesus was the divine Messiah) and greed (he wanted compensation for his evil deed). Because he had no faith, his remorse led to despair and its natural end: suicide.

2. Peter - Peter's denial of Jesus was caused by fear (threat of arrest and death) and pride (he thought he was strong).

His sorrow and repentance led to restoration because despite his human weaknesses, he believed.

Faith is what determined the outcome of both Judas and Peter, and will do so for the outcome of our lives as well.

Reading Assignment: Luke 23:26-24:43

Discussion Questions

1. Prepare a 5-minute communion devotional that focuses on one of the 7 events in the Passion of the Lord.

   o   Present your devotional to the class.

2. Class feedback for each devotional:

	GOOD	FAIR	NEEDS IMPROVEMENT
A. PRESENTATION			
B. EFFECTIVENESS			
C. AUTHENTICITY			

CHAPTER 13
THE CONSUMMATION
- PART 2

LUKE 23:26-24:53

Let's review our outline one last time:

1. The Beginning – 1:1-3:38
2. Jesus in Galilee – 4:1-9:50
3. Jesus Facing Jerusalem – 9:51-18:30
4. Jesus Entering Jerusalem – 18:31-21:38
5. **The Consummation – 22:1-24:53**

I mentioned the fact that we followed a geographical outline of Jesus' ministry in our study because Luke, in wanting to establish a historical narrative of Jesus' life and ministry for his reader, Theopholis, does so by framing events in Jesus' life using two factors:

1. **Time** - of year or festival or history depending on who ruled politically or who led religiously (i.e. governors, high priests, etc.) which can be verified historically.

2. **Place** - where things happened so that the various incidents are grouped based on where Jesus was at

the time. This is how our outline has been developed.

Unlike Matthew and Mark, and later, John, who each have a theological theme for their records (i.e. Matthew - Jesus is the Jewish Messiah; Mark - Jesus is divine; John - Jesus is both man and God), Luke's goal is to set Jesus, the Son of God, into a historical context; and for this the actual time and place where the events of Jesus' life and ministry take place need to be mentioned.

Now, as far as our study of Luke's gospel is concerned, we are reviewing the last three of the 10 final events of His Passion (suffering). The 10 passion events that Luke recounts are:

1. Gethsemane
2. Betrayal and arrest
3. Peter's denial
4. Trial before Annas, Caiaphas and the council
5. Trial before Pilate – 1
6. Jesus before Herod
7. Trial before Pilate – 2
8. Torture and cross
9. Death of Jesus
10. Burial of Jesus

In the previous chapter we reviewed Pilate's failed attempts to save Jesus and his cowardly acquiescence to the Jewish leaders and mob to have Jesus, a man he knew to be innocent, executed. Let us now examine the last three events in Jesus' passion of the cross, and the glorious conclusion to Luke's gospel.

The Passion, Part II – 23:26-56

8. Torture and the Cross

> ²⁶When they led Him away, they seized a man, Simon of Cyrene, coming in from the country, and placed on him the cross to carry behind Jesus. ²⁷And following Him was a large crowd of the people, and of women who were mourning and lamenting Him. ²⁸But Jesus turning to them said, "Daughters of Jerusalem, stop weeping for Me, but weep for yourselves and for your children. ²⁹For behold, the days are coming when they will say, 'Blessed are the barren, and the wombs that never bore, and the breasts that never nursed.' ³⁰Then they will begin to say to the mountains, 'Fall on us,' and to the hills, 'Cover us.' ³¹For if they do these things when the tree is green, what will happen when it is dry?" ³²Two others also, who were criminals, were being led away to be put to death with Him.
>
> - Luke 23:26-32

Luke forgoes any description of the scourging and psychological abuse administered by the soldiers prior to Jesus' execution. This torture, however, takes its toll as the Romans press Simon, an innocent bystander, to carry the cross for the exhausted Jesus. Mark names two of Simon's sons who later become prominent members of the church (Mark 15:21).

The women "mourning and lamenting" were expressing the traditional bewailing for a person who was as good as dead. Judging by Jesus' answer to their cries, these women were not His disciples because He tells them to stop mourning Him and begin mourning for themselves, a prophetic reference to the terrible suffering and destruction that will take place in 70 AD when the Roman army will destroy both the city and its people. The green wood mentioned is Jesus in His sinlessness and the dry wood is the Jewish nation in its guilt. The inferred question is, "If this is what happens to the innocent, imagine what will happen to the guilty?"

Luke mentions the two criminals that Pilate sends to be executed with Jesus. This is done as a show of contempt for the Jews (i.e. this is what I think of your king).

9. The Crucifixion (23:33-49)

Note that Luke's description of this event is entirely made up of reactions, not actions.

> When they came to the place called The Skull,
> there they crucified Him and the criminals, one on
> the right and the other on the left.
> - Luke 23:33

The opening verse sets the scene in the briefest way possible: Jesus is crucified with thieves crucified to His right and left. Perhaps Luke knew that his Gentile reader was familiar with this Roman style of execution and needed no explanations.

Jesus' Reaction

> But Jesus was saying, "Father, forgive them; for
> they do not know what they are doing." And they
> cast lots, dividing up His garments among
> themselves.
> - Luke 23:34

Jesus will speak several times, but His first reaction is to plead to God on behalf of those who have put Him on this cross. God answered this prayer because a few weeks later Peter would be offering God's forgiveness to these very same people as he preached the gospel from the Pilgrim Gate at the temple in Jerusalem (Acts 2:14-42). Who knows how many in this crowd at the cross were among the 3000 baptized on Pentecost Sunday?

The clothing and effects of the condemned were the property of the soldiers tasked with the execution.

The People

> And the people stood by, looking on.
> - Luke 23:35a

Luke will mention the crowd later on, but at the moment he says that they are mainly quiet. Now that the awful reality of what they had demanded stands before them, they are reduced to silence. After all, crucified and slowly dying in excruciating pain before their eyes was not a murderer or thief but the teacher from Galilee, a Jew like themselves, put to death before them by pagan soldiers.

Jewish Rulers

> And even the rulers were sneering at Him, saying, "He saved others; let Him save Himself if this is the Christ of God, His Chosen One."
> - Luke 23:35b

The ones who spoke did so in cruelty actually mocking a dying man. They use His crucifixion as the final evidence for their accusation that He was an imposter. "If He is the Messiah (Christ of God) let Him save Himself from this execution." The insinuation is that since He cannot do this it proves that His claim of saving others is also false. The blasphemy here is not only against the Son but also against the Father who has sent the Son to seek and save the lost (Luke 19:10; John 20:21).

Roman Soldiers

> [36]The soldiers also mocked Him, coming up to Him, offering Him sour wine, [37]and saying, "If You are the King of the Jews, save Yourself!" [38]Now there was also an inscription above Him, "THIS IS THE KING OF THE JEWS."
> - Luke 23:36-38

The soldiers' insults are directed at Jesus but meant for the Jewish people as a whole. Being stationed in Judea was not the best assignment. These men were far from Rome and Roman society, among a rebellious people with a fanatical devotion to their strange religion. The inscription above the cross said, "This is the king of the Jews," but the sentiment behind the inscription said, "This is what we think of and what we do to anyone who declares that he is the king of the Jews or king of anything else for that matter." It was a brutal show of force and a warning by the Imperial Roman Army to other would-be troublemakers.

The Two Thieves

> [39]One of the criminals who were hanged there was hurling abuse at Him, saying, "Are You not the Christ? Save Yourself and us!" [40]But the other answered, and rebuking him said, "Do you not even fear God, since you are under the same sentence of condemnation? [41]And we indeed are suffering justly, for we are receiving what we deserve for our deeds; but this man has done nothing wrong." [42]And he was saying, "Jesus, remember me when You come in Your kingdom!" [43]And He said to him, "Truly I say to you, today you shall be with Me in Paradise."
> - Luke 23:39-43

Luke spends time describing the reaction of the two convicted thieves hung on either side of Him. Matthew and

Mark say that Jesus was being reviled by both thieves at first. We get an idea of what was being said since Luke preserves some of the dialogue. One thief incorporates what the Jewish leaders are saying by goading Jesus to save Himself along with both of them, if He is indeed the Messiah. We often think that the other thief did nothing special in coming to Christ, he simply asked and was saved. However, the change of heart in defending Jesus required him to rebuke the other criminal and contradict the soldiers as well as the Jewish leaders in order to ask the Lord for mercy. He was a thief, but somehow he knew of the kingdom to come (as a Jew he was probably referring to the kingdom at the end of the world) and he wanted to be part of that.

We note that Jesus promises the thief that he would be in Paradise (heaven) with Him (Jesus) that very day. In saying this, Jesus not only forgives the man his sins but also utters a prophecy. Normally it took three to four days for a person to die from crucifixion, however, the Jews had Pilate instruct his soldiers to break the legs of the men on the cross in order to hasten their death since it was unacceptable to have a public execution on the Sabbath. Once their legs were broken the crucified men could not support themselves to breathe so they quickly died of suffocation. The thief had no way of knowing that he would die so soon and thus be with Jesus on that same day, making Jesus' words both an absolution of sin as well as a prophecy.

The argument that the thief on the cross was saved without being baptized thus nullifying the need for baptism in the process of salvation is answered in the following way:

In the gospel of Mark we read about the time when Jesus healed a paralytic and also forgave his sins.

> [10]But so that you may know that the Son of Man has authority on earth to forgive sins"—He said to the paralytic, [11]"I say to you, get up, pick up your pallet and go home."
> - Mark 2:10-11

While among us Jesus often forgave sins by the simple exercise of His will. He, as the Son of God, had the divine authority to grant this and we see Him doing for the thief on the cross what He did for the paralytic (simply forgive his sins without reference to baptism). However, after His resurrection and before His ascent into heaven He left His Apostles with final instructions concerning salvation now that He would no longer be on earth with them in bodily form. These instructions included the baptism (immersion) in water of repentant believers.

> [18]And Jesus came up and spoke to them, saying, "All authority has been given to Me in heaven and on earth. [19]Go therefore and make disciples of all the nations, baptizing them in the name of the Father and the Son and the Holy Spirit,
> - Matthew 28:18-19

> [15]And He said to them, "Go into all the world and preach the gospel to all creation. [16]He who has believed and has been baptized shall be saved; but he who has disbelieved shall be condemned.
> - Mark 16:15-16

We note that Peter follows these instructions when he preaches his first sermon on Pentecost Sunday.

> Peter said to them, "Repent, and each of you be baptized in the name of Jesus Christ for the forgiveness of your sins; and you will receive the gift of the Holy Spirit.
> - Acts 2:38

It is fitting that Jesus' final act of ministry before His death would be the transfer of one more repentant believer from the kingdom of darkness into the kingdom of light (heaven/paradise - Colossians 1:13).

The Centurion

> [44]It was now about the sixth hour, and darkness fell over the whole land until the ninth hour, [45]because the sun was obscured; and the veil of the temple was torn in two. [46]And Jesus, crying out with a loud voice, said, "Father, into Your hands I commit My spirit." Having said this, He breathed His last. [47]Now when the centurion saw what had happened, he began praising God, saying, "Certainly this man was innocent."
> - Luke 23:44-47

Luke only describes two of the signs that occurred at Jesus' death:

1. **Darkness** - from noon until three in the afternoon, as a sign of divine judgment for what has taken place - the execution of the Son of God, the light of the world.

2. **Tearing of the veil** - inside the temple itself there was a heavy veil that separated the inner room (Holy of Holies) from the outer room (Holy Place). The Ark of the Covenant covered by the "mercy seat" was inside the Holy of Holies where the High Priest would enter once per year to offer sacrifices making atonement for his sins and those of the people. The significance of the torn curtain was that there would no longer be a restriction (symbolized by the curtain) to the throne of God's grace (represented by the Holy of Holies where God met with the high priest once per year). The way was now open and accessible to all through faith in Jesus Christ (Hebrews 10:19-20).

Matthew (Matthew 27:50-53) records that there was also an earthquake at that time, and after His resurrection many other believers were raised from the dead and appeared to people in Jerusalem. Luke reports that after witnessing Jesus' death on the cross, the centurion in charge of the detail is himself converted. Mark quotes him as saying,

"Truly this man was the Son of God" (Mark 15:39). So the Jews were silent and the Jewish leaders were cruel and mocking, but the actual crucifixion brought two sinful souls to salvation: the thief who died with Jesus and the centurion who executed them both.

The Jewish Crowds

> And all the crowds who came together for this spectacle, when they observed what had happened, began to return, beating their breasts.
> - Luke 23:48

The people who had rejected Jesus now mourned His passing. Luke notes that they came out to see a show/spectacle, but were less enthusiastic after actually witnessing the cruelty and brutality of Jesus' execution.

The Believers and Disciples

> And all His acquaintances and the women who accompanied Him from Galilee were standing at a distance, seeing these things.
> - Luke 23:49

There is no comment as to their feelings or expressed thoughts, only that they were witnesses of Jesus' death. Notice that Luke does not include the names or references to any of the Apostles that may have been present.

The Burial (23:50-56)

Luke only mentions Joseph of Arimathea, a member of the Sanhedrin who had not supported the condemnation of Jesus, as the one who buried the Lord. He also refers to the women who noted the place of burial with plans to return after the Sabbath had passed to properly prepare the Lord's body for its repose. Luke may have limited this information sensing that Theophilus, a Gentile, would have little interest in the details of Jewish burial customs.

The Resurrection

[1]But on the first day of the week, at early dawn, they came to the tomb bringing the spices which they had prepared. [2]And they found the stone rolled away from the tomb, [3]but when they entered, they did not find the body of the Lord Jesus. [4]While they were perplexed about this, behold, two men suddenly stood near them in dazzling clothing; [5]and as the women were terrified and bowed their faces to the ground, the men said to them, "Why do you seek the living One among the dead? [6]He is not here, but He has risen. Remember how He spoke to you while He was still in Galilee, [7]saying that the Son of Man must be delivered into the hands of sinful men, and be crucified, and the third day rise again." [8]And they remembered His words, [9]and returned from the tomb and reported all these things to the eleven and to all the rest. [10]Now they were Mary Magdalene and Joanna and Mary the mother of James; also the other women with them were telling these things to the apostles. [11]But these words appeared to them as nonsense, and they would not believe them. [12]But Peter got up and ran to the tomb; stooping and looking in, he saw the linen wrappings only; and he went away to his home, marveling at what had happened.
- Luke 24:1-12

There are many artistic renditions of Jesus' resurrection showing frightened soldiers fleeing or an angel rolling away the stone in order to free the Lord from the tomb. The biblical sequence, however, is the following:

1. Early Sunday morning Jesus resurrects and leaves the tomb. No one is aware of this. None of the gospels

describe the event, only the things that happened afterwards to prove that the resurrection actually took place.

2. There was an earthquake which coincided with the descent of an angel who rolled away the stone covering the tomb's entrance in order to show that it was already empty (not to let Jesus out), and the angel then sitting on that stone.

3. The soldiers guarding the tomb fainted.

4. The women arrive and find the tomb empty, which is where Luke picks up his story.

5. The angel speaks to the women (Luke adds that there were two angels) and confirms that Jesus previously spoke of His resurrection while He was alive. The women then leave to find the Apostles in order to tell them what they have seen.

6. Luke reports that there is disbelief among the Apostles at this news but nevertheless Peter and John rush to the tomb to see for themselves.

After these events take place, the gospel writers (and Paul) will record a number of other appearances by the risen Jesus to various individuals:

1. Mary Magdalene – Mark 16:9, John 20:11-18

2. Other women – Matthew 28:8-10

3. Peter – Luke 24:34

4. Two disciples on the road to Emmaus
   – Mark 16:12-13, Luke 24:13-35

We no longer know where Emmaus is located, but it is estimated that it was some five to seven miles from Jerusalem. Luke writes that two disciples were on their way home discussing what they had recently witnessed in

Jerusalem. Jesus joined them at some point but they were prevented from recognizing Him. They tell Him that they were hoping Jesus would have been the Messiah, but now that He has been tortured and killed, they are not so sure. They hoped that the Messiah would be like David, a great warrior king. In the Old Testament, however, Isaiah (Isaiah 53:1-12) presented the Messiah as a figure of suffering and servanthood (many Jews see this as a personification of their nation as a whole, even to this day).

Jesus explains to these disciples that the Messiah would have two profiles:

1. **Suffering Servant** - Jesus' suffering was not a failure or mistake but, according to Isaiah, a complete fulfillment of the Messiah's mission.

2. **Glorious Savior** - As David defeated Israel's enemies, Jesus with His death and resurrection will defeat mankind's greatest enemy: death.

When darkness approached, Jesus went into their home to share a meal. As He broke and blessed the bread, Luke describes the moment that "...their eyes were opened," and they recognized Him at which point He vanished from their sight. The disciples are filled with joy and return to Jerusalem that very night to tell the Apostles of their experience.

The Apostles, the Disciples From Emmaus and Other Disciples – 24:36-49

Luke couples the appearance of Jesus to the disciples from Emmaus to His next appearance before these same disciples now that they have returned to Jerusalem to find the Apostles.

> [36]While they were telling these things, He Himself stood in their midst and said to them, "Peace be to you." [37]But they were startled and frightened and thought that they were seeing a spirit. [38]And He

said to them, "Why are you troubled, and why do doubts arise in your hearts? [39]See My hands and My feet, that it is I Myself; touch Me and see, for a spirit does not have flesh and bones as you see that I have." [40]And when He had said this, He showed them His hands and His feet. [41]While they still could not believe it because of their joy and amazement, He said to them, "Have you anything here to eat?" [42]They gave Him a piece of a broiled fish; [43]and He took it and ate it before them.
- Luke 24:36-43

The Lord confirms the witness of these two as well as that of the women by now appearing to the Apostles while they are together, and we find out from Mark and John (Mark 16:14, John 20:24-31) that only Thomas was not present.

In verses 44-49, Jesus provides for the Apostles the teaching and information He had given to the two disciples from Emmaus. Luke also gives a short summary of the great commission which is more fully stated in Matthew 28:18-20 and Mark 16:16-18. At this appearance Luke sets up a bridge for the next letter that he will write to Theopholis called, the Acts of the Apostles. He does so by noting Jesus' instruction to the Apostles to remain in Jerusalem until they receive power from on high. Luke includes no further information and leaves his reader anxious to see what this might mean. Other appearances by Jesus, but not recorded by Luke were:

1. Thomas (John 20:24-31)
2. The Apostles together in Galilee
   (Matthew 28:18-20; Mark 16:16-20)
3. The Apostles at the Sea of Galilee (John 21:1-25)
4. Non-gospel appearances (I Corinthians 15:6-8)
5. 500 disciples
6. James, His earthly brother
7. Paul, after His ascension

Apostles at His Ascension

> [50]And He led them out as far as Bethany, and He lifted up His hands and blessed them. [51]While He was blessing them, He parted from them and was carried up into heaven. [52]And they, after worshiping Him, returned to Jerusalem with great joy, [53]and were continually in the temple praising God.
> - Luke 24:50-53

Luke, as he has done throughout his gospel, mentions the place of Jesus' ascension, Bethany, only a few miles from Jerusalem. The Apostles' natural inclination when the Lord was gone the first time was to return home to family, friends and work (fishing). But Luke notes that after Jesus ascends, they return to Jerusalem where He previously instructed them to remain until they were empowered by the Holy Spirit to carry out their great commission of preaching the gospel to every tribe and tongue. In this way Luke neatly closes out his account of Jesus' life, death, resurrection and ascension, and sets the stage for the story of how the Apostles (notably Peter and Paul), through the power of the Holy Spirit, will establish the church that, 2000 years later, we are members of today.

Discussion Questions

1. Which of the eight reactions to Jesus' death do you identify with most as a sinner? Why?

2. Summarize as briefly as possible the answer to the "Thief on the Cross" statement that baptism is not necessary.

3. In your opinion, why didn't Jesus give the leadership role in the church to women since women were far more faithful to Him than men and He appeared to women first after His resurrection.

   o   Discuss

ACTS

CHAPTER 14
THE MINISTRY OF PETER
PETER'S FIRST SERMON

ACTS 1:1-2:47

Luke's first letter to Theophilus is normally found in the gospel section of the New Testament along with Matthew, Mark and John because in this letter Luke describes the birth, life, death and resurrection of Jesus as do the other gospel writers. The book of Acts (Luke's second letter to this Gentile official written somewhere between 60-68 AD), which comes after the four gospels, stands alone as a history book and is followed by the rest of the New Testament made up of letters (epistles) from the Apostles Paul, Peter and other contributors to the canon. In this second letter to Theophilus, Luke describes the people and events that contributed to the establishment and development of the church which began on Pentecost Sunday (Pentecost is a Greek translation of the Hebrew word "weeks").

The timing for the feast of Pentecost was as follows:

Immediately after the Passover (on a Friday) there was a period of seven days where no leaven was to be eaten or kept in the house. That seven days led to another Sabbath day (Saturday) when this feast was completed. On the following day (Sunday) the Jews celebrated the Feast of

First Fruits where they brought in the first part of their spring crop (usually barley) and made an offering to the Lord before they themselves ate from this yield (Leviticus 23:10-11).

The next feast on the Jewish religious calendar was the Feast of Weeks (Greek - Pentecost) where the people counted seven weeks (seven Sabbaths) plus one day (totaling 50 days) and gave thanks for the much greater harvest that occurred at that time of year (late summer).

JEWISH TIMELINE

PASSOVER UNLEAVENED BREAD		SABBATH DAY	FEAST OF FIRSTFRUITS		FEAST OF WEEKS (HEBREW) PENTECOST (GREEK)
	7 DAYS	SAT.	SUN.	50 DAYS (7 WEEKS + 1 DAY)	SUN.

CHRISTIAN TIMELINE

LAST SUPPER GETHSEMANE	CRUCIFIXION BURIAL	SABBATH	RESURRECTION	JESUS' APPEARANCES ASCENSION	APOSTLES WAIT IN JERUSALEM	PENTECOST HOLY SPIRIT DESCENDS
THURS.	FRI.	SAT.	SUN.	40 DAYS	10 DAYS	SUN.

It is against this backdrop of a yearly Jewish celebration taking place in Jerusalem (Luke, as always, is interested in providing historical and cultural markers) that the writer of Acts begins to instruct his audience of one concerning the establishment, growth and spread of the Christian church throughout the Roman Empire.

Outline - Acts

1. The Ministry of Peter - Acts 1:1-12:25

1. Peter's First Sermon – Acts 1:1-2:47
2. Peter's Post-Pentecost Ministry – Acts 3:1-4:37
3. Persecution of Peter and the Apostles – Acts 5:1-42
4. Persecution of the Church I – Acts 6:1-7:60
5. Persecution of the Church II – Acts 8:1-9:43
6. Peter Preaches to the Gentiles – Acts 10:1-12:25

2. The Ministry of Paul - Acts 13:1-28:31

7. Paul's First Missionary Journey – Acts 13:1-15:35
8. Paul's Second Missionary Journey – Acts 15:36-18:22
9. Paul's Third Missionary Journey – Acts 18:23-21:14
10. Paul's Arrest and Imprisonment I – Acts 21:15-23:11
11. Paul's Arrest and Imprisonment II – Acts 23:12-25:22
12. Paul's Arrest and Imprisonment III – 25:23-26:32
13. Paul's Journey to Rome – Acts 27:1-28:31

The book of Acts is easy to outline because it details the ministry of Peter and Paul in a straightforward narrative style. This is why it is called the "Acts" of the Apostles, and not the thoughts or theology of the Apostles. Luke records many teachings by Peter, Paul and others (e.g. Stephen) in his letter, but these sections are subordinate and in service to the "actions" of the Apostles and other early church characters who, against great odds, spread the gospel and planted the church in the pagan world of the first century.

Luke begins with Peter's ministry as he is the first to preach the gospel in the power of the Holy Spirit. We see him proclaiming a resurrected Jesus to the Jews and converts to

Judaism who had come to Jerusalem to celebrate the Feast of Pentecost. Later on, Peter is directed by God to bring the gospel to non-Jews as well. Luke then moves on seamlessly to describe the dynamic conversion of the most unlikely Apostle, Saul of Tarsus. This man was a Jewish Pharisee bent on destroying what he believed was a heretical sect of Judaism that worshipped Jesus as the divine Messiah. Luke completes his letter by detailing the incredible ministry of Saul, now Paul the Apostle, as he takes the gospel beyond Judea and Samaria to every corner of the Roman Empire and beyond.

The Ministry of Peter – Acts 1:1-12:25

Peter's First Sermon (Acts 1:1-2:27)

Review and Ascension

> The first account I composed, Theophilus,
> - Acts 1:1a

The fact that Luke refers to his reader by his name, Theophilus, and not his title (Most Excellent) suggests that this man had been converted since the writing of Luke's first letter. In that society it would have been highly improper to omit his reader's title unless their relationship had changed somehow. In the same way, it would have been unusual for Luke to use a formal title when speaking to a brother in Christ because these were set aside when believers addressed one another in the church.

> [1b]about all that Jesus began to do and teach, [2]until the day when He was taken up to heaven, after He had by the Holy Spirit given orders to the apostles whom He had chosen. [3]To these He also presented Himself alive after His suffering, by many convincing proofs, appearing to them over a period of forty days and speaking of the things

> concerning the kingdom of God. [4]Gathering them together, He commanded them not to leave Jerusalem, but to wait for what the Father had promised, "Which," He said, "you heard of from Me; [5]for John baptized with water, but you will be baptized with the Holy Spirit not many days from now."
>
> - Acts 1:1b-5

Luke summarizes Jesus' life and ministry with just a few words and focuses on events that took place between His resurrection and ascension:

1. His dynamic appearances during a 40-day period.

2. His teachings concerning the kingdom.

3. His instructions to the Apostles to remain in Jerusalem and not return home to Galilee as they had done after His crucifixion.

4. His promise that they would be baptized with the Holy Spirit in the near future.

There is often confusion about the nature of what Jesus is referring to here so let us briefly review the topic of baptism with the Holy Spirit by establishing and reviewing two particular terms:

Empower: When the Holy Spirit grants supernatural ability.

For example: The Holy Spirit enables someone to perform great or complex tasks.

> [1]Now the Lord spoke to Moses, saying, [2]"See, I have called by name Bezalel, the son of Uri, the son of Hur, of the tribe of Judah. [3]**I have filled him with the Spirit of God** in wisdom, in understanding, in knowledge, and in all kinds of craftsmanship, [4]to make artistic designs for work in

gold, in silver, and in bronze, [5]and in the cutting of stones for settings, and in the carving of wood, that he may work in all kinds of craftsmanship.
- Exodus 31:1-5

Or, the Holy Spirit empowers someone to perform miracles (e.g. Moses). Or, the Holy Spirit empowers someone to see visions or speak from God.

[1]Now **the Spirit of God came on Azariah** the son of Oded, [2]and he went out to meet Asa and said to him, "Listen to me, Asa, and all Judah and Benjamin: the Lord is with you when you are with Him. And if you seek Him, He will let you find Him; but if you forsake Him, He will forsake you.
- II Chronicles 15:1-2

In the year of King Uzziah's death **I saw the Lord sitting on a throne**, lofty and exalted, with the train of His robe filling the temple.
- Isaiah 6:1

Or, the Holy Spirit empowers someone for leadership (e.g. David).

Then Samuel took the horn of oil and anointed him in the midst of his brothers; and the **Spirit of the Lord came mightily upon David** from that day forward. And Samuel arose and went to Ramah.
- I Samuel 16:13

The Bible refers to this "empowering" work of the Holy Spirit in different ways. For example, "filled with the Spirit" (Exodus 31:5 - craftsmen who built the tabernacle); "Perform [...] all the miracles I have given you the power to do." (Exodus 4:21 - Moses); "The Spirit of God came upon..." (II Chronicles 15:1 - Azariah); "The Spirit of the Lord came mightily upon..." (I Samuel 16:13 - David).

This empowering was given only to certain ones for a time, enabling them to carry out a task or mission from God. For example, David asks God not to remove the Spirit from him (Psalms 51:11), and Samson was empowered by God with great strength but lost it because of sin (Judges 16). The Spirit empowered some people for certain tasks, but it was always temporary. The great promise of the Old Testament was that when the Messiah would come, He would usher in a time when all of God's people would have a portion of the Holy Spirit, not only a few like prophets and kings as was the case in the Old Testament. Peter quotes the prophet Joel who spoke of this some eight centuries before Christ came.

> [28]"It will come about after this
> That **I will pour out My Spirit on all mankind**;
> And your sons and daughters will prophesy,
> Your old men will dream dreams,
> Your young men will see visions.
> [29]"Even on the male and female servants
> I will pour out My Spirit in those days.
> - Joel 2:28-29

This promise of the Spirit was going to be different somehow. Everyone would have it, both men and women, as well as old and young would know and speak God's word and see the vision of heaven described there, not just the prophets. Most important, the Spirit would always be with you. This measure of the Spirit would not be empowerment, it would be called **indwelling**.

Indwelling: The Holy Spirit dwelling within each believer.

The Holy Spirit living within the believer not simply enabling him to do, see or say something in service to God, but existing within a person in order to transform that individual into the image of Christ. Empowering enabled certain people to do great things and the Old Testament is filled with stories of what these people did in service to God (Moses, Joshua, David, the Prophets, as well as the Apostles and certain individuals in the early church for a short time). Indwelling, on the other hand, enabled people to become Christlike, to become living sacrifices, to become eternal beings. Paul describes in detail what the indwelling does for the Christian in Romans 8. Indwelling is also referred to in a variety of ways:

> And when He had said this, He breathed on them (the Apostles) and said to them, **"Receive the Holy Spirit."**
> - John 20:22

This event does not refer to empowering because the Apostles do not speak in tongues as a result. The miraculous ability to speak in tongues only came on Pentecost Sunday when they were empowered to do so by the Holy Spirit. What John describes here is the moment when the Apostles received the indwelling of the Holy Spirit.

> Peter said to them, "Repent, and each of you be baptized in the name of Jesus Christ for the forgiveness of your sins; and **you will receive the gift of the Holy Spirit.**
> - Acts 2:38

In this passage Luke is describing when the people received the indwelling of the Holy Spirit (when repentant believers were baptized in Jesus' name). Peter was not promising the "empowering" of those who responded to the gospel because none of the 3000 baptized that day exhibited any miraculous power.

The confusion between the two occurs because the Bible uses the same term when referring to both empowering or indwelling. We have to examine carefully the context in which the term is used in order to understand if the writer is referring to empowerment or indwelling. Here are a few examples to show the difference.

> "As for me, I baptize you with water for repentance, but He who is coming after me is mightier than I, and I am not fit to remove His sandals; **He will baptize you with the Holy Spirit.**
> -Matthew 3:11

When John the Baptist used the term (baptized with the Holy Spirit) he was referring to the indwelling of the Spirit that Jesus, as the Messiah, would bring.

> for John baptized with water, **but you will be baptized with the Holy Spirit** not many days from now."
> - Acts 1:5

When, however, Jesus uses the term in Acts 1:5 in reference to what would happen to His Apostles, He is speaking of the empowerment they were to receive in order to preach, to speak in tongues, to do great miracles (e.g. Peter raising the dead), to plant and grow the church while enduring great persecution. The Lord is not promising indwelling here because He has already given them the indwelling of the Holy Spirit in John 20:22.

Let us, therefore, keep these two definitions in mind as we go on because they will help us understand the passages in Acts that deal with the Holy Spirit.

> [6]So when they had come together, they were asking Him, saying, "Lord, is it at this time You are restoring the kingdom to Israel?" [7]He said to them, "It is not for you to know times or epochs which the Father has fixed by His own authority; [8]but you will receive power when the Holy Spirit has come upon you; and you shall be My witnesses both in Jerusalem, and in all Judea and Samaria, and even to the remotest part of the earth."
> [9]And after He had said these things, He was lifted up while they were looking on, and a cloud

> received Him out of their sight. [10]And as they were
> gazing intently into the sky while He was going,
> behold, two men in white clothing stood beside
> them. [11]They also said, "Men of Galilee, why do
> you stand looking into the sky? This Jesus, who
> has been taken up from you into heaven, will come
> in just the same way as you have watched Him go
> into heaven."
> - Acts 1:6-11

Their question about the restoration of the kingdom shows
that they are still under the false notion of a glorious
restoration of the Jewish state (and their place in it). Jesus
does not bother to point out their error, instead He does two
other things:

1. He states that the knowledge of when the end of the
   Jewish kingdom will take place, or the end of the world
   for that matter, is beyond man's grasp, only God knows
   when these things will happen and they were to stop
   speculating and questioning Him about these things.

2. He outlines and reviews their mission. They will receive
   empowerment ("Holy Spirit will come upon you"). They
   are to witness what they have seen to the world
   beginning in Jerusalem.

Luke repeats the description of Jesus's ascension, this time
adding the information about the angels who prophecy
concerning His return.

The Upper Room (Acts 1:12-26)

The book of Acts provides an intimate look at the activity that
took place among the Apostles and disciples between the
time of Jesus' ascension and the descent of the Holy Spirit
on Pentecost Sunday.

1. The Apostles (11) gathered with the women who had
   supported and followed Jesus, Mary His mother, His

brothers and other disciples. Luke notes that they begin devoting themselves to prayer and waiting.

2. Peter takes the lead by putting into Scriptural context the actions and death of Judas, otherwise this could have become a reason for doubt and a point of discouragement. Peter's comment explains that what Judas did and how his life ended served God's purpose and was spoken of by the prophets. It was not a failure on their part or a mark on Jesus' mission.

3. They, through prayer, put forward two qualified men who had been faithful disciples from Jesus' baptism to His ascension. After casting lots, Matthias is chosen to replace Judas.

The Day of Pentecost (Acts 2:1-12)

[1]When the day of Pentecost had come, they were all together in one place. [2]And suddenly there came from heaven a noise like a violent rushing wind, and it filled the whole house where they were sitting. [3]And there appeared to them tongues as of fire distributing themselves, and they rested on each one of them. [4]**And they were all filled with the Holy Spirit and began to speak with other tongues,** as the Spirit was giving them utterance. [5]Now there were Jews living in Jerusalem, devout men from every nation under heaven. [6]And when this sound occurred, the crowd came together, and were bewildered because each one of them was hearing them speak in his own language. [7]They were amazed and astonished, saying, "Why, are not all these who are speaking Galileans? [8]And how is it that we each hear them in our own language to which we were born?
- Acts 2:1-8

They were "filled with the Holy Spirit" meaning that they received empowerment and the visible signs of this were the "tongues of fire" appearing over their heads and the sudden miraculous ability to speak languages that were previously unknown to them. They were from Galilee and spoke Aramaic in their daily lives, and Hebrew for their religious practices.

Pentecost was an important feast that brought Jews from all over the world to Jerusalem for this event. Luke records over a dozen language groups gathered and each heard the Apostles speaking in their native tongues. I mention this because there is the effort by charismatic groups to claim that they have reproduced this miracle in the modern age, however, the sounds they make (which they claim are "tongues") are unintelligible and make no sense. The usual explanation is that only God understands what they are saying or that they are speaking in the tongues of angels. This, of course, is contrary to the grammar and context of the passage.

1. **Grammar**: Tongue ("*glossa*" in Greek) refers to the physical tongue and by extension a known language.

2. **Context**: In verse 8 the crowd says that they heard the Apostles speak in their own language, and Luke names over a dozen languages that were used.

To summarize, the Apostles receive empowerment and that power is seen (tongues of fire) and heard (Jewish men miraculously preaching in languages they did not know). This phenomenon done in fulfillment of a prophecy concerning the time when the Messiah would come.

> In the Law it is written, "By men of strange tongues and by the lips of strangers I will speak to this people, and even so they will not listen to Me," says the Lord.
> - I Corinthians 14:21

Peter's Sermon (Acts 2:13-42)

> But others were mocking and saying, "They are full
> of sweet wine."
> - Acts 2:13

Luke sets the stage for Peter's first sermon by describing a
reaction that some had to the miracle just witnessed: "The
Apostles are drunk." Peter draws the crowd's attention by
answering this charge with his powerful Pentecost sermon.
This sermon can be divided into three sections:

Witness of the Holy Spirit (Acts 2:14-21)

Peter begins his sermon by crediting the Spirit of God for the
miracle of tongues they have just witnessed. He declares
that what they have both seen and heard is the phenomenon
that would accompany the coming of the Messiah according
to the prophets, and he quotes the prophet Joel 2:28-32 to
make his point.

Witness of the Gospel (Acts 2:22-41)

> [22]"Men of Israel, listen to these words: Jesus the
> Nazarene, a man attested to you by God with
> miracles and wonders and signs which God
> performed through Him in your midst, just as you
> yourselves know— [23]this Man, delivered over by
> the predetermined plan and foreknowledge of God,
> you nailed to a cross by the hands of godless men
> and put Him to death. [24]But God raised Him up
> again, putting an end to the agony of death, since it
> was impossible for Him to be held in its power.
> - Acts 2:22-24

Peter proclaimed the simple facts of the gospel message:
Jesus, proven to be God's anointed One through miracles,
wonders and signs; Jesus, crucified unjustly by sinful men,
all done according to God's foreknowledge and plan; Jesus,

resurrected by God, according to prophecy about Him (and Peter quotes David, Psalms 16:8-11, again to make the point that all of this was according to God's will and foretold by the prophets).

> [29]"Brethren, I may confidently say to you regarding the patriarch David that he both died and was buried, and his tomb is with us to this day. [30]And so, because he was a prophet and knew that God had sworn to him with an oath to seat one of his descendants on his throne, [31]he looked ahead and spoke of the resurrection of the Christ, that He was neither abandoned to Hades, nor did His flesh suffer decay. [32]This Jesus God raised up again, to which we are all witnesses. [33]Therefore having been exalted to the right hand of God, and having received from the Father the promise of the Holy Spirit, He has poured forth this which you both see and hear. [34]For it was not David who ascended into heaven, but he himself says:
> 'The Lord said to my Lord,
> "Sit at My right hand,
> [35]Until I make Your enemies a footstool for Your feet."'
> [36]Therefore let all the house of Israel know for certain that God has made Him both Lord and Christ—this Jesus whom you crucified."
> - Acts 2:29-36

Peter fortifies his gospel message with a deeper explanation concerning the resurrection, for this was a new element (they understood the idea of substitutionary death as an atonement for sin), however the idea, not to mention the possibility, of resurrection was new to them. None of the animals they had sacrificed over the centuries ever came back to life.

Peter explains that David prophesied about this very event and corrects their understanding of two passages where the

Jews thought that David was referring to himself but in reality was referring to Jesus:

1. Psalm 16:8-11, where David speaks of the promise of his resurrection. Peter says that this actually points to Christ who will make David's resurrection possible with His own.

2. Psalm 110:1, which Jews saw as a promise God made to David concerning his reign and power over his enemies. Jesus Himself corrected them of this idea when He asked the Pharisees a question about this passage that they could not answer, "If David calls Him Lord, how is He his Son?" (Matthew 22:45). Peter provides the answer by explaining that in this passage the Father is talking to the Son (Jesus), not David. God said to Jesus, sit at my right hand (power) and I will make your enemies your footstool (you will win over the Devil, death and unbelieving Jews through resurrection).

He summarizes his argument with a damning conclusion: This Jesus, anointed by God, spoken of by the prophets, witnessed by miracles, seen resurrected by us, ascended to heaven and who has sent the Holy Spirit to do what you have heard and seen today, who has now been declared Lord and Christ by God: **You killed Him!**

> [37]Now when they heard this, they were pierced to the heart, and said to Peter and the rest of the apostles, "Brethren, what shall we do?" [38]Peter said to them, "Repent, and each of you be baptized in the name of Jesus Christ for the forgiveness of your sins; and you will receive the gift of the Holy Spirit. [39]For the promise is for you and your children and for all who are far off, as many as the Lord our God will call to Himself." [40]And with many other words he solemnly testified and kept on exhorting them, saying, "Be saved from this perverse generation!" [41]So then, those who had

received his word were baptized; and that day
there were added about three thousand souls.
-Acts 2:37-41

Those who accept/believe the witness of the Spirit and the
message of the gospel respond. Peter, according to the
instructions given him and the other Apostles in Matthew
28:18-19 and Mark 16:15-16, tells them how they are to obey
the gospel.

[18]And Jesus came up and spoke to them, saying,
"All authority has been given to Me in heaven and
on earth. [19]Go therefore and make disciples of all
the nations, baptizing them in the name of the
Father and the Son and the Holy Spirit,
- Matthew 28:18-19

[15]And He said to them, "Go into all the world and
preach the gospel to all creation. [16]He who has
believed and has been baptized shall be saved;
but he who has disbelieved shall be condemned.
- Mark 16:15-16

They express their faith in Jesus as Lord and Christ by
repenting of their sins and being baptized (immersed in
water - the Pool of Siloam nearby as well as the water basin
near the Pilgrim Gate where pilgrims purified themselves
before entering the holy city of Jerusalem). Peter teaches
that at their baptism these people would receive both the
forgiveness of sins and the gift of the Holy Spirit (indwelling).
Luke does not provide details as to how the indwelling Spirit
affects the believer. Much of this information is contained in
Paul's epistles to the Romans (chapter 8) and Galatians
(chapter 5).

Three thousand people were baptized by the 12 on that day
(Acts 2:41) and since then we continue to preach the same
gospel message with the same instructions to those who
believe (repent and be baptized in Jesus' name for the

forgiveness of sin and you will receive the gift of the Holy Spirit).

Witness of the Church

> [42]They were continually devoting themselves to the apostles' teaching and to fellowship, to the breaking of bread and to prayer.
> [43]Everyone kept feeling a sense of awe; and many wonders and signs were taking place through the apostles. [44]And all those who had believed were together and had all things in common; [45]and they began selling their property and possessions and were sharing them with all, as anyone might have need. [46]Day by day continuing with one mind in the temple, and breaking bread from house to house, they were taking their meals together with gladness and sincerity of heart, [47]praising God and having favor with all the people.
> - Acts 2:42-47a

Luke summarizes the early activity, organization and enthusiasm of the first Christian church. Note carefully the outline of and inspired biblical pattern laid out for church ministry, organization and growth in these few lines of Scripture. If you look carefully you will note five different ministries begin and develop, as well as a compact summary of the relationship between ministry and church growth.

1. **Evangelism** (Acts 2:12-41): They were preaching the gospel of Christ to the lost and baptizing repentant believers.

2. **Education** (Acts 2:42a): They were teaching the converts to know and obey the words of Christ.

3. **Fellowship** (Acts 2:42b): They were integrating these new Christians into the body of Christ.

4. **Worship** (Acts2:42c): They were organizing the church for Christian worship (Lord's Supper, etc.).

5. **Service** (Acts 2:43-47a): The church began to pool its resources to care for the needs of the brethren and the community in the name of Christ.

Luke does not provide details on how all of this was done, only a brief overall sketch of the early church's five areas of ministry. In the final verse of this section the inspired writer reveals the biblical approach to church growth.

> And the Lord was adding to their number day by day those who were being saved.
> - Acts 2:47b

When you take the entire section together you see that when the church is active in preaching to the lost, teaching the saved, practicing fellowship, worship and service, Jesus then adds to His church. In other words, when the church ministers, the Lord adds to its number.

Lessons

1. Pray while you wait.

The Apostles remained in prayer while they waited for the Holy Spirit, and this kept them focused and ready when they were empowered. Waiting on the Lord is not a passive thing. Positive, productive waiting is accomplished through prayer, worship and service so that we can stay spiritually focused and avoid foolish complaining or premature surrender.

2. Some people need more encouragement than others.

Three thousand were baptized on Pentecost Sunday but there were more than 3000 people there. In the face of disbelief and rejection from people who may understand the gospel but refuse to respond, do what Peter did ("he kept on exhorting them" - verse 40), keep proclaiming the message, some will eventually respond.

3. Focus on ministry, not growth.

Our task is to be active in the five areas of ministry, learn how to carry these out more effectively and keep these ministries operating simultaneously. Jesus' task is adding to the church. More effective ministry equals more growth.

For more information on church growth see
the series "Unlimited Growth" on BibleTalk.tv

Reading Assignment: Acts 3:1-4:37

Discussion Questions

1. What two ways was the promise of the Holy Spirit fulfilled on Pentecost Sunday and why is there often confusion about these blessings?

2. How would you demonstrate from Acts chapter 2 that the gift of tongues given to the Apostles is different from what charismatics claim today as speaking in tongues?

3. Summarize Peter's use of David's Psalms in his argument to the Jews that Jesus was the Messiah.

CHAPTER 15
PETER'S POST PENTECOST MINISTRY

ACTS 3:1-4:37

Let us take a look at where we are in our outline:

I. Ministry of Peter – 1:1-12:19

1. Peter's First Sermon – 1:1-2:4

In this section, Luke describes the waiting Apostles receiving empowerment as the Holy Spirit comes upon them on Pentecost Sunday. We read Peter's first gospel sermon and the thousands who responded in repentance and baptism. Luke then describes the forming and development of the early church as it practiced the five basic biblical ministries of the church: evangelism, teaching, fellowship, worship and service. Luke concludes this first section by declaring that the Lord added to His church as the Apostles ministered to the people. This leads to the next section of the book.

2. Peter's Post-Pentecost Ministry – 3:1-4:37

Luke describes how Peter reacts when the religious leaders forbid him to preach the gospel or witness concerning Jesus' resurrection.

Healing the Man Crippled from Birth

[1]Now Peter and John were going up to the temple at the ninth hour, the hour of prayer. [2]And a man who had been lame from his mother's womb was being carried along, whom they used to set down every day at the gate of the temple which is called Beautiful, in order to beg alms of those who were entering the temple. [3]When he saw Peter and John about to go into the temple, he began asking to receive alms. [4]But Peter, along with John, fixed his gaze on him and said, "Look at us!" [5]And he began to give them his attention, expecting to receive something from them. [6]But Peter said, "I do not possess silver and gold, but what I do have I give to you: In the name of Jesus Christ the Nazarene—walk!" [7]And seizing him by the right hand, he raised him up; and immediately his feet and his ankles were strengthened. [8]With a leap he stood upright and began to walk; and he entered the temple with them, walking and leaping and praising God. [9]And all the people saw him walking and praising God; [10]and they were taking note of him as being the one who used to sit at the Beautiful Gate of the temple to beg alms, and they were filled with wonder and amazement at what had happened to him.
- Acts 3:1-10

Luke wastes no time commenting on the events of Pentecost. He moves his story along by recounting an event that was as great as the Pentecost miracle, but involved only one man. The first thing that strikes the reader concerning this account is the sureness of the miracle:

- The beggar was well known by the people, having been infirmed from birth.

- The infirmity was complete (could not walk) and we see this as he had to be carried to and from his usual spot each day at one of the temple gates.

- He is healed and immediately walks into the temple with the Apostles, praising God and literally jumping for joy.

- The people who knew and saw him regularly witnessed the before and after of his healing.

- They may have wondered how he was healed but there was no doubt that he was indeed healed of an incurable condition.

As verse 10 indicates (the people were filled with wonder at what they had seen), this miracle sets the scene for Peter's first defense of the gospel before the Jewish leadership. The miracle of tongues may have been baffling to some, and others found ways of denying it (i.e. the Apostles were drunk), however, this miracle was indisputably clear in its power and result as well as its source: Jesus Christ. Peter did not even ask if the man believed or not, he pronounced him healed in the name of Jesus (by the authority of) and the man's infirmity was gone.

Response of the Jewish People and Leaders (3:11-4:37)

In Acts 2, Luke summarizes the activity of the early church in Jerusalem as the day of Pentecost came and went, and life returned to normal.

> [43]Everyone kept feeling a sense of awe; and many wonders and signs were taking place through the apostles. [44]And all those who had believed were together and had all things in common; [45]and they began selling their property and possessions and were sharing them with all, as anyone might have need. [46]Day by day continuing with one mind in the temple, and breaking bread from house to house, they were taking their meals together with gladness and sincerity of heart, [47]praising God and

having favor with all the people. And the Lord was adding to their number day by day those who were being saved.
- Acts 2:43-47

In the following chapter he doubles back and focuses on the healing of one man and the events that took place as a result of this miracle:

Peter's Second Sermon (3:11-26)

[11]While he was clinging to Peter and John, all the people ran together to them at the so-called portico of Solomon, full of amazement. [12]But when Peter saw this, he replied to the people, "Men of Israel, why are you amazed at this, or why do you gaze at us, as if by our own power or piety we had made him walk? [13]The God of Abraham, Isaac and Jacob, the God of our fathers, has glorified His servant Jesus, the one whom you delivered and disowned in the presence of Pilate, when he had decided to release Him. [14]But you disowned the Holy and Righteous One and asked for a murderer to be granted to you, [15]but put to death the Prince of life, the one whom God raised from the dead, a fact to which we are witnesses. [16]And on the basis of faith in His name, it is the name of Jesus which has strengthened this man whom you see and know; and the faith which comes through Him has given him this perfect health in the presence of you all.
- Acts 3:11-16

As in the case of the Apostles speaking in tongues, this undeniable miracle draws a large crowd. In the same way that people wondered about the Apostles speaking in foreign languages through the power of the Holy Spirit, they are now amazed (literal translation - "dumbfounded") and waiting for an explanation. They saw and believed the what, they now wanted to know the "how."

This presents a second opportunity for Peter to address a large crowd with the gospel message and he follows the pattern used in his Pentecost sermon. He begins by establishing Jesus as the source of spiritual power, demonstrated in the miracle, by virtue of the fact that He is God's Messiah. He reminds them of their culpability in sending their own Savior to the cross in exchange for a notorious murderer. He proclaims the resurrection of Jesus and the fact that he and John were eye witnesses of this great miracle. Peter finishes by giving glory to Jesus for the healing of the lame man. This, then, is the "how."

In Acts 2:40, Luke writes that after initially preaching to the crowd on Pentecost Sunday, Peter "kept on exhorting them." In other words, he continued to make arguments and encouragements for people to respond in obedience to the gospel message. In Acts 2, Luke does not provide any more information as to the nature of these exhortations, only the results (3000 baptized, verse 41). In Acts 3, however, Luke continues to record Peter's sermon in addition to the results it received.

> [17]"And now, brethren, I know that you acted in ignorance, just as your rulers did also. [18]But the things which God announced beforehand by the mouth of all the prophets, that His Christ would suffer, He has thus fulfilled. [19]Therefore repent and return, so that your sins may be wiped away, in order that times of refreshing may come from the presence of the Lord;
> - Acts 3:17-19

In these verses, Peter mitigates their failure in receiving Jesus by stating that they did this in ignorance as His rejection and death were spoken of by the prophets. Their sins did not surprise God and as grave as they were, God was nevertheless offering them and their leaders forgiveness and the peace that the forgiven enjoy.

> [20]and that He may send Jesus, the Christ appointed for you, [21]whom heaven must receive until the period of restoration of all things about which God spoke by the mouth of His holy prophets from ancient time. [22]Moses said, 'The Lord God will raise up for you a prophet like me from your brethren; to Him you shall give heed to everything He says to you. [23]And it will be that every soul that does not heed that prophet shall be utterly destroyed from among the people.' [24]And likewise, all the prophets who have spoken, from Samuel and his successors onward, also announced these days. [25]It is you who are the sons of the prophets and of the covenant which God made with your fathers, saying to Abraham, 'And in your seed all the families of the earth shall be blessed.'
> - Acts 3:20-25

Here Peter turns their attention from the present judgment to the judgment to come at the end of the world when Jesus returns. He emphasizes the fact that Jesus, who was raised from the dead and ascended into heaven, will return to restore all things. This restoration would include the proper order with God/Christ and the church ruling; the old heaven and earth replaced by the new heaven and earth; and Satan and disbelievers punished. The final restoration, he says, was spoken of by the prophets and was offered first to you, the Jewish people.

> For you first, God raised up His Servant and sent Him to bless you by turning every one of you from your wicked ways."
> - Acts 3:26

He sums everything up in verse 26 by reiterating that Jesus' resurrection (the proof that He was the divine Messiah) was given to them first with the purpose of turning them away from their sins and saving them from the present and future judgment to come.

The second event that took place as a result of the healing...

Peter and John Arrested

> [1]As they were speaking to the people, the priests and the captain of the temple guard and the Sadducees came up to them, [2]being greatly disturbed because they were teaching the people and proclaiming in Jesus the resurrection from the dead. [3]And they laid hands on them and put them in jail until the next day, for it was already evening
> - Acts 4:1-3

While Peter is speaking, he and John are interrupted and arrested by:

- **Priests**: Several priests that belonged to the 24 groups of priests who were selected by lot to conduct services at the temple on various days. For example, Zachariah, John the Baptist's father.

> [8]Now it happened that while he was performing his priestly service before God in the appointed order of his division, [9]according to the custom of the priestly office, he was chosen by lot to enter the temple of the Lord and burn incense.
> - Luke 1:8-9

- **Captain of the Temple Guard:** Levites who served as temple police: guarding entrances, closing gates on the Sabbath, ensuring laws concerning movement and conduct in the temple area were obeyed.

- **Sadducees:** Wealthy priests who were part of the Sanhedrin (ruling council).

The Sadducees, being of the highest rank, probably instigated the arrest, and did so not because there was disorder or too big a crowd, but because of what was being taught. As the principal groups that argued for Jesus' execution, any talk of His resurrection and the subsequent growth of His movement would ultimately come back on them. They feared a loss of authority and position, and the privileges that came with these. They also denied the existence of spirits, angels or afterlife and only accepted the first five books of the Bible as authority, so a "risen Savior" would also disprove their teaching position on miracles and the afterlife.

Although few in number, the Sadducees wielded tremendous influence because they commanded great wealth and social position, and in addition to these, the family of the high priest belonged to their group. (Lenski, p. 153)

> But many of those who had heard the message
> believed; and the number of the men came to be
> about five thousand.
> - Acts 4:4

Luke, as he does for the Pentecost sermon, records the response of the crowd and the number who became Christians (2000 plus). He simply mentions that they went from 3000 to 5000 men, a way of giving a general estimate of the rate of growth (2000 men, not counting women and youth). He does not mention baptism and the need to confess Christ because this has already been described as necessary in the process of conversion. Faith is expressed by confessing Christ, repentance and baptism. There is no need to continually repeat this every time a writer is describing a person's conversion (otherwise the Bible would be thousands of pages long). Luke merely states the conclusion and response to Peter's sermon: 2000 plus people were converted.

A third event resulting from Peter's preaching...

Trial Before Jewish Leaders (4:5-22)

> [5]On the next day, their rulers and elders and
> scribes were gathered together in Jerusalem; [6]and
> Annas the high priest was there, and Caiaphas and
> John and Alexander, and all who were of high-
> priestly descent. [7]When they had placed them in
> the center, they began to inquire, "By what power,
> or in what name, have you done this?" [8]Then
> Peter, filled with the Holy Spirit, said to them,
> "Rulers and elders of the people, [9]if we are on trial
> today for a benefit done to a sick man, as to how
> this man has been made well, [10]let it be known to
> all of you and to all the people of Israel, that by the
> name of Jesus Christ the Nazarene, whom you
> crucified, whom God raised from the dead—by this
> name this man stands here before you in good
> health. [11]He is the stone which was rejected by
> you, the builders, but which became the chief
> corner stone. [12]And there is salvation in no one
> else; for there is no other name under heaven that
> has been given among men by which we must be
> saved."
> - Acts 4:5-12

Although Peter and John are brought before the Jewish
leaders for questioning and possible imprisonment, Luke
shows that this occasion quickly becomes the scene for
Peter's third sermon. This is given to a much smaller crowd,
but one with the most wealth and power in Israel.

As is Luke's custom, he provides historical and personal
detail by naming some of the prominent men present and
their positions:

- **Rulers**: High priests and family, Annas and Caiaphas
  (Annas' son-in-law). All Sadducees.

- **Elders**: Chief men appointed to the Sanhedrin (70-72 rulers/elders/scribes). John and Alexander.

- **Scribes**: Rabbis/lawyers (Pharisees).

Note that they ask Peter and John the same questions they had posed Jesus when they had confronted Him in the temple courtyard (Matthew 21:23 - "By what authority are you doing these things?"). Peter's response or sermon is the direct fulfillment of what Jesus prophesied in Luke 12:11-12.

> [11]When they bring you before the synagogues and the rulers and the authorities, do not worry about how or what you are to speak in your defense, or what you are to say; [12]for the Holy Spirit will teach you in that very hour what you ought to say."
> - Luke 12:11-12

Luke even says as much when prefacing Peter's remarks by saying that he was speaking by the power of the Holy Spirit (verse 8).

Luke records the heart of Peter's sermon:

1. The miracle was done by the power and authority of Jesus Christ.

2. The rulers were responsible for His execution by crucifixion.

3. God raised this Jesus from the dead.

4. That the leaders would reject the One chosen by God (Messiah) was spoken of by the prophet David (Psalms 118:22). This would have been especially galling to hear since the high priest and other priests in the Sanhedrin were Sadducees who did not believe in resurrection or afterlife.

5. Peter finishes with a summary statement that makes Jesus and faith in Him the exclusive pathway to salvation. A statement that continues to offend to this

day because it makes Christianity an exclusive religion: Only Jesus and no other can save.

> [13]Now as they observed the confidence of Peter and John and understood that they were uneducated and untrained men, they were amazed, and began to recognize them as having been with Jesus. [14]And seeing the man who had been healed standing with them, they had nothing to say in reply. [15]But when they had ordered them to leave the Council, they began to confer with one another, [16]saying, "What shall we do with these men? For the fact that a noteworthy miracle has taken place through them is apparent to all who live in Jerusalem, and we cannot deny it. [17]But so that it will not spread any further among the people, let us warn them to speak no longer to any man in this name." [18]And when they had summoned them, they commanded them not to speak or teach at all in the name of Jesus. [19]But Peter and John answered and said to them, "Whether it is right in the sight of God to give heed to you rather than to God, you be the judge; [20]for we cannot stop speaking about what we have seen and heard." [21]When they had threatened them further, they let them go (finding no basis on which to punish them) on account of the people, because they were all glorifying God for what had happened; [22]for the man was more than forty years old on whom this miracle of healing had been performed.
> - Acts 4:13-22

The leaders would now have wanted to punish and silence them but for three reasons could not:

1. They could not deny Peter's sermon. Many in the city thought the same about Jesus and they had no rebuttal to Peter's argument based on Scripture (Jesus was the rejected Messiah according to Psalms 118:22).

2. They could not deny the obvious miracle. They may have even known or recognized this crippled beggar now completely healed standing before them.

3. They could not deny the Apostles their freedom. Taking action against them would create a riot and this would demonstrate to the Roman government that they were not able to maintain order and thus might lose the favored positions they held made possible by their Roman overlords.

In verses 23-31, Luke records the joy, praise and prayer that the church experiences after the release of Peter and John. Remember that only a few weeks before, Jesus had been brought to stand before these very same men and had subsequently been crucified. The Apostles and the church gained great confidence after this event.

> And when they had prayed, the place where they had gathered together was shaken, and they were all filled with the Holy Spirit and began to speak the word of God with boldness.
> - Acts 4:31

The Church Flourishes (4:32-37)

The story of Peter and John's defense of the gospel and release sparks a surge in the growth and development of the church along with the expanded ministry of all the Apostles. Luke describes the benevolent work of the church and the generosity of its members.

Luke uses this occasion to introduce a prominent character who will appear later on when he begins to describe Paul's ministry: Joseph, a Levite (temple worker/security) from Cyprus (foreign born Jew), called Barnabas (son of encouragement). He was the first temple official converted by the Apostles.

Lessons

Jesus Does Not Need Someone's Faith to Act

Our faith in Jesus is important but not the determining factor for His actions. His will is the determining factor in what He does, not how great our faith is. Strong faith helps us to know and accept His will and helps us to persevere when we do not understand or disagree with His will. My prayer of faith hopes that His will is done and that I can trust and rejoice in it even if I do not always understand it.

Keep the Gospel Simple

In Acts 4:8-12, Peter makes five important points in five verses of text that take 40 seconds to read. My point here is that when we are evangelizing someone we should not begin by "explaining" the gospel, we should just "preach" it: the life, death and resurrection of Christ and our response to this. You can then answer questions, challenges and explain in more detail. When it comes to the gospel, first proclaim, then explain.

Discussion Questions

1. In your opinion, what parts of Peter's first and second sermon were the same? What parts were different?

2. How would you explain the fact that Peter only mentions baptism in his first sermon on Pentecost Sunday but not in his preaching to the crowd after healing the crippled beggar?

3. Name and describe three things that prevented the Jewish leaders from believing in Jesus. Name three things that, in your opinion, prevent people from believing in Him today.

CHAPTER 16
PERSECUTION OF PETER AND APOSTLES

ACTS 5:1-42

Let us review our outline as we follow the first section of Acts dealing primarily with the ministry of the Apostle Peter.

1. Peter's First Sermon – Acts 1:1-2:47

2. Peter's Post-Pentecost Ministry – Acts 3:1-4:37

3. **Persecution of Peter and the Apostles** – Acts 5:1-42

We left off at the point where the church in Jerusalem was rejoicing and experiencing spiritual power at the release of Peter and John by the Jewish leaders. This joy would soon turn to concern as a new wave of persecution would be experienced by Peter and the Apostles.

Ananias and Sapphira – 5:1-11

> [36]Now Joseph, a Levite of Cyprian birth, who was also called Barnabas by the apostles (which translated means Son of Encouragement), [37]and who owned a tract of land, sold it and brought the

money and laid it at the apostles' feet.
- Acts 4:36-37

In this passage we read about the joy and spiritual momentum the church experienced as a result of Peter's bold witness before and after his release by the Jewish leaders. This enthusiasm motivated the members of the church to give generously in order to care for the needs of the young and growing congregation. Into this period of joyful liberality, Luke inserts an unusual episode of fraud perpetuated by a husband and wife who were also members of this very same assembly.

[1]But a man named Ananias, with his wife Sapphira, sold a piece of property, [2]and kept back some of the price for himself, with his wife's full knowledge, and bringing a portion of it, he laid it at the apostles' feet. [3]But Peter said, "Ananias, why has Satan filled your heart to lie to the Holy Spirit and to keep back some of the price of the land? [4]While it remained unsold, did it not remain your own? And after it was sold, was it not under your control? Why is it that you have conceived this deed in your heart? You have not lied to men but to God." [5]And as he heard these words, Ananias fell down and breathed his last; and great fear came over all who heard of it. [6]The young men got up and covered him up, and after carrying him out, they buried him.
- Acts 5:1-6

Note several things about this action and why it was so serious:

- They were pretending to duplicate the giving done by Barnabas (give all the proceeds of a land sale to the church).

- The man and his wife plotted the fraud in advance and together. They planned to sell the land, keep a portion for themselves and give the balance to the church pretending that they were turning over all the proceeds as a gift.

- The sin was not the fact that they kept some of the money for themselves. Peter said that the land and money was rightly theirs and in their control. The sin was creating the lie concerning their giving. They pretended to give all their proceeds but in fact kept some of it back for themselves.

- The gravity of the sin was not based on them keeping the money, but as Peter states, believing they could lie to the Holy Spirit and think they would get away with this.

- Their failing was not greed, their failing was faith. Their faith in Christ was so weak, and they themselves so jaded that they could actually come up with a devious scheme like this in order to be praised as generous by other Christians.

- Ananias dies instantly and goes to judgment without a chance to repent, change or grow. Note that the effect on the church is no longer enthusiasm and spiritual power but that of fear; fear for what has just happened before them and possibly fear as they searched their own hearts and actions for signs of greed and insincerity.

[7]Now there elapsed an interval of about three hours, and his wife came in, not knowing what had happened. [8]And Peter responded to her, "Tell me whether you sold the land for such and such a price?" And she said, "Yes, that was the price." [9]Then Peter said to her, "Why is it that you have agreed together to put the Spirit of the Lord to the test? Behold, the feet of those who have buried your husband are at the door, and they will carry you out as well." [10]And immediately she fell at his feet and breathed her last, and the young men came in and found her dead, and they carried her out and buried her beside her husband. [11]And

> great fear came over the whole church, and over
> all who heard of these things.
> - Acts 5:7-11

Note that Peter gives Sapphira a chance to confess the wrong, repent and receive forgiveness, but she doubles down on the lie and experiences the same fate as her husband. Note also that Peter confronts her with her sins (conspire to defraud the church, lie to the Holy Spirit). This time Luke says that fear not only came on those who heard about this incident but also over the entire church. This is the first time in the book of Acts that this term "church" is used (from the Greek - "the called out". Originally referring to those called to serve as city leaders, eventually used exclusively in connection with the body of believers in Christ).

Growth of the Church – 5:12-16

After describing this particular episode, Luke provides a wider view of the situation in Jerusalem as the church was experiencing dramatic growth largely due to the dynamic ministry of Peter and the Apostles.

> [12]At the hands of the apostles many signs and
> wonders were taking place among the people; and
> they were all with one accord in Solomon's
> portico. [13]But none of the rest dared to associate
> with them; however, the people held them in high
> esteem.
> - Acts 5:12-13

Luke describes the location where the church met (Solomon's Porch) an open promenade in the Temple complex which could accommodate thousands of people. He notes the unity of the young church as well as its favor with the people, even though they were afraid to join them on account of the Jewish leaders.

> [14]And all the more believers in the Lord, multitudes
> of men and women, were constantly added to their
> number, [15]to such an extent that they even carried
> the sick out into the streets and laid them on cots
> and pallets, so that when Peter came by at least
> his shadow might fall on any one of them. [16]Also
> the people from the cities in the vicinity of
> Jerusalem were coming together, bringing people
> who were sick or afflicted with unclean spirits, and
> they were all being healed.
> - Acts 5:14-16

Here we see the widening influence of the Apostles' work as
their healing ministry opened the door of opportunity for
reaching people who lived beyond the city of Jerusalem. This
fulfilled Jesus' promise in Acts 1:8, that they would be His
witnesses in Jerusalem, in all Judea (which was now
happening) and Samaria, even to the remotest parts of the
earth (Paul's ministry).

Persecution – 5:17-42

Second Arrest

> [17]But the high priest rose up, along with all his
> associates (that is the sect of the Sadducees), and
> they were filled with jealousy. [18]They laid hands on
> the apostles and put them in a public jail. [19]But
> during the night an angel of the Lord opened the
> gates of the prison, and taking them out he
> said, [20]"Go, stand and speak to the people in the
> temple the whole message of this Life." [21]Upon
> hearing this, they entered into the temple about
> daybreak and began to teach.
> Now when the high priest and his associates
> came, they called the Council together, even all the
> Senate of the sons of Israel, and sent orders to the
> prison house for them to be brought. [22]But the
> officers who came did not find them in the prison;

and they returned and reported back, [23]saying,
"We found the prison house locked quite securely
and the guards standing at the doors; but when we
had opened up, we found no one inside." [24]Now
when the captain of the temple guard and the chief
priests heard these words, they were greatly
perplexed about them as to what would come of
this. [25]But someone came and reported to them,
"The men whom you put in prison are standing in
the temple and teaching the people!"
- Acts 5:17-25

They had been arrested before (Acts 4:3) and warned not to
preach Christ. As more and more people were converted
and met in the temple area, the leaders were not only
jealous but fearful that this movement would threaten their
authority and position. After the Apostles' first arrest they
were released with a warning. This time they are
miraculously freed by an angel and told to continue with their
preaching. When the leaders send for them, the guards not
only report that they are gone, but that the Apostles had
returned to the temple to preach.

Third Arrest

[26]Then the captain went along with the officers and
proceeded to bring them back without violence (for
they were afraid of the people, that they might be
stoned).
[27]When they had brought them, they stood them
before the Council. The high priest questioned
them, [28]saying, "We gave you strict orders not to
continue teaching in this name, and yet, you have
filled Jerusalem with your teaching and intend to
bring this man's blood upon us." [29]But Peter and
the apostles answered, "We must obey God rather
than men. [30]The God of our fathers raised up
Jesus, whom you had put to death by hanging Him
on a cross. [31]He is the one whom God exalted to
His right hand as a Prince and a Savior, to grant

repentance to Israel, and forgiveness of sins. [32]And we are witnesses of these things; and so is the Holy Spirit, whom God has given to those who obey Him."
- Acts 5:26-32

Peter's Defense

They arrest them once again, with care this time fearing the people, and bring them before the Jewish leaders to be questioned. At their first arrest the leaders wanted to know, "By what authority do you do these things?" (preach and heal). At that time Peter answered:

- By Jesus' authority.

- Who you crucified.

- That God raised.

- He is the Messiah according to prophecy ("the stone rejected by the builders").

- He is the only Savior of all men.

This time their tone is different, almost self-defensive, "Why do you continue doing this (preach and heal), do you want to have us bear the guilt for Jesus's death?" They were being disingenuous since they knew exactly what they had done in order to force Pilate into executing Jesus unjustly.

Peter's answer repeats some of the points from his previous appearance before them:

- This teaching and healing power is from God.

- It was you, the leaders, who put Him to death. This sin is yours.

- God, however, raised Jesus up.

At this point Peter adds more information to his response:

- Jesus is now in heaven occupying a place of authority and power at the right hand of God.

- Ironically, if they are guilty, Jesus is the only one that they, as Jews, can appeal to for forgiveness, the one they killed.

- The teaching and miracles they see are a result of the Holy Spirit who empowers them and indwells all who believe and obey the gospel.

We see in this short excerpt Peter's boldness and insight growing. For example, he refuses to stop preaching and healing; he continues to accuse them of killing Jesus, their Messiah; he proclaims Jesus as the only Savior of both Jews and Gentiles; he reveals His position in heaven; and he claims that He is the source of their power to preach and heal. Peter, not groveling and fearful before them, causes jealousy and anger among them but also forces these men to stop and think about what they must do.

Gamaliel's Counsel

[33]But when they heard this, they were cut to the quick and intended to kill them. [34]But a Pharisee named Gamaliel, a teacher of the Law, respected by all the people, stood up in the Council and gave orders to put the men outside for a short time. [35]And he said to them, "Men of Israel, take care what you propose to do with these men. [36]For some time ago Theudas rose up, claiming to be somebody, and a group of about four hundred men joined up with him. But he was killed, and all who followed him were dispersed and came to nothing. [37]After this man, Judas of Galilee rose up in the days of the census and drew away some people after him; he too perished, and all those who followed him were scattered. [38]So in the present case, I say to you, stay away from these men and let them alone, for if this plan or action is of men, it will be overthrown; [39]but if it is of God,

> you will not be able to overthrow them; or else you
> may even be found fighting against God."
> - Acts 5:33-39

Gamaliel was an expert in the Law and teacher who was a member of the Sanhedrin. His intervention saved their lives because Peter's reply had brought the council members into a murderous rage. Peter must have known that the content and boldness of his response would probably get them killed, but he spoke out anyways. What is interesting here is that God used one of the men that opposed the Apostles to actually save them. You never know how God will rescue you, but He will.

Gamaliel's advice (wait and see, don't do anything rash) is accepted by the other leaders. The Bible mentions him as Paul's teacher before he was converted (Acts 22:3) but has no other references to him after that. According to Photios (a 9th century church leader), Gamaliel, along with his two sons, was eventually baptized by Peter and John, and died in 52 AD.

Punishment by the Council

> [40]They took his advice; and after calling the apostles in, they flogged them and ordered them not to speak in the name of Jesus, and then released them. [41]So they went on their way from the presence of the Council, rejoicing that they had been considered worthy to suffer shame for His name. [42]And every day, in the temple and from house to house, they kept right on teaching and preaching Jesus as the Christ.
> - Acts 5:40-42

The leaders follow Gamaliel's counsel to prudence, but in a repeated effort to frighten and discourage the Apostles they warn them to stop their preaching and reinforce this warning by torturing them. Flogging or flaying was 39 strikes on the back and sides with rods (Matthew 10:17; II Corinthians 11:24). Note that all the Apostles endured this beating. Their reaction was the complete opposite of what the Jewish leaders expected: fear, discouragement, doubting their cause and mission. Luke writes that on the contrary, they rejoiced because this event proved several things:

1. They were sincerely faithful. Taking this beating and receiving these threats without losing faith proved the quality and strength of their belief.

2. This event also proved the sureness of Jesus' word and promise.

> [16]"Behold, I send you out as sheep in the midst of wolves; so be shrewd as serpents and innocent as doves. [17]But beware of men, for they will hand you over to the courts and scourge you in their synagogues; [18]and you will even be brought before governors and kings for My sake, as a testimony to them and to the Gentiles. [19]But when they hand you over, do not worry about how or what you are to say; for it will be given you in that hour what you are to say. [20]For it is not you who speak, but it is the Spirit of your Father who speaks in you.
> - Matthew 10:16-20

The bad thing that He said would happen did take place but so did the promise to know what to say when the critical moment arrived.

3. Their actions demonstrated the weakness of the opposition. Peter had now spoken before the Jewish leaders twice and both times they had no counterargument to his preaching of the gospel. These supposed teachers, wise men, leaders of Israel, had no answer to the accusations and proclamations of a humble fisherman from Galilee.

4. God considered them worthy (faithful) enough to suffer for the name of Christ. They did not invite rejection and violence but when it happened because of their faith, they were fully assured that they were following Jesus' lead who also had suffered for the doing of God's will.

Since the beating was administered in the presence of the Sanhedrin, the joyful reaction of the Apostles must have been disquieting to these men looking on.

Luke ends this section by noting a new element in the development of the early church, house to house teaching and preaching. This was probably done for two reasons:

1. The congregation was becoming too large to effectively minister to by coming together in a single place.

2. To avoid the mounting opposition of the Jewish leaders who controlled the temple area where the church met.

Lessons

God Knows

Peter knew about the deception of Ananias and Sapphira because it was revealed to him by God's Spirit. It is amazing how believers, who should know better, think they can hide their sins or motivations from God. In the end it is not our spouses or friends or even ourselves that will judge us, it is the all-knowing God who will judge.

> But I tell you that every careless word that people speak, they shall give an accounting for it in the day of judgment.
> - Matthew 12:36

There is Always a Cost

Luke writes that many were becoming Christians but the majority of the people, even though they respected them, would not join them. It was commendable that the people respected the church but respect does not save you or forgive your sins. Faith and obedience does that. Even though these people respected the sincerity, spirituality and lovingkindness of the disciples, they would not pay the price (faith and possible rejection by their family and friends). And so, they were left to observe and admire something they would never have, a Spirit-filled and eternal life.

God is Stronger

We need to remember, in times of trouble and sorrow, that God is stronger than what opposes us. We may not be stronger than what is hurting us, but He is. Luke describes the battle lines in Acts: Jewish leadership, tradition, Roman Empire, pagan world against the 12 Apostles and a young church. With the accuracy of hindsight we know that each of these were eventually overtaken to make way for Jesus' word and His church. John says, *"greater is He who is in you than he who is in the world."* (I John 4:4). Keep this in mind when discouraged: the Spirit of God that dwells in you is greater than the spirit of the one who rules this world. This may not always be evident, but the final proof of it will be seen when He will raise us from the dead and destroy the evil one and all that opposes us, once and forever.

Discussion Questions

1. In what ways do we "lie" to the Holy Spirit today? What would be the proper repentance for this?

2. In the face of such strong evidence, why do you think the Jewish leaders continued to disbelieve? In your opinion what is the reason that people today believe or reject Christ when presented a similar gospel and arguments?

3. Describe a way or an instance when you suffered for Christ and how you felt afterwards. How was your faith affected?

CHAPTER 17
PERSECUTION OF THE CHURCH
- PART 1

ACTS 6:1-7:60

So far in his record, Luke has focused his attention on Peter the Apostle's ministry and persecution at the hands of the Jewish leaders. Beginning in this chapter, Luke brings the church and its inner workings to the foreground. Let us look at our outline to see what point we have reached in our study.

1. Peter's First Sermon – Acts 1:1-2:47

2. Peter's Post Pentecost Ministry – Acts 3:1-4:37

3. Persecution of Peter and the Apostles – Acts 5:1-42

4. **Persecution of the Church** - Acts 6:1-7:60

Luke will now describe people and events that were part of the first congregation of the church in Jerusalem.

The Choosing of the Seven – 6:1-7

The Problem

> Now at this time while the disciples were increasing in number, a complaint arose on the

> part of the Hellenistic Jews against the native
> Hebrews, because their widows were being
> overlooked in the daily serving of food.
> - Acts 6:1

It seems that after they were set free from confinement by the religious leaders, the Apostles continued their work in Jerusalem where it is estimated that the church grew to about 25,000 people. We read previously that certain members sold their land and donated the proceeds to the church, and here we see that some of this money was used to provide food for poor widows. I have done a quick count and in my congregation of about 400 people we have 25 widows. Using this ratio, a congregation of 25,000 would have some 1,500 widows. Apparently this distribution and care was taking place on a daily basis which would have been an expensive and time consuming ministry.

The Hellenistic Jews were not Greek converts to Judaism, they were Jews who were born outside of Israel. Note that Luke refers to the Jews born in Israel as "native" Hebrews in order to make the distinction between these two groups. We do not know why the widows of the Hellenistic Jews were being neglected, perhaps the rapid growth of the church caused some to be overlooked, perhaps the Hellenistic Jews were sensitive to the fact that all the church leaders (Apostles) were native Hebrews and any difference in the treatment of their people was seized upon. Luke does not comment on the legitimacy of their complaint, only that things finally came to a head because their concern reached the ears of the Apostles.

The Solution

> So the twelve summoned the congregation of the
> disciples and said, "It is not desirable for us to
> neglect the word of God in order to serve tables.
> - Acts 6:2

It seems that the Apostles themselves were actively involved in caring for the widows at this point and conclude that this task was crowding out their more important work as leaders and teachers in the church. Even today, elders and preachers often find themselves overloaded with tasks not connected with their primary work of teaching, preaching and ministering the Word to the flock. Luke states that this problem moved them to begin delegating some of the benevolent tasks that they had been doing, and thus a ministry structure was put into place in the young church.

> [3]Therefore, brethren, select from among you seven men of good reputation, full of the Spirit and of wisdom, whom we may put in charge of this task. [4]But we will devote ourselves to prayer and to the ministry of the word." [5]The statement found approval with the whole congregation; and they chose Stephen, a man full of faith and of the Holy Spirit, and Philip, Prochorus, Nicanor, Timon, Parmenas and Nicolas, a proselyte from Antioch. [6]And these they brought before the apostles; and after praying, they laid their hands on them.
> - Acts 6:3-6

Luke carefully lays out the process that they followed:

1. The Apostles established the qualifications for those to be chosen. To begin with, they specified that men only were to be considered for this role (the term used referred to males and not people in general). They could have established a precedent here for females to serve as deacons but they chose not to. They were to choose seven men because the Apostles determined that seven men would be required to do this job properly. These needed to be spiritually mature men (full of the Spirit) and ones who possessed wisdom (they knew how to apply or use the knowledge they had). Many times, we choose a person who is a good carpenter or bookkeeper in seeking men to serve as

deacons thinking that job skill or training are the primary qualities this brother should have. Note that Peter only names spirituality and wisdom as the things to look for in a potential deacon.

2. The Apostles instructed the church to select the candidates for deacons. The church had to choose men who were both spiritual and wise to be considered for the role of deacon (a Greek word meaning waiter, servant or minister).

3. The Apostles would then authorize the men selected and vetted by the congregation to serve. This they did by prayer and the laying on of their hands in order to commend these individuals into their ministry as deacons.

The Results

> The word of God kept on spreading; and the number of the disciples continued to increase greatly in Jerusalem, and a great many of the priests were becoming obedient to the faith.
> - Acts 6:7

The Apostles returned to their essential work of prayer and teaching. We see the results of this renewed effort as Luke records the continued growth of the church. Luke also mentions that the gospel was impacting the higher levels of society and religion as a good number of priests were turning to Christ as well.

Persecution Begins – 6:8-7:60

Stephen's Arrest

> [8]And Stephen, full of grace and power, was performing great wonders and signs among the

> people. [9]But some men from what was called the Synagogue of the Freedmen, including both Cyrenians and Alexandrians, and some from Cilicia and Asia, rose up and argued with Stephen. [10]But they were unable to cope with the wisdom and the Spirit with which he was speaking. [11]Then they secretly induced men to say, "We have heard him speak blasphemous words against Moses and against God." [12]And they stirred up the people, the elders and the scribes, and they came up to him and dragged him away and brought him before the Council.
> - Acts 6:8-12

Luke writes that beyond his work as a deacon, Stephen also performed miracles and thus became the first member of the church, aside from the Apostles, to do so. We learn later on that the ability to speak in tongues, heal others and work miracles was transferred to believers by the laying on of the Apostle's hands (Acts 8:14-18). This is how Stephen received his ability to do these things.

He was wise and spiritually mature which explains his ability to preach, teach and debate with the Hellenists. Stephen himself was a Hellenistic Jew converted to Christianity and was now attacked by other Hebrew Hellenists who considered him a traitor for his conversion. They tried debating him and were unsuccessful so they resorted to the same tactics used to have Jesus arrested and executed. They stirred up the people with lies and this provided the Jewish leaders an opportunity to arrest him.

The Trial

> [13]They put forward false witnesses who said, "This man incessantly speaks against this holy place and the Law; [14]for we have heard him say that this Nazarene, Jesus, will destroy this place and alter the customs which Moses handed down to us."

> [15]And fixing their gaze on him, all who were sitting in the Council saw his face like the face of an angel.
> - Acts 6:13-15

Once before the Jewish leaders, several charges are brought against him which are nearly the same as the ones brought against Jesus (it worked then, why not now?). Luke records the various accusations (without evidence) made by false witnesses who lied in order to secure his conviction. Very much like Jesus, Stephen did not debate or defend himself against his accusers. Perhaps included in the Lord's promise to provide His disciples with the wisdom to give a proper answer when questioned also came the ability to know when to say nothing as well.

Stephen's Response (7:1-53)

> [1]The high priest said, "Are these things so?"
> [2]And he said, "Hear me, brethren and fathers! The God of glory appeared to our father Abraham when he was in Mesopotamia, before he lived in Haran, [3]and said to him, 'Leave your country and your relatives, and come into the land that I will show you.'
> - Acts 7:1-3

Prodded by the high priest to speak and answer the charges, which would have been useless since the purpose of the hearing was to find him guilty and execute him, Stephen instead proceeds to recite the story of the Jewish people. He begins with Abraham and his initial call by God to leave his home (Mesopotamia - Iraq) and go to the land of Canaan (Israel). He summarizes their history and heroes, as well as God's dealing with them as His chosen nation. Stephen then brings the story to the present day and concludes with the same accusation that Peter made when he and the other Apostles were dragged before these very same men.

> ^{51}"You men who are stiff-necked and uncircumcised in heart and ears are always resisting the Holy Spirit; you are doing just as your fathers did. ^{52}Which one of the prophets did your fathers not persecute? They killed those who had previously announced the coming of the Righteous One, whose betrayers and murderers you have now become; ^{53}you who received the law as ordained by angels, and yet did not keep it."
> - Acts 7:51-53

His accusations are harsh but true:

1. They were stubborn, hard-hearted and completely unspiritual.
2. They were disobedient, resisting God's Spirit.
3. They were as evil and disobedient as their forefathers.
4. They not only killed the prophet (John the Baptist) sent to announce the coming of the Messiah, they also killed the Messiah Himself (Jesus).
5. They received the divinely appointed Law but did not honor or keep it.

Stephen's inditement of them is complete: guilty in the past (their ancestors rejected and killed the prophets sent to them), and guilty in the present (of rejecting and killing their own Messiah). He leaves out the future because the judgment to come for their sins is evident if not spoken.

Stephen's Death (7:54-60)

> Now when they heard this, they were cut to the quick, and they began gnashing their teeth at him.
> - Acts 7:54

His accusations hit home and the Jewish leaders experience extreme emotion (cut to the quick/sawn in two/gnashing of teeth/grinding one's teeth in suppressed rage). Despite this, however, they do not make a move against him as he is still able to speak.

> [55]But being full of the Holy Spirit, he gazed intently into heaven and saw the glory of God, and Jesus standing at the right hand of God; [56]and he said, "Behold, I see the heavens opened up and the Son of Man standing at the right hand of God."
> - Acts 7:55-56

In His mercy and knowing what is to come, God gives Stephen a vision of the heaven he is about to enter as his reward for being faithful unto death. Note that Luke mentions that Jesus is standing at the right hand of God twice, thus signifying His authority (right hand). Some commentators (Lenski, p. 304) suggest that Jesus is standing to welcome the first saint and martyr to reach heaven since the church was established on Pentecost Sunday.

> But they cried out with a loud voice, and covered their ears and rushed at him with one impulse.
> - Acts 7:57

It is one thing to accuse them to their faces of rejecting the Messiah. After all, Peter had done the same and every one of the 25,000 disciples in Jerusalem shared in his accusation by accepting Christ. Now, however, this man was claiming to actually see both God and Jesus in heaven. In their estimation, this was blasphemy! Stephen was raising himself up as one who could see God in the heavens. They would hear no more and in a rage moved to silence him.

> [58]When they had driven him out of the city, they began stoning him; and the witnesses laid aside their robes at the feet of a young man named Saul. [59]They went on stoning Stephen as he called on the Lord and said, "Lord Jesus, receive my

spirit!" [60]Then falling on his knees, he cried out with a loud voice, "Lord, do not hold this sin against them!" Having said this, he fell asleep.
- Acts 7:58-60

Note that the "trial" did not follow the normal procedure with a vote or a 24-hour cooling off period before pronouncing sentence, especially one requiring an execution. I've mentioned in our study of Luke's gospel that the Jews were not permitted to execute criminals, they had to go through the Roman officials as they had done with Jesus. However, this was no longer a trial to seek justice but an angry mob taking the law into their own hands and murdering someone in an act of rage. I believe, however, that there were no repercussions for two reasons:

1. Stephen was not a high-profile person like Jesus and had not come to the attention of Herod or Pilate.

2. Even if Christians complained and brought charges, they could not do so to the Jewish leaders for obvious reasons, and dared not approach Pilate after what happened to Jesus.

Luke chooses to introduce Saul (Paul) at this point as one who minded the cloaks of those stoning Stephen. The witnesses were those who testified against Stephen. According to the Law these men were required to cast the first stones as the ones who had witnessed the crime for which the person was being executed (Deuteronomy 17:6). In this case, these people were adding murder to the sin of perjury they had already committed.

Stephen is not afraid of dying because he is absolutely sure where he is going, to the point where he calls on the Lord to receive his spirit. He fell "asleep" signifying that he entered the period of waiting until the return of Jesus. And, what must have been hard for the Jews to bear, Stephen's final words are not a cry for help or a curse on his attackers but, like Jesus, a plea to God to forgive those who are in the process of killing him.

In this way God provides us with a model for those who would suffer a martyr's death:

1. Do not act like your executioners.
2. Keep your eyes of faith on Jesus.
3. Do not exchange a few more years of life on this earth for an early departure for heaven.
4. Forgive those who are taking your life because in doing so you may have a chance to see them in heaven one day.

Lessons

Satan Always Finds a Way

Notice that it does not take long before Satan begins his attacks on the young church in Jerusalem.

- Peter is arrested in an effort to silence him.
- All of the Apostles are arrested in order to remove the church's leadership.
- Some begin to stir up trouble in the benevolence ministry.
- The Jews attack a dynamic servant of the church who is having an impact on the people in the name of Christ.

It began almost from the beginning and has continued throughout history to this very day. Satan continually attacks the church, especially when it is growing and bearing fruit.

We Will All See What Stephen Saw

Stephen saw Jesus at the right hand of God just moments before he fell asleep (the kind of death believers experience as they await Jesus' return and their awakening from sleep).

We will both see and hear Jesus at the right hand of God saying, *"Well done good and faithful servant."* This is what we will experience a moment after being awakened by an angel's trumpet and the call of the Lord when He returns. Stephen was only a man, but as the first Christian to die, God has shown all of us through him what to expect after death no matter how we die (a time of peaceful sleep, then the resurrection and the ability to see and hear Jesus Himself welcome us to heaven).

Reading Assignment: Acts 8:1-9:43

Discussion Questions

1. On average women are usually more faithful and active in the church. Why then do you think God entrusted the leadership of the church to men?

2. In your opinion, what does your church need to do to recruit qualified deacons?

3. Describe ways that Satan has attacked your church and how it dealt with this. Could the church have avoided trouble? How?

CHAPTER 18
PERSECUTION OF THE CHURCH
- PART 2

ACTS 8:1-9:43

In the previous chapter, we read about the beginning of the persecution of the church as Peter and the Apostles were arrested and beaten, and Stephen was stoned to death. This violence will continue as a persecution of the entire church, not only its leaders, ensues. Let us check with our outline to situate where we are in our study.

1. Peter's First Sermon – Acts 1:1-2:47
2. Peter's Post-Pentecost Ministry – Acts 3:1-4:37
3. Persecution of Peter and the Apostles – Acts 5:1-42
4. Persecution of the Church – Acts 6:1-7:60
5. **Persecution of the Church Part II – Acts 8:1-9:43**

We pick up the story in chapter 9 with the introduction of Saul, an early persecutor of the church.

Persecution and Scattering of the Church

Saul's Persecution

> [1]Saul was in hearty agreement with putting him to
> death. And on that day a great persecution began
> against the church in Jerusalem, and they were all
> scattered throughout the regions of Judea and
> Samaria, except the apostles. [2]Some devout men
> buried Stephen, and made loud lamentation over
> him. [3]But Saul began ravaging the church, entering
> house after house, and dragging off men and
> women, he would put them in prison.
> - Acts 8:1-3

Note what Luke says about Saul's attitude and actions:

1. He enthusiastically agreed with the killing of Stephen.

2. Since this was so, it was natural for him to want to
   destroy all Christians in the same manner.

3. On the day of Stephen's death, Saul begins a
   persecution campaign without restraint or mercy. Both
   men and women are dragged from their homes and
   imprisoned.

Luke mentions that it was this persecution that sent
Christians fleeing from Jerusalem to other, safer parts of the
country (i.e. Samaria where the Sanhedrin had no authority).
Stephen is properly buried and the Apostles, not afraid of
Saul, remain in Jerusalem because that is where the bulk of
the church remains and where their work is centered.

Philip in Samaria (8:4-40)

> [4]Therefore, those who had been scattered went
> about preaching the word. [5]Philip went down to the
> city of Samaria and began proclaiming Christ to

them. [6]The crowds with one accord were giving attention to what was said by Philip, as they heard and saw the signs which he was performing. [7]For in the case of many who had unclean spirits, they were coming out of them shouting with a loud voice; and many who had been paralyzed and lame were healed. [8]So there was much rejoicing in that city.
- Acts 8:4-8

Luke now introduces another main character of the early church: Philip, who along with Stephen was one of the original seven deacons. The persecution sends him to Samaria (a place he would not have visited as a Jew). However, as a Christian, he not only travels there but begins to share the gospel with these people that the Jews had no contact or dealings with. The Holy Spirit empowers Philip to perform signs and healings (a power he received through the laying on of the Apostles' hands - Acts 6:6) as a dynamic way to confirm the Word that he spoke, and the people there responded.

[9]Now there was a man named Simon, who formerly was practicing magic in the city and astonishing the people of Samaria, claiming to be someone great; [10]and they all, from smallest to greatest, were giving attention to him, saying, "This man is what is called the Great Power of God." [11]And they were giving him attention because he had for a long time astonished them with his magic arts. [12]But when they believed Philip preaching the good news about the kingdom of God and the name of Jesus Christ, they were being baptized, men and women alike. [13]Even Simon himself believed; and after being baptized, he continued on with Philip, and as he observed signs and great miracles taking place, he was constantly amazed.
- Acts 8:9-13

At this point Luke focuses on one convert in particular, Simon, a magician. He was highly regarded as a practitioner of the black arts. Magic is the attempt to manipulate or influence the "spirit world" for your benefit or the harm of others by doing something in the material world (i.e. carrying a lucky penny thinking the spirits will bring good fortune).

The Bible forbids all forms of magic and the occult (Exodus 7:11-12; Deuteronomy 18:9-12; Galatians 5:19-21). Here are some general definitions of these practices with Scriptures that forbid them:

1. **Enchantments:** Practice of magical arts
   – Deuteronomy 18:10-12

2. **Witchcraft:** Soothsaying/magic – II Chronicles 33:6

3. **Sorcery:** Same as witchcraft – Jeremiah 27:9

4. **Divination:** Fortune telling – II Kings 17:17

5. **Wizardry:** Male witch – Exodus 22:18

6. **Necromancy:** Séance/communication with the dead
   – I Chronicles 10:13-14

7. **Charming:** Casting spells – Isaiah 19:3

8. **Star Gazing:** Astrology – Isaiah 47:12-15

9. **Imagery:** Use of images from these practices for logos/decoration

These are forbidden by God because whether they realize it or not, the people who use magic are actually appealing to Satan and his power to accomplish their desired ends. The only appeal to the spirit world blessed by God is prayer offered to Himself through faith in Jesus (Luke 11:9; John 14:13). God refers to all occult practices as an abomination (Deuteronomy 18:10-12).

Luke writes that like all disciples, Simon believes the gospel and is baptized as a result (verse 13).

> [14]Now when the apostles in Jerusalem heard that Samaria had received the word of God, they sent them Peter and John, [15]who came down and prayed for them that they might receive the Holy Spirit. [16]For He had not yet fallen upon any of them; they had simply been baptized in the name of the Lord Jesus. [17]Then they began laying their hands on them, and they were receiving the Holy Spirit.
>
> - Acts 8:14-17

This passage is better understood if we review again the meaning of the two terms describing the work of the Holy Spirit:

1. **Indwelling**: The Holy Spirit dwells within the believer. This takes place at baptism (Acts 2:38).

2. **Empowering**: The Holy Spirit empowers someone to do miracles, speak in tongues, etc. (Acts 2:1-13).

Sometimes the writers use an expression (i.e. receiving the Holy Spirit) that refers to one of these two things (indwelling or empowering) but the reader has to examine the text to know which he is referring to. In verses 16-17, Luke writes that the Samaritans had been baptized in the name of Jesus, therefore at that moment, according to Acts 2:38, they also received the indwelling of the Holy Spirit. This being so, the other blessing of the Spirit (that they "receive the Holy Spirit" refers to the "empowering by the Holy Spirit"), since they had already received the "indwelling" at baptism. Note that they received empowerment at the laying on of the Apostles' hands. Philip sent for the Apostles because he could administer the water baptism that would bring them the indwelling of the Spirit, but only the Apostles could transfer the empowerment of the Holy Spirit through the imposition or laying on of their hands.

This is an important point to understand because it is the basis for the teaching on modern-day miracles. Here is the breakdown of this teaching:

1. The Holy Spirit empowered only the Apostles (and, as we will learn later in chapter 10, Cornelius) with the ability to speak in tongues, heal and do miracles.

2. The Apostles (as we see here) also had the ability to transfer this empowerment to speak in tongues, heal, etc. to other disciples through the laying on of their hands.

3. These disciples, however, who had received this empowerment from the Apostles, did not have the ability to empower others by the laying on of their hands. This is why even though Philip himself could perform signs and wonders, he could not enable other disciples to do the same. Only the Apostles could do this and for this reason they came to help Philip and empowered his converts to practice spiritual gifts. With the death of the Apostles the performance of miracles diminished and eventually ceased because the way to receive the empowerment ended with their passing.

> [18]Now when Simon saw that the Spirit was bestowed through the laying on of the apostles' hands, he offered them money, [19]saying, "Give this authority to me as well, so that everyone on whom I lay my hands may receive the Holy Spirit." [20]But Peter said to him, "May your silver perish with you, because you thought you could obtain the gift of God with money! [21]You have no part or portion in this matter, for your heart is not right before God. [22]Therefore repent of this wickedness of yours, and pray the Lord that, if possible, the intention of your heart may be forgiven you. [23]For I see that you are in the gall of bitterness and in the bondage of iniquity." [24]But Simon answered and said, "Pray to the Lord for me yourselves, so that nothing of what you have said may come upon me."
> - Acts 8:18-24

4. Simon sees that the transfer of spiritual power is accomplished by the laying on of hands. He realizes this when he notices that those on whom the Apostles laid hands began speaking in tongues and doing the things that Philip had done. He makes the connection between the laying on of the hands of the Apostles and empowerment.

5. Since the disciples who were empowered could not pass on this spiritual gift, and the Apostles eventually died, with time there was no one left in the church who had the empowerment or could pass it on to others.

6. Paul teaches that these abilities and powers would eventually disappear once the full revelation from God was recorded and preserved (I Corinthians 13:8-10).

This is the short teaching version of the reason we do not believe that God empowers people today with the ability to speak in tongues, heal or do miracles. He can if He wants to, but according to Scripture, He does not. The Bible contains all that we need to win souls, build the church and mature Christians (II Timothy 3:15-16; II Peter 1:3; Romans 1:16). Those who claim to have this power do so in opposition to Scripture and have difficulty in demonstrating objectively that their power and healing are similar to that demonstrated in the New Testament. For example, the miracle of tongues in the Bible is described as the ability to speak in various human languages not known or studied by the speaker. Modern day Charismatics do not and have never been able to do this.

We read that Simon makes the mistake of trying to purchase this power from the Apostles, falling back into his old ways where magicians bought and sold their tricks and deceptions from one another. Peter severely rebukes him and admonishes him to repent immediately for such a serious sin (to buy the blessing of God). He was probably spared because he was a young Christian and acted impetuously. The gall of bitterness and the bondage of iniquity are two references that mean the same thing, Simon's sinful attitude (gall of bitterness - bad fruit) is a bond that firmly holds him. His response shows that he takes this seriously and appeals to the Apostles for their help in prayer.

Philip and the Ethiopian Eunuch (8:25-40)

Luke includes a second account of Philip's ministry, this time to a Gentile convert to Judaism from Africa. We read that Philip's evangelism ministry was quite dynamic in that he was already reaching out beyond the boundaries of the Jewish nation with the gospel message, first to the Samaritans and now to this foreign Gentile proselyte to the Jewish faith. He is directed by an angel to this man who was a "keeper of the treasure" for the Queen of Ethiopia. This person was not only a convert to Judaism but of a different race as well.

Luke recounts how Philip rode along with this person and answered his questions concerning the Scripture he was reading. Philip uses this opportunity to preach the gospel to him and the eunuch responds immediately.

> [34]The eunuch answered Philip and said, "Please tell me, of whom does the prophet say this? Of himself or of someone else?" [35]Then Philip opened his mouth, and beginning from this Scripture he preached Jesus to him. [36]As they went along the road they came to some water; and the eunuch said, "Look! Water! What prevents me from being baptized?" [37][And Philip said, "If you believe with all your heart, you may." And he answered and said, "I believe that Jesus Christ is the Son of God."] [38]And he ordered the chariot to stop; and they both went down into the water, Philip as well as the eunuch, and he baptized him.
> - Acts 8:34-38

Note that the eunuch's initial response after hearing the gospel was to inquire about baptism. This shows three things:

1. The command to be baptized is part of the preaching of the gospel.

2. Being baptized is part of one's response of faith to the gospel.

3. The baptism taught and administered was a water baptism. Also, an immersion since both men went down into the water.

One other point not mentioned was that his deformity as a eunuch only allowed this man to be considered a "proselyte of the gate" by the Jews and thus barred from entering the courtyard area where other Gentile proselytes could worship (Deuteronomy 23:1). The eunuch's conversion to Christianity, however, transformed him from being one who could only go to the gate of the Temple but no further, to becoming the actual temple of the Holy Spirit through Christ (I Corinthians 6:19-20).

The Conversion of Saul – 9:1-19

Luke now shifts the focus of his narrative from the work of Peter and the early church to the conversion of its chief antagonist leading the persecution against them, Saul of Tarsus.

> [1]Now Saul, still breathing threats and murder against the disciples of the Lord, went to the high priest, [2]and asked for letters from him to the synagogues at Damascus, so that if he found any belonging to the Way, both men and women, he might bring them bound to Jerusalem.
> - Acts 9:1-2

Saul was not merely an opponent of the religion and had theoretical objections to Christianity, he was out to destroy it as a religion and kill or imprison those who practiced it. He had been confining his attacks in and around Jerusalem, but was now expanding his aggression outside of the city and nation.

That he sought authorization from the Jewish leaders to arrest and imprison Jewish converts in another city confirms two things:

1. The Jewish leadership was complicit in the persecution of Christians.

2. Saul was their official leader in charge of this effort.

> [3]As he was traveling, it happened that he was approaching Damascus, and suddenly a light from heaven flashed around him; [4]and he fell to the ground and heard a voice saying to him, "Saul, Saul, why are you persecuting Me?" [5]And he said, "Who are You, Lord?" And He said, "I am Jesus whom you are persecuting, [6]but get up and enter the city, and it will be told you what you must do." [7]The men who traveled with him stood speechless, hearing the voice but seeing no one. [8]Saul got up from the ground, and though his eyes were open, he could see nothing; and leading him by the hand, they brought him into Damascus. [9]And he was three days without sight, and neither ate nor drank.
> - Acts 9:3-9

God chose the gospel's chief enemy to bring the gospel to the Gentiles. Paul's encounter with Christ stops his persecution and renders him helpless. He spends several days fasting and praying, as a devout Jew would do in these circumstances. God gives him three days to ponder Jesus' question, "Why are you persecuting Me?" Saul was so sure of his mission (destroy Christianity because it is false and a threat to Judaism) that he was willing to kill and imprison both men and women, all in good conscience. Saul must have also wondered what God would have him do.

Luke now introduces another character and the task he is given to perform.

> ¹⁰Now there was a disciple at Damascus named Ananias; and the Lord said to him in a vision, "Ananias." And he said, "Here I am, Lord." ¹¹And the Lord said to him, "Get up and go to the street called Straight, and inquire at the house of Judas for a man from Tarsus named Saul, for he is praying, ¹²and he has seen in a vision a man named Ananias come in and lay his hands on him, so that he might regain his sight." ¹³But Ananias answered, "Lord, I have heard from many about this man, how much harm he did to Your saints at Jerusalem; ¹⁴and here he has authority from the chief priests to bind all who call on Your name." ¹⁵But the Lord said to him, "Go, for he is a chosen instrument of Mine, to bear My name before the Gentiles and kings and the sons of Israel; ¹⁶for I will show him how much he must suffer for My name's sake." ¹⁷So Ananias departed and entered the house, and after laying his hands on him said, "Brother Saul, the Lord Jesus, who appeared to you on the road by which you were coming, has sent me so that you may regain your sight and be filled with the Holy Spirit." ¹⁸And immediately there fell from his eyes something like scales, and he regained his sight, and he got up and was baptized; ¹⁹and he took food and was strengthened.
> - Acts 9:10-19

In this section Luke gives some background information on Ananias, and his struggle to believe God concerning Saul and what He wanted Ananias to do. In chapter 22 we find out that Ananias preached the gospel to Paul and baptized him. Yet another biblical example of a person immediately responding to the gospel with baptism as the initial expression of their faith in Jesus.

If you put this account together with the one in chapter 22, there is an order in Saul's conversion that emerges:

1. He is called (miraculously).
2. He is taught (the gospel).
3. He is baptized (to remove sin, especially the murder of Stephen and others).
4. He begins to minister (too soon).

By removing Saul as an aggressor, the church once again enjoys a period of peace and growth.

Saul Begins His Ministry

[20]and immediately he began to proclaim Jesus in the synagogues, saying, "He is the Son of God." [21]All those hearing him continued to be amazed, and were saying, "Is this not he who in Jerusalem destroyed those who called on this name, and who had come here for the purpose of bringing them bound before the chief priests?" [22]But Saul kept increasing in strength and confounding the Jews who lived at Damascus by proving that this Jesus is the Christ.
[23]When many days had elapsed, the Jews plotted together to do away with him, [24]but their plot became known to Saul. They were also watching the gates day and night so that they might put him to death; [25]but his disciples took him by night and let him down through an opening in the wall, lowering him in a large basket.
- Acts 9:20-25

Saul, because of his notoriety and grasp of the Scriptures, immediately becomes a defender of the faith and is successful as a preacher. Just as Jesus and Peter did (not Philip because he preached in areas where the Jewish leaders had no authority: Samaria and Damascus), Saul runs into opposition from the leading Jews who are plotting to kill him for preaching Christ. They resort to this because they are unwilling and unable to debate, humiliate or distract him. Luke describes how Saul became stronger as their attacks grew more vicious. Eventually it becomes necessary for him to escape and his friends lower him over the city wall in a basket so he can leave Damascus and safely make his way to Jerusalem.

Saul Joins the Disciples in Jerusalem

[26]When he came to Jerusalem, he was trying to associate with the disciples; but they were all afraid of him, not believing that he was a disciple. [27]But Barnabas took hold of him and brought him to the apostles and described to them how he had seen the Lord on the road, and that He had talked to him, and how at Damascus he had spoken out boldly in the name of Jesus. [28]And he was with them, moving about freely in Jerusalem, speaking out boldly in the name of the Lord. [29]And he was talking and arguing with the Hellenistic Jews; but they were attempting to put him to death. [30]But when the brethren learned of it, they brought him down to Caesarea and sent him away to Tarsus. [31]So the church throughout all Judea and Galilee and Samaria enjoyed peace, being built up; and going on in the fear of the Lord and in the comfort of the Holy Spirit, it continued to increase.
- Acts 9:26-31

Some scholars believe that Saul returned to Jerusalem after a one to three-year period. Communication being what it was in those days, the news of him and his conversion may have been carried back in bits and pieces. Suddenly, however, he reappears and immediately wants to worship and associate with the saints but they were afraid, not believing that he was converted. They may have thought that this was a trick to spy on them and continue the persecution.

Barnabas (Acts 4:36-37), who has access to the Apostles, brings him before them to substantiate his story. Once they give him their blessing, Paul is accepted and continues his teaching ministry among the Jews as he had done in Damascus. Of course the same thing that had happened there, a plot to kill him, takes place in Jerusalem this time organized by the Hellenistic Jews (same group that attacked Stephen). Luke writes that the brethren brought him out of the city and sent him back to the friendlier confines of Tarsus, his home town.

Luke finishes this section by describing the peace and growth the church experienced now that their chief opponent, Saul, had been converted and was ministering far away in the north. Saul had stopped persecuting the church and by his absence was no longer a lightening rod for his previous masters among the Jewish leadership in attacking the believers in Jerusalem. Without Saul to create friction the church could grow in peace.

Peter's Ministry Continues – 9:31-43

Luke now switches back to focus on Peter and his ministry. He will take up Saul's progress again in the future but there are still important events in Peter's ministry he wishes to record.

The first of these is the healing of a paralyzed man who is made well as Peter invokes the name of Jesus. This occurred in the town of Lydda and the people there believed in Jesus at the preaching and healing ministry of Peter. He was then called to Joppa, a town nearby where a disciple named Tabitha (Greek - Dorcas) had died. The brethren appealed to Peter to come despite the fact that she was already dead. Peter arrives and immediately, to the joy of the disciples, raises her from the dead. This news causes many in that town to believe in Jesus as well.

These two scenes give us insight into the apostolic ministry carried out by Peter:

1. He travelled throughout Judea preaching and performing miracles.

2. His miraculous powers were unlimited. He healed an unbeliever with a word. He brought a believer back from the dead with only a word.

3. He was not an administrator/CEO type of leader, he was a shepherd and proclaimer type of leader.

In the next session, Luke will describe one of the most significant events in Peter's ministry as an Apostle.

Lessons

All Roads Lead to Jesus

In teaching the eunuch, Philip began in the book of Isaiah and showed how his prophecies pointed to Jesus. Everything in the Bible is about, supports, leads to and explains the person and ministry of Christ. If, after reading the Bible, you arrive at the conclusion that Jesus is not the divine Savior, you have read the Bible incorrectly.

We All Become Christians in the Same Way

You will note that all the way through the book of Acts people became Christians by faith in Christ expressed in repentance and baptism (i.e. the 3000 at Pentecost were baptized - Acts 2:41; the Samaritans were baptized - Acts 8:16; the Ethiopian eunuch was baptized - Acts 8:26-40; Saul the Jewish Pharisee was baptized - Acts 9:18). The argument over the necessity of baptism is not one that the early church had. The New Testament is very clear on this topic and provides at least ten examples in the book of Acts alone that show people who are converting to Christianity being baptized.

Discussion Questions

1. In your opinion, what are the major differences between the deacons we read about in the book of Acts and the deacons in the church today? Why is this so?

2. What is the difference between the indwelling and the empowering of the Holy Spirit? List the way that the Holy Spirit influences us today as Paul explains it in Romans 8.

3. Many claim that baptism is a "work of the Law" and thus not necessary to be saved. How would you answer this teaching (use specific scriptures)?

CHAPTER 19
PETER PREACHES TO THE GENTILES

ACTS 10:1-12:25

This is the final section of the book of Acts that deals primarily with Peter's ministry in and around Jerusalem. Peter has been privileged to be the first to preach the full gospel on Pentecost Sunday, and Luke completes his review by describing the events that precede and follow this Apostle's preaching to the Gentiles for the first time as well. So far the Apostles and their disciples have been preaching to Jews and Gentile converts to Judaism (i.e. Philip and the eunuch). Peter, however, will break through this wall of separation (Jew/Gentile) and bring the gospel to a Roman soldier thus opening the door for Paul and others to freely proclaim the Good News to all men regardless of culture, gender, religion or position in society.

Cornelius

> [1]Now there was a man at Caesarea named Cornelius, a centurion of what was called the Italian cohort, [2]a devout man and one who feared God with all his household, and gave many alms to the Jewish people and prayed to God continually. [3]About the ninth hour of the day he clearly saw in a vision an angel of God who had just come in and said to him, "Cornelius!" [4]And fixing his gaze on him and being much alarmed, he

> said, "What is it, Lord?" And he said to him, "Your prayers and alms have ascended as a memorial before God. [5]Now dispatch some men to Joppa and send for a man named Simon, who is also called Peter; [6]he is staying with a tanner named Simon, whose house is by the sea." [7]When the angel who was speaking to him had left, he summoned two of his servants and a devout soldier of those who were his personal attendants, [8]and after he had explained everything to them, he sent them to Joppa.
> - Acts 10:1-8

The Jews had two classes of converts (Lenski, p.67):

1. **Proselytes of the Gate:** These converts were not subject to circumcision and observed only a limited portion of the Law forbidding idolatry, blasphemy, disobedience to judges, murder, fornication/incest, theft and eating of blood. The eunuch that Philip baptized was one of these as was Cornelius, probably because he was a Roman soldier and a foreigner.

2. **Proselyte of Righteousness:** These were Gentiles that became complete Jews, accepting circumcision, and were subject to all of the Law. They were permitted to enter and worship at the Temple (in the Court of the Gentiles).

Although he was a Proselyte of the Gate, Luke describes Cornelius (centurion is a Roman officer over 100 soldiers) as being:

- Devout/pious: A proselyte who worshiped the God of the Jews and led his household in that direction.

- Benevolent: He used his position and wealth to benefit the poor thus confirming that his faith was sincere.

- Spiritually minded: He wanted a spiritual relationship with God and pursued it through prayer.

His prayers are answered as God gives him instructions to bring Peter to his home. Note that the angel could have preached the gospel to him then and there, but that task was given by God to men not angels, so that even if it was more complicated to arrange, Cornelius sends for Peter.

Peter

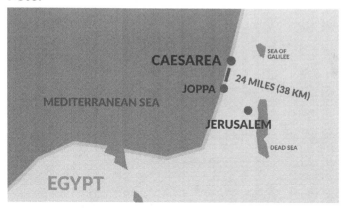

^{9}On the next day, as they were on their way and approaching the city, Peter went up on the housetop about the sixth hour to pray. ^{10}But he became hungry and was desiring to eat; but while they were making preparations, he fell into a trance; ^{11}and he saw the sky opened up, and an object like a great sheet coming down, lowered by four corners to the ground, ^{12}and there were in it all kinds of four-footed animals and crawling creatures of the earth and birds of the air. ^{13}A voice came to him, "Get up, Peter, kill and eat!" ^{14}But Peter said, "By no means, Lord, for I have never eaten anything unholy and unclean." ^{15}Again a voice came to him a second time, "What God has cleansed, no longer consider unholy." ^{16}This happened three times, and immediately the object was taken up into the sky.
- Acts 10:9-16

God provides a vision where Peter is commanded to eat food that Jews were not permitted to eat according to Jewish food laws. The Lord had prepared Cornelius for Peter's visit with the appearance of an angel who gave him specific instructions. God also prepares Peter so that he will be able to carry out God's mission despite the challenges it will present him as a faithful Jew.

Jewish ceremonial and food laws were given to the Jews by God in order to make a distinction between themselves as God's people and other nations (Gentiles) who were not. For example, the whole world labored seven days per week, but the Jews were different in that they devoted one day (Sabbath) to the Lord and rested. The other nations ate every kind of food. Jews were different because what they did or did not eat was guided by their law given to them by God. Once Christ came, the way to be separated from the world was to follow Him and submit to the direction of the Holy Spirit who leads Christians through His Word (New Testament) spoken by Christ and taught by His Apostles (Acts 2:42).

The problem for Peter as well as the other Apostles was that the practices that they had followed as Jews (food laws, Sabbath day observations, etc.) were now taken away or fulfilled by Jesus, but they were slow to understand. This included the rules concerning their association with Gentiles. For example, they could not enter a Gentile's home or share a meal with them, nor could the Gentiles enter a Jew's home or the Temple.

In the vision of the clean and unclean food and the command to eat, God was teaching Peter two things:

1. God had the authority to establish laws, change laws, or suspend laws because He was God, the giver of laws.

2. He was now amending the law concerning food, declaring that all food was to be considered "clean" and thus could be eaten freely by Jewish Christians (something Jesus had already declared in Mark 7:19).

> [17]Now while Peter was greatly perplexed in mind as to what the vision which he had seen might be, behold, the men who had been sent by Cornelius, having asked directions for Simon's house, appeared at the gate; [18]and calling out, they were asking whether Simon, who was also called Peter, was staying there. [19]While Peter was reflecting on the vision, the Spirit said to him, "Behold, three men are looking for you. [20]But get up, go downstairs and accompany them without misgivings, for I have sent them Myself." [21]Peter went down to the men and said, "Behold, I am the one you are looking for; what is the reason for which you have come?" [22]They said, "Cornelius, a centurion, a righteous and God-fearing man well spoken of by the entire nation of the Jews, was divinely directed by a holy angel to send for you to come to his house and hear a message from you." [23]So he invited them in and gave them lodging.
> - Acts 10:17-23a

Peter, still trying to absorb the meaning of the vision, is told that the men sent by Cornelius are at the gate and he should welcome them. Peter greets them and after hearing the reason for their journey invites them to spend the night with him and Simon's family. Peter may not have understood the full impact of the vision but nevertheless obeyed God's instructions to invite the Gentiles in, despite his discomfort.

Peter Meets Cornelius

> [23b]And on the next day he got up and went away with them, and some of the brethren from Joppa accompanied him. [24]On the following day he entered Caesarea. Now Cornelius was waiting for them and had called together his relatives and close friends. [25]When Peter entered, Cornelius met him, and fell at his feet and worshiped him. [26]But

> Peter raised him up, saying, "Stand up; I too am just a man." [27]As he talked with him, he entered and found many people assembled. [28]And he said to them, "You yourselves know how unlawful it is for a man who is a Jew to associate with a foreigner or to visit him; and yet God has shown me that I should not call any man unholy or unclean. [29]That is why I came without even raising any objection when I was sent for. So I ask for what reason you have sent for me."
>
> [30]Cornelius said, "Four days ago to this hour, I was praying in my house during the ninth hour; and behold, a man stood before me in shining garments, [31]and he said, 'Cornelius, your prayer has been heard and your alms have been remembered before God. [32]Therefore send to Joppa and invite Simon, who is also called Peter, to come to you; he is staying at the house of Simon the tanner by the sea.' [33]So I sent for you immediately, and you have been kind enough to come. Now then, we are all here present before God to hear all that you have been commanded by the Lord."
>
> - Acts 10:23[b]-33

Luke describes both Cornelius' preparations for Peter's visit (he had no doubt would come). There is also a marvelous image of these two pious and humble men deferring to one another. Cornelius, a Roman Centurion, kneeling in front of this Galilean fisherman in front of his family and friends. And the servant of the Lord refusing this type of homage declaring the truth that before God both of them were only men (sinful men).

Peter begins by speaking to the obvious issue, "What are a group of Jewish men doing visiting/entering the house of a Gentile?," something that everyone knew was not permitted for a Jew. He does not describe his vision, as Cornelius will do in a moment, but demonstrates that he has understood the meaning of the vision God gave him and that he has obeyed it. Cornelius explains his own vision and how this has led to Peter's arrival in his home. The stage has now been set for the first instance where the gospel will be proclaimed to the Gentiles.

Peter Preaches to the Gentiles (10:34-43)

Peter's lesson assumes that his hearers are all familiar with the facts of the gospel as were most of the people who lived in that area and knew of Jesus, His ministry, as well as His death and reports of His resurrection. He also includes the new information given him by God in the vision that the gospel is for all, not only the Jews to whom he had been preaching since Pentecost. His main point is that he and the Apostles are actual witnesses of the death, burial and resurrection of Jesus.

> [39]We are witnesses of all the things He did both in the land of the Jews and in Jerusalem. They also put Him to death by hanging Him on a cross. [40]God raised Him up on the third day and granted that He become visible, [41]not to all the people, but to witnesses who were chosen beforehand by God, that is, to us who ate and drank with Him after He arose from the dead. [42]And He ordered us to preach to the people, and solemnly to testify that this is the One who has been appointed by God as Judge of the living and the dead. [43]Of Him all the prophets bear witness that through His name everyone who believes in Him receives forgiveness of sins."
> - Acts 10:39-43

Response to Peter's Preaching (10:44-48)

> [44]While Peter was still speaking these words, the Holy Spirit fell upon all those who were listening to the message. [45]All the circumcised believers who came with Peter were amazed, because the gift of the Holy Spirit had been poured out on the

> Gentiles also. ⁴⁶For they were hearing them
> speaking with tongues and exalting God. Then
> Peter answered,
> - Acts 10:44-46

Before Peter can finish by encouraging his audience to
repent and be baptized as he did with the crowd on
Pentecost Sunday, Cornelius and the other hearers begin
speaking in tongues and praising God. Luke describes this
phenomenon as, "the gift of the Holy Spirit poured out on the
Gentiles."

Think back to other times in the book of Acts when the Holy
Spirit was mentioned and answer this question, "What has
just happened here: empowerment by the Holy Spirit or
indwelling of the Holy Spirit?" The answer is: empowerment.
The Holy Spirit empowered these people to speak in
tongues. I believe this happened in order to convince those
that did not have a vision (like Peter's companions) that God
was extending the gospel to the Gentiles, not only to the
Jews. There were many prophets who said that this would
be so (Micah 4:2; Zechariah 8:22; Amos 9:12) including
Jesus Himself in Mark 13:10.

> ⁴⁷"Surely no one can refuse the water for these to
> be baptized who have received the Holy Spirit just
> as we did, can he?" ⁴⁸And he ordered them to be
> baptized in the name of Jesus Christ. Then they
> asked him to stay on for a few days.
> - Acts 10:47-48

Peter now finishes his lesson by directing these new
believers to be baptized because if there were any who
doubted that the gospel was also for the Gentiles, their
questions had been answered by the Holy Spirit Himself
when He empowered these people to speak in tongues.
Peter mentions that they had received the empowerment by
the Holy Spirit just like the Apostles did, without human
intervention (no laying on of hands). He also insists that they

be baptized in order to obey the gospel and receive the indwelling of the Holy Spirit (Acts 2:38).

And so God uses the appearance of an angel, a special vision and the empowering of Gentiles to direct Peter to open the gospel to non-Jews. We find out that all of this and more would be necessary to convince the early church, made up exclusively of Jewish Christians, to accept this directive from God.

Peter Reports to Jerusalem – 11:1-18

Luke describes Peter's return to the church in Jerusalem and his explanation of the breakthrough for the gospel message now brought to Gentiles. Upon his return he faces a skeptical reaction from the Jewish Christians who are concerned that he has associated with and preached to Gentiles. These Jews had become Christians but were emotionally and culturally still operating from a Jewish worldview. Peter then reviews his vision and the vision that had prompted Cornelius to send for him in the first place, along with what took place while he preached to them, and the church concluded that this was from God.

It is interesting to note that Peter, the Apostle, was still subject to explaining his actions to the church to guarantee and prove that what he had done was from God and not his own initiative. Today, leaders and teachers are accountable to the church which uses the Scriptures to judge their teachings and ministry (II Timothy 2:15).

The Church at Antioch – 11:19-30

[19]So then those who were scattered because of the persecution that occurred in connection with Stephen made their way to Phoenicia and Cyprus and Antioch, speaking the word to no one except to Jews alone. [20]But there were some of them, men of Cyprus and Cyrene, who came to Antioch and began speaking to the Greeks also, preaching

> the Lord Jesus. [21]And the hand of the Lord was with them, and a large number who believed turned to the Lord. [22]The news about them reached the ears of the church at Jerusalem, and they sent Barnabas off to Antioch. [23]Then when he arrived and witnessed the grace of God, he rejoiced and began to encourage them all with resolute heart to remain true to the Lord; [24]for he was a good man, and full of the Holy Spirit and of faith. And considerable numbers were brought to the Lord.
> - Acts 11:19-24

Here we see God's providential care ordering events in favor of His kingdom on earth, the church. Peter has opened the door to the Gentiles. Christians, forced out of Jerusalem, preach to Gentiles while on their travels. This news reaches the leaders in Jerusalem, who have already given their blessing to the evangelization of the Gentiles. Barnabas, who has proven his faithfulness and generosity to the church, is sent to help teach these brethren who have formed or joined the church at Antioch. Luke writes that Barnabas' ministry there was successful and the church grew.

> [25]And he left for Tarsus to look for Saul; [26]and when he had found him, he brought him to Antioch. And for an entire year they met with the church and taught considerable numbers; and the disciples were first called Christians in Antioch.
> - Acts 11:25-26

Growing churches need ministers, so Barnabas finds Saul since, as a Roman citizen, he will be effective in teaching these Gentile converts. We can understand that the name "Christian" was coined at Antioch since they had a mixed cultural group (Jew and Gentile) who needed a concise name that would eliminate any cultural, social or former religious identity from them. The term "Christian" accomplished these goals perfectly.

> ²⁷Now at this time some prophets came down from Jerusalem to Antioch. ²⁸One of them named Agabus stood up and began to indicate by the Spirit that there would certainly be a great famine all over the world. And this took place in the reign of Claudius. ²⁹And in the proportion that any of the disciples had means, each of them determined to send a contribution for the relief of the brethren living in Judea. ³⁰And this they did, sending it in charge of Barnabas and Saul to the elders.
> - Acts 11:27-30

A true test of fellowship arises, this time for the Gentile Christians. A famine is predicted by one of the prophets from Jerusalem who also brings a request for assistance. This was the first example of inter-congregational cooperation for the purpose of assistance and benevolence. The challenge for Antioch was if the Gentile brethren would send money to their Jewish brothers and sisters who, before becoming Christians, had despised them. The challenge for the Jewish Christians in Jerusalem was the reverse, would they receive charity from Gentiles, even if they had confessed Christ?

The answer is found in verse 29, where Luke reports that all who had the ability (both Jew and Gentile) gave, and the two main teachers: Barnabas (named first because he is still discipling Saul at this point) and Saul are entrusted with delivering the gift to the church in Jerusalem. The way that all of this was handled was a testimony that the Apostles in Jerusalem and the teachers (Barnabas and Saul) from Antioch were succeeding in their teaching and preaching ministries.

Peter's Arrest and Delivery – 12:1-25

> ¹Now about that time Herod the king laid hands on some who belonged to the church in order to mistreat them. ²And he had James the brother of John put to death with a sword. ³When he saw that

it pleased the Jews, he proceeded to arrest Peter also. Now it was during the days of Unleavened Bread. [4]When he had seized him, he put him in prison, delivering him to four squads of soldiers to guard him, intending after the Passover to bring him out before the people. [5]So Peter was kept in the prison, but prayer for him was being made fervently by the church to God.
- Acts 12:1-5

Luke chooses to end his narrative of Peter's ministry with his arrest by Herod and miraculous deliverance by the hand of an angel. Luke also adds more early church historical information by including the death of the Apostle James. The church in Jerusalem is undergoing severe trials and challenges at this time:

1. Challenges brought about by rapid growth (several thousand people added in only a few years).

2. Demanding benevolence needs (requiring seven deacons to operate a food service for widows).

3. Local famine on the general population (prophesied by Agabus).

4. Persecution of the church beginning with Stephen's death and the dispersion of many members.

Now Luke adds that James is killed and Peter arrested, not by the Jewish religious leaders but by King Herod this time. This was not Herod Antipas who had questioned Jesus and only ruled in the northern region of Galilee. This was Herod Agrippa I, a grandson of Herod the Great, who now ruled all of the region and was seated in Jerusalem. He had Peter arrested to curry favor with the Jewish leaders.

In Acts 12:6-19, Luke mentions that despite their many trials and discouragements, the church prayed for Peter's release. Peter's miraculous escape made possible by an angel is described in the kind of detail that could have only been provided by an eyewitness. Luke also adds a humorous account of how a young maid's excitement left Peter standing out in the street knocking on the door of Mary's (John Mark's mother) house while she ran in to announce that Peter was at the door. Peter is finally let in and instructs the brethren to inform James (the Lord's brother, not the Apostle that had been killed by Herod) and others of his freedom. Peter probably went into hiding to avoid Herod's efforts at recapturing him. Luke mentions Peter again in chapter 15 where he and others discuss certain issues taking place at the church in Antioch.

Acts 12:20-23: As an epilogue, Luke adds a few verses describing Herod's death soon after Peter's escape. This produced a lull in the on-going persecution of the church and Luke ends the section about Peter's ministry on a positive and hopeful note.

> [24]But the word of the Lord continued to grow and to be multiplied. [25]And Barnabas and Saul returned from Jerusalem when they had fulfilled their mission, taking along with them John, who was also called Mark.
> - Acts 12:24-25

Lessons

Obey What You Know

We do not always have all the facts or clearly see God's overall plan or purpose for us when making decisions about obeying His will in a matter. In this type of situation it is wise to obey or follow the ways or commands of the Lord that we know and are sure of. After all, we live by faith, not by sight. Sometimes we just have to obey and pray that God will provide us with understanding at some point. Imagine if Peter had been stubborn, not understanding God's greater plan, and refused (as was his life-long custom) to mix with Gentiles? God would have used another servant and another way to bring the gospel to the Gentiles, but think of the opportunity and blessings Peter would have forfeited!

God Blesses Those Who Bless

In Acts 10:4, Luke says that Cornelius' prayers and alms (giving to the needy) were recognized by God. It was not that his piety and benevolence saved him, it was that his good works were seen as sincere, and in return God gave him the opportunity to hear the gospel. There is a lesson here for both the good person who is a Christian and the good person who is not:

1. The Christian needs to remember that it is not a person's goodness or generosity that saves them, it is the gospel and obedience to it. In speaking of personal righteousness the prophet Isaiah says, *"all our righteous deeds are like a filthy garment."* (Isaiah 64:6). As Christians we should not assume that good, kind and generous people are somehow excused from hearing and obeying the gospel message. *"All have sinned and fallen short of the glory of God"* (Romans 3:23).

2. There is also a lesson for the good and upstanding person that never harmed anyone and always did their best. These should not depend on their own goodness to save them if they are not Christians. The reward for your good life is not salvation. God's reward to the "good" person is exposure to the message of the gospel. You can only offer up the sacrifice of Christ (through faith expressed in repentance and baptism) in exchange for eternal life with God, because He will not accept your life, no matter how good you believe it to be.

Discussion Questions

1. Who, in your opinion, is the most difficult type of person to convert?

   o Atheist

   o Agnostic

   o Other religion (than Christianity)

   o Christian in name only

   o Other _____

     ▪ Why?

     ▪ What would be your approach?

2. What religious traditions in the Churches of Christ need to be changed / updated / eliminated? How would you do this? Replaced with what?

3. In your opinion, what is the greatest danger facing the church today? How should the church deal with it?

CHAPTER 20
THE MINISTRY
OF PAUL
PAUL'S FIRST
MISSIONARY JOURNEY

ACTS 13:1-15:35

We have concluded Luke's description of Peter's ministry among the Jews and the calling that he received from God to bring the gospel to the Gentiles. After Pentecost it seemed that the Apostles understood the great commission to be that they preach to all the Jews in the world. It took a miraculous event (Cornelius speaking in tongues) to convince Peter to not only preach to the Gentiles but to offer them the same salvation through faith, expressed in repentance and baptism, that he had offered the crowd he was preaching to on the day of Pentecost. This breakthrough encouraged others to bring the gospel to the Gentiles. Luke will describe one such effort in the area of Antioch, where Barnabas and Paul had an extensive preaching ministry among this mixed Jewish and Gentile congregation.

Let's take a quick look at our outline and note that we are beginning the second section of this book where Luke will deal primarily with Paul's ministry and travels.

1. Peter's First Sermon – Acts 1:1-2:47

2. Peter's Post-Pentecost Ministry – Acts 3:1-4:37

3. Persecution of Peter and the Apostles – Acts 5:1-42

4. Persecution of the Church – Acts 6:1-7:60

5. Persecution of the Church Part II – Acts 8:1-9:43

6. Peter Preaches to the Gentiles – Acts 10:1-12:25

7. **Paul's First Missionary Journey – Acts 13:1-15:35**

Luke has set the geographical scene, Antioch, as well as the historical moment, after Peter's contact with Cornelius. At this time Barnabas and Paul have gained considerable experience not only in working together but working with Jewish as well as Gentile converts to Christianity. They were able to meet each group's particular religious and cultural needs.

Paul's First Missionary Journey – 13:1-14:28

A Call to Ministry

> [1]Now there were at Antioch, in the church that was there, prophets and teachers: Barnabas, and Simeon who was called Niger, and Lucius of Cyrene, and Manaen who had been brought up with Herod the tetrarch, and Saul. [2]While they were ministering to the Lord and fasting, the Holy Spirit said, "Set apart for Me Barnabas and Saul for the work to which I have called them." [3]Then, when they had fasted and prayed and laid their hands on them, they sent them away.
> - Acts 13:1-3

What we read here is really the third step in Paul's call to ministry. His call to ministry sets a pattern for those who feel they are called to full-time ministry but are not sure if their calling is a legitimate one from God.

When studying Paul's life we see three stages in his call to ministry:

1. **The Calling:** This describes the way God has called/directed/led a person into full-time ministry. Paul was called in a miraculous way (blinded, heard the voice of the Lord, healed of this blindness - Acts 9:3-9; 17) but the manner of his calling is the exception, not the rule. For most people the calling begins as a desire or opportunity to serve in some way that grows stronger with time. In many instances it takes the form of positive feedback from church members or leaders who see talent in a person and encourage them to develop and use that skill in service to the Lord. Many ministers go into full-time ministry because they see a great need that the church (or the lost) have and feel compelled to step up and fill the gap (even if they do not feel qualified). Whatever the way a person is called, one feature is the same for all: the feeling that God's call does not go away until it is answered. Some battle with it for years and even when they choose to do something else with their lives, continue to feel that calling from time to time.

2. **The Consecration:** The consecration (or setting apart) is the time that the called person spends in preparation for their ministry. In Paul's case there was a period of approximately 10-12 years between his calling and the beginning of his ministry to the Gentiles on his first missionary journey. During that time he spent three years in the desert of Arabia being taught by the Spirit of Christ (Galatians 1:11-17), he travelled to Jerusalem, then returned to teach in his home town of Tarsus for an additional four years (Acts 9:30), he was then recruited by Barnabas to come and teach at the Antioch church for an entire year. Finally, he and Barnabas escorted food and relief supplies to Jerusalem after a two year famine had gripped the country (Acts 12:25). Paul's

consecration period saw him being taught by the Lord, teaching at the church at Antioch, traveling and meeting with various Apostles and church leaders, and managing a benevolence program to help the church in Jerusalem. A ten-year period of training and preparation for the ministry he was originally called to at the time of his conversion. Today, we have preacher training schools operated by various congregations in our brotherhood, there are also colleges and universities where a person with a calling can receive training to prepare him or her (many types of full-time ministries are open to women) to prepare someone with a calling for ministry. The confusion some have is thinking that they must begin their ministry the moment they receive the call. The consecration time is important because it usually serves to confirm if ministry is truly one's calling.

3. **The Commendation:** The commendation to ministry is what is taking place in Acts 13:1-3. The Holy Spirit, through the church (its leaders and teachers) commend, send or authorize Paul and Barnabas to take the gospel to the world. This scene teaches us that God works through His church. The Lord had called Paul on the road to Damascus but when the time came for him to fulfill his ministry, God used the church to commend him since Paul could not commend himself. The point here is that no one appoints themselves to positions in the church. For example, there are no self-appointed elders in the church (these are appointed and trained by evangelists - Acts 14:23; Titus 1:5). There are no self-appointed evangelists in the church (these are appointed by elders - I Timothy 4:14). There are no self appointed deacons in the church (these are selected by the church and confirmed by the elders - Acts 6:3-6). There are no self-appointed missionaries in the church (these are trained by the church and sent by the church leadership - Acts 13:1-3). We see this taking place with Paul and Barnabas as the first missionaries confirmed and sent by the church, and this method continues to this day in the Lord's church. It is not a certificate of studies or a college degree that authorizes a person to

be an evangelist or teacher or missionary. It is the commendation by the church that sends or confirms both the calling and the consecration to the Lord's service in and for His church.

The First Missionary Journey – 13:4-14:28

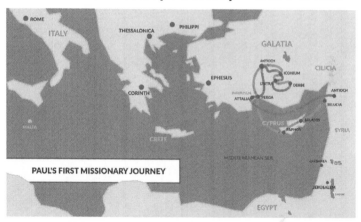

PAUL'S FIRST MISSIONARY JOURNEY

Here's a geographic overview of Paul's first mission trip:

Cyprus (13:4)

Luke writes that Paul, Barnabas and his cousin, John Mark, leave from the port city of Selucia, near Antioch and sail to the island of Cyprus where Barnabas was from (Acts 4:32).

Salamis (13:5)

Their first stop was the friendly confines of the local synagogue where Barnabas was probably known and welcomed to speak. At this point they are reaching out to the Jews since this was the opportunity open to them.

Paphos (13:6-12)

> [6]When they had gone through the whole island as far as Paphos, they found a magician, a Jewish

false prophet whose name was Bar-Jesus, [7]who was with the proconsul, Sergius Paulus, a man of intelligence. This man summoned Barnabas and Saul and sought to hear the word of God. [8]But Elymas the magician (for so his name is translated) was opposing them, seeking to turn the proconsul away from the faith. [9]But Saul, who was also known as Paul, filled with the Holy Spirit, fixed his gaze on him, [10]and said, "You who are full of all deceit and fraud, you son of the devil, you enemy of all righteousness, will you not cease to make crooked the straight ways of the Lord? [11]Now, behold, the hand of the Lord is upon you, and you will be blind and not see the sun for a time." And immediately a mist and a darkness fell upon him, and he went about seeking those who would lead him by the hand. [12]Then the proconsul believed when he saw what had happened, being amazed at the teaching of the Lord.
- Acts 13:6-12

Note that their work on the island was so successful that the governor sent for them to hear the gospel message. The fact that Barnabas is mentioned first suggests that he was the leader and chief speaker at this point. The name "Elymas" meant "expert" so this magician was called, Bar-Jesus the Expert. He had the favor of the governor and interfered with their mission so Paul denounced him, and Bar-Jesus was rendered blind for a period of time, the first miracle credited to Paul. The governor was converted and Luke mentions that it was the teaching of the Lord that amazed him, not the blinding of the magician. The miracle confirmed the teaching, and the teaching produced the conversion.

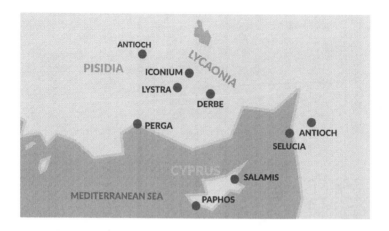

Perga

> Now Paul and his companions put out to sea from
> Paphos and came to Perga in Pamphylia; but John
> left them and returned to Jerusalem.
> - Acts 13:13

Luke names Paul first denoting that after their work in
Cyprus (especially the miracle done through him) Paul is
now the leader of the mission. John Mark leaves them to
return to Jerusalem, probably because he lacked the
courage to travel on in an unknown land. Note that it was
Barnabas and Paul (in that order) that had been called by
the Spirit to undertake this mission. John Mark was added by
Barnabas, his cousin, not by the Holy Spirit. God knew that
John Mark was not ready, however, it took Barnabas, John
Mark and Paul a little longer to discover this as well.

Pisidian Antioch (13:14-52)

Paul and Barnabas do no work in Perga but make their way
north to the city of Antioch located on the border of Pisidia,
thus named to differentiate it from the city of Antioch located
in Syria from which they had come. Here Luke gives a
detailed account of Paul's preaching and the reaction of the
people to his and Barnabas' ministry.

> [14]But when the apostles Barnabas and Paul heard
> of it, they tore their robes and rushed out into the
> crowd, crying out [15]and saying, "Men, why are you
> doing these things? We are also men of the same
> nature as you, and preach the gospel to you that
> you should turn from these vain things to a living
> God, who made the heaven and the earth and the
> sea and all that is in them. [16]In the generations
> gone by He permitted all the nations to go their
> own ways;
> - Acts 14:14-16

Luke describes the method Paul used in preaching the
gospel among the Jews and converts to the Jewish faith.
The service was led by elders or officials who would invite
visiting rabbis to speak. Paul, the famous student of
Gamaliel, and Barnabas a Levite and resident of Jerusalem,
were both known among the Jews and so Paul was asked to
speak.

Luke records the teaching that was probably a basic lesson
that Paul preached when addressing a Jewish audience.
Paul's lesson has four parts and could be entitled, "Israel's
Savior is Jesus Christ" (Lenski, p. 516).

1. Israel's history leads to Jesus (13:17-25)

> And while John was completing his course, he kept
> saying, 'What do you suppose that I am? I am not
> He. But behold, one is coming after me the sandals
> of whose feet I am not worthy to untie.'
> - Acts 13:25

2. Israel rejected the Savior spoken of by the prophets and
sent by God (13:26-29)

> When they had carried out all that was written
> concerning Him, they took Him down from the

cross and laid Him in a tomb.
- Acts 13:29

3. God fulfilled His promises to Israel by raising Him from the dead (13:30-37)

> [32]And we preach to you the good news of the promise made to the fathers, [33]that God has fulfilled this promise to our children in that He raised up Jesus, as it is also written in the second Psalm, 'You are My Son; today I have begotten You.'
> - Acts 13:32-33

4. In Jesus alone is forgiveness and salvation (13:38-41)

> [38]Therefore let it be known to you, brethren, that through Him forgiveness of sins is proclaimed to you, [39]and through Him everyone who believes is freed from all things, from which you could not be freed through the Law of Moses.
> - Acts 13:38-39

In the following verses a familiar pattern emerges where Paul's words draw large crowds which, in turn, antagonize the Jewish leaders who begin attacking him. Many Jews and Gentile converts to Judaism decide to follow Paul and his teachings to the point where the Apostle declares openly that because of Jewish rejection and persecution he will now focus his ministry on the Gentiles. This produces joy and enthusiasm among the Gentiles because God has offered salvation to them making them equal partners with Jewish Christians in God's kingdom, the church.

Iconium, Lystra, Derbe (14:1-21a)

Luke mentions several towns where they continued preaching and teaching. He focuses on two places:

1. Iconium (14:1-7): The same pattern appears here as their preaching divides the audience (some believe, others do not). The Jews then step up their opposition by enlisting Gentiles who form a mob to stone Paul and Barnabas who are then forced to escape to another one of the cities mentioned in verse 6.

2. Lystra (14:8-20a): Luke describes a second miracle performed by Paul (healing of a man lame from birth) which causes a stir in the crowd who think Paul and Barnabas are incarnations of their pagan gods Zeus (Greek god of sky and thunder) and Hermes (son of the Greek god Zeus).

> [14]But when the apostles Barnabas and Paul heard of it, they tore their robes and rushed out into the crowd, crying out [15]and saying, "Men, why are you doing these things? We are also men of the same nature as you, and preach the gospel to you that you should turn from these vain things to a living God, who made the heaven and the earth and the sea and all that is in them. [16]In the generations gone by He permitted all the nations to go their own ways; [17]and yet He did not leave Himself without witness, in that He did good and gave you rains from heaven and fruitful seasons, satisfying your hearts with food and gladness." [18]Even saying these things, with difficulty they restrained the crowds from offering sacrifice to them.
> - Acts 14:14-18

Paul begins preaching to these Gentiles using the situation at hand as a starting point.

> [19]But Jews came from Antioch and Iconium, and having won over the crowds, they stoned Paul and dragged him out of the city, supposing him to be dead. [20]But while the disciples stood around him, he got up and entered the city.
> - Acts 14:19-20a

However, the Apostle has no chance to continue as the Jews from other cities begin following him from town to town. Paul has been harassed and chased, but this time the Jews manage to capture and stone him on the spot, then drag his body outside the city leaving him there for dead. Luke simply states that Paul, surrounded by disciples (gathered there to bury him), awakens (no mention of a miracle so he was probably unconscious) and returns to the city.

3. Derbe (20b-21a): Luke briefly mentions that Paul and Barnabas go to this city to preach and they have many converts but no opposition.

Lystra, Iconium, Antioch (14:21b-23)

At this point they begin to backtrack and revisit the young churches that they planted during this first two-year mission trip (44-46 AD).

> When they had appointed elders for them in every church, having prayed with fasting, they commended them to the Lord in whom they had believed.
> - Acts 14:23

Many Jewish converts had the moral and spiritual maturity to serve as elders in these churches. They may have had leadership positions in their synagogues before their conversion. Christianity was the fulfillment of their Jewish faith and the knowledge of the gospel was the final mystery that completed all that they had learned and believed as Jews. In that first generation church many Jewish converts continued to practice their Jewish faith and held to the Jewish religious calendar (containing feast days, etc.). With time and the destruction of the Temple by the Romans in 70 AD the distinction and practice of these two faiths became quite separate, with Christianity being recognized as a stand alone faith and not simply a sect connected to the Jewish religion.

Pamphylia, Perga, Attalia, Antioch (14:24-28)

Luke continues naming the various stops along their route home to Antioch in Syria. He writes that Paul and Barnabas gather the church that had originally sent them out in order to give them a report of their work, especially the breakthrough they had in preaching to and converting Gentiles.

This sets up the next scene where Luke describes an important meeting and decision concerning the Gentiles and their entry into the church.

The Jerusalem Council – 15:1-35

In Acts 15:1-35, Luke summarizes the issue and the approach to its resolution in the first two verses.

The Issue

> Some men came down from Judea and began teaching the brethren, "Unless you are circumcised according to the custom of Moses, you cannot be saved."
> - Acts 15:1

Jewish Christians from Jerusalem (Acts 15:5 - Pharisees converted to Christianity) come to Antioch teaching that Gentiles had to first adhere to Jewish laws of conversion before they could become Christians. This meant that they had to first be circumcised before they could be baptized.

If you were a Jewish Pharisee converted to Christ, this idea was quite logical. Judaism came first, Jesus was a Jew, Christianity was simply an extension of the Jewish faith, so adhering to Jewish law and custom before identifying as a Christian made sense. For them, baptism was simply an add-on.

The problem with this teaching was that it did not understand Christianity's relationship to Judaism:

1. Judaism was a vehicle designed to deliver Jesus, the Son of God and Savior of mankind, to the world.

> Do not think that I came to abolish the Law or the Prophets; I did not come to abolish but to fulfill.
> - Matthew 5:17

Judaism's rituals, laws and practices were meant to be a preview of what was to come: Jesus dying on the cross as a perfect sacrifice to save mankind from condemnation due to sin. These Jewish Christians thought that their religion was the substance of God's will when in fact it was only the shadow of what God had planned to do through Jesus Christ: offer Himself as a perfect sacrifice to atone for the sins of mankind and then offer redemption to both Jews and Gentiles based on faith in Him as the Son of God.

2. This teaching was dangerous because it substituted a salvation based on Law (be circumcised, obey food and other laws) in order to be worthy of becoming a Christian. They were replacing a gospel based on grace and faith, "I am saved because I believe in Jesus and express my faith through repentance and baptism" (Acts 2:38); this was being replaced with, "I am saved because I obey the Law" (circumcision and the rules of Judaism). In other words, I am saved because I do things, instead of I am saved because I believe in Jesus.

The Solution (15:2-35)

> And when Paul and Barnabas had great dissension and debate with them, the brethren determined that Paul and Barnabas and some others of them should go up to Jerusalem to the apostles and elders concerning this issue.
> - Acts 15:2

Since Antioch was a church consisting of both Jews and Gentiles, and since much of Paul's ministry involved outreach to non-Jews, much was at stake here.

Note the different parties (the missionaries, Jewish Christian teachers, elders of the church, and Apostles) gathered to discuss this issue. This was not decided by an executive group or Peter as some kind of chief Apostle. Luke writes that there was extensive discussion and he records part of Peter's argument.

> [10]Now therefore why do you put God to the test by placing upon the neck of the disciples a yoke which neither our fathers nor we have been able to bear? [11]But we believe that we are saved through the grace of the Lord Jesus, in the same way as they also are."
> - Acts 15:10-11

He also argues that bringing the gospel to the Gentiles was part of God's plan recorded in the Scriptures.

> [14]Simeon has related how God first concerned Himself about taking from among the Gentiles a people for His name. [15]With this the words of the Prophets agree, just as it is written,
> - Acts 15:14-15

In the end all agree to continue preaching to the Gentiles with a caution for them to avoid sexual immorality, which was part of the Gentile lifestyle, and care to respect certain Jewish sensitivities towards eating meat previously offered in pagan sacrifices and then sold in the public market, along with the eating of blood which was forbidden for Jews. These were given to guarantee peace in an assembly where both Jews and Gentiles worshiped and often ate fellowship meals together. So you have the problem stated, debated and ultimately resolved according to God's word, then recorded in a letter to the Antioch church and sent back with Paul, Barnabas and brethren from the church in Jerusalem.

Luke finishes this section by recording the joyful reaction of the Gentile Christians at the news that they were not to be subjected to the Jewish Law, and were accepted by no less than the Apostles themselves as equal and full members of God's church along with their Jewish brethren who also had been converted.

The final scene sees Paul and Barnabas remaining in Antioch busy teaching and preaching to the brethren there.

Reading Assignment: Acts 15:36-18:22

Discussion Questions

1. Have you ever felt a calling to serve the Lord in a greater way? How did He call you? What was your response?

2. Have you ever failed in ministry? Explain how. What did you learn from the experience?

3. Explain how each part of Paul's basic four-part sermon to the Jews would be relevant to a Gentile audience today.

CHAPTER 21
PAUL'S SECOND MISSIONARY JOURNEY

ACTS 15:36-18:22

In the previous chapter we left off at the scene where the Apostles and elders in Jerusalem had defused an extremely divisive situation at the church in Antioch by sending a letter instructing these brethren that, contrary to certain incorrect teachings, Gentile converts to Christianity did not need to be circumcised before they could become Christians. This idea had been promoted by Jewish Pharisees who themselves had converted to Christianity but wanted to impose their former Jewish legalism on Gentile proselytes. Their idea was that in order to become a Christian, which was an offshoot of Judaism, you needed to keep the Jewish Law and the most obvious sign of this was the rite of circumcision. This false idea was repudiated by the leaders in Jerusalem and they informed the brethren of their decision in a letter delivered by Paul, Barnabas, Silas and Barsabbas.

Their decision also confirmed and approved the work that Paul and Barnabas had done among the Gentiles and gave it legitimacy among the brotherhood, otherwise there would not have been a second or third missionary effort. After delivering the letter to the church, Luke writes that Paul, Barnabas and now Silas remained in Antioch teaching the church there, probably reinforcing the ideas sent in the letter and undoing some of the doctrinal confusion caused by the teachers of the circumcision. This issue, however, would continue to plague the early church (Paul speaks of it in Galatians 5:12 and in the letter to the Colossians 2:11-17).

Paul's Second Missionary Journey – 15:36-18:22

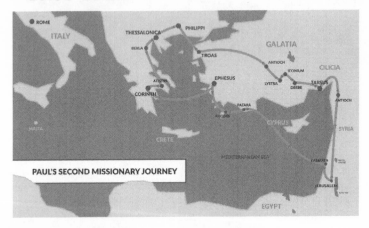

PAUL'S SECOND MISSIONARY JOURNEY

Dispute (15:36-40)

After a time in Antioch, Paul proposes that he and Barnabas return to the field in order to strengthen the churches they planted on their previous journey. Barnabas and Paul have a disagreement over bringing Barnabas' cousin, John Mark, with them. The issue is settled as Paul chooses Silas to work with him, and Barnabas takes John Mark under his wing and returns to the work in Cyprus, his previous home.

This is only speculation, but it seems that Paul had outgrown the mentor-student relationship that he had with Barnabas. Silas, referred to as a prophet in verse 32, was a more suitable partner for him now. John Mark, on the other hand, still affected by his failure to keep up on the first journey but willing to try again, was in need of a good teacher and mentor like Barnabas. Through God's providential care an incident that threatened to break up one team of missionaries actually produced two teams, and we know that John Mark went on to serve both Paul and then Peter in later years (writing the Gospel of Mark which was primarily a summary of Peter's experiences with Jesus).

Timothy is Recruited

[41]And he was traveling through Syria and Cilicia, strengthening the churches.
[1]Paul came also to Derbe and to Lystra. And a disciple was there, named Timothy, the son of a Jewish woman who was a believer, but his father was a Greek, [2]and he was well spoken of by the brethren who were in Lystra and Iconium. [3]Paul wanted this man to go with him; and he took him and circumcised him because of the Jews who were in those parts, for they all knew that his father was a Greek. [4]Now while they were passing through the cities, they were delivering the decrees which had been decided upon by the apostles and elders who were in Jerusalem, for them to observe. [5]So the churches were being strengthened in the faith, and were increasing in number daily.
- Acts 15:41-16:5

We see that at the beginning of their journey their objectives were twofold:

1. To read and explain the letter sent by the Apostles to the churches concerning circumcision.

2. To strengthen the faith of young Christians in the churches that Paul and Barnabas had originally planted.

Timothy joins their mission and was given the tasks originally done by John Mark. Note that despite championing the right of Gentiles to become Christians without the obligation to be circumcised, Paul does circumcise Timothy (whose father was Greek and a non-believer). This was necessary, not for

Timothy to become a Christian as he was already a member of the church, but required to enter synagogues where the uncircumcised were not permitted, and where Paul often preached. In addition to this, it was known that Timothy's father was a Gentile.

The Spirit's Guidance

> [6]They passed through the Phrygian and Galatian region, having been forbidden by the Holy Spirit to speak the word in Asia; [7]and after they came to Mysia, they were trying to go into Bithynia, and the Spirit of Jesus did not permit them; [8]and passing by Mysia, they came down to Troas. [9]A vision appeared to Paul in the night: a man of Macedonia was standing and appealing to him, and saying, "Come over to Macedonia and help us." [10]When he had seen the vision, immediately we sought to go into Macedonia, concluding that God had called us to preach the gospel to them.
> - Acts 16:6-10

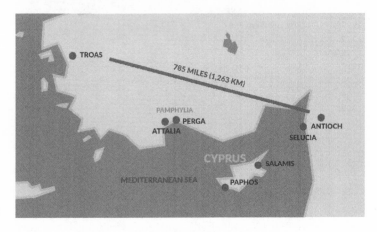

From their starting point of Antioch in Syria, the distance to the city of Troas is approximately 785 miles (1263 kilometers). Luke describes the trip in a few verses, but their overland route could have taken them several months. The Roman road system permitted fairly safe travel and people like Paul walked some 15-20 miles per day (24-32 kilometers), staying in inns, homes of friends or synagogues.

Aside from the work in the churches that they had established on their first trip, much of their journey turns out to be a failed attempt to go eastward. The "Spirit preventing them" could mean a variety of setbacks or obstacles that kept them from preaching the gospel in that region. For example, washed out bridges, no available synagogues, illness or insufficient finances could explain their lack of success. Once they arrived at the coastal city of Troas, however, Paul has a vision that finally provides the direction they were seeking. The dream is general in nature (come to Macedonia), but no details of who to contact or where to go specifically are provided. Paul's faith, however, is strong enough to act based on this limited instruction.

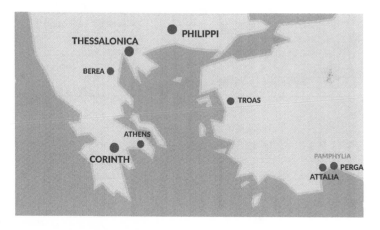

Philippi (16:11-40)

In his vision, Paul sees a man of Macedonia calling out to him for help. The Apostle and his companions set out from Troas and head for Philippi, which was a leading city in the Macedonian region. Once there, they seek out a place where Jews might gather and thus provide him with an opportunity to preach.

> [13]And on the Sabbath day we went outside the gate to a riverside, where we were supposing that there would be a place of prayer; and we sat down and began speaking to the women who had assembled.
> [14]A woman named Lydia, from the city of Thyatira, a seller of purple fabrics, a worshiper of God, was listening; and the Lord opened her heart to respond to the things spoken by Paul. [15]And when she and her household had been baptized, she urged us, saying,
>
> "If you have judged me to be faithful to the Lord, come into my house and stay." And she prevailed upon us.
> - Acts 16:13-15

In the following verses (Acts 16:16-24) Luke describes an incident that resembles what took place in Cyprus during the first missionary journey. There Paul struck blind a sorcerer who was trying to hinder his work. In Philippi he casts out an evil spirit from a girl who had been following them and drawing attention to their ministry. Paul, not wanting a witness from a girl possessed of an evil spirit, quiets her by casting it out. This led to a riot stirred up by the girl's handlers who made a living using her occult skills. Paul and Silas are dragged before the judge, beaten and then put into prison with their feet locked in stocks. The only difference here is that their imprisonment was not caused by the Jews this time.

> [25]But about midnight Paul and Silas were praying and singing hymns of praise to God, and the prisoners were listening to them; [26]and suddenly there came a great earthquake, so that the foundations of the prison house were shaken; and immediately all the doors were opened and everyone's chains were unfastened. [27]When the jailer awoke and saw the prison doors opened, he

drew his sword and was about to kill himself, supposing that the prisoners had escaped. [28]But Paul cried out with a loud voice, saying, "Do not harm yourself, for we are all here!" [29]And he called for lights and rushed in, and trembling with fear he fell down before Paul and Silas, [30]and after he brought them out, he said, "Sirs, what must I do to be saved?"

[31]They said, "Believe in the Lord Jesus, and you will be saved, you and your household." [32]And they spoke the word of the Lord to him together with all who were in his house. [33]And he took them that very hour of the night and washed their wounds, and immediately he was baptized, he and all his household. [34]And he brought them into his house and set food before them, and rejoiced greatly, having believed in God with his whole household.
- Acts 16:25-34

Notice that the jailor had some knowledge of the faith because the earthquake and the fact that none of the prisoners escaped moved him to ask the same question that the crowd on Pentecost Sunday asked of Peter, "Brethren what shall we do?" (Acts 2:37).

Luke records only a summary of what Paul taught him. Notice, however, that the very first thing the jailor does after confessing his faith in Christ is submit to baptism, just like the crowd in Jerusalem on Pentecost Sunday. Luke does not mention Paul teaching the jailor and his household about baptism, but the fact that this is the first thing he does after acknowledging his belief tells us that baptism was part of the gospel message.

[35]Now when day came, the chief magistrates sent their policemen, saying, "Release those men." [36]And the jailer reported these words to Paul, saying, "The chief magistrates have sent to release you. Therefore come out now and go in peace." [37]But Paul said to them, "They have

> beaten us in public without trial, men who are
> Romans, and have thrown us into prison; and now
> are they sending us away secretly? No indeed! But
> let them come themselves and bring us out." [38]The
> policemen reported these words to the chief
> magistrates. They were afraid when they heard
> that they were Romans, [39]and they came and
> appealed to them, and when they had brought
> them out, they kept begging them to leave the
> city. [40]They went out of the prison and entered the
> house of Lydia, and when they saw the brethren,
> they encouraged them and departed.
> - Acts 16:35-40

An interesting postscript here is that when the magistrates
sought to release Paul and his co-worker quietly, he reminds
them of his Roman citizenship and the illegal manner in
which they were treated, and thus refuses to go unless
publicly set free by the judges themselves. He did this to
guard against someone, in a future attack, accusing him of
escaping from jail instead of his lawful release. And so, he
and Silas leave the jail publicly and legally. They then pay a
farewell visit to Lydia and move on to another location in
order to preach the gospel.

Thessalonica

> [1]Now when they had traveled through Amphipolis
> and Apollonia, they came to Thessalonica, where
> there was a synagogue of the Jews. [2]And
> according to Paul's custom, he went to them, and
> for three Sabbaths reasoned with them from the
> Scriptures, [3]explaining and giving evidence that the
> Christ had to suffer and rise again from the dead,
> and saying, "This Jesus whom I am proclaiming to
> you is the Christ." [4]And some of them were
> persuaded and joined Paul and Silas, along with a
> large number of the God-fearing Greeks and a
> number of the leading women. [5]But the Jews,
> becoming jealous and taking along some wicked

men from the market place, formed a mob and set the city in an uproar; and attacking the house of Jason, they were seeking to bring them out to the people. [6]When they did not find them, they began dragging Jason and some brethren before the city authorities, shouting, "These men who have upset the world have come here also; [7]and Jason has welcomed them, and they all act contrary to the decrees of Caesar, saying that there is another king, Jesus." [8]They stirred up the crowd and the city authorities who heard these things. [9]And when they had received a pledge from Jason and the others, they released them.
- Acts 17:1-9

Do we see a pattern here?

1. Paul arrives at a city and finds a place where he can preach.

2. Some believe and others do not.

3. Those who believe follow Paul and receive more teaching, those who disbelieve cause trouble.

4. Paul leaves or escapes, and the cycle repeats itself in another location.

Despite the trouble, however, a church is planted in Thessalonica.

Berea (Acts 17:10-14)

Berea is the exception to this cycle that proves the rule. The Jews in this place are eager to hear Paul and consider everything according to Scripture. Many Jews are converted along with Greek proselytes to Judaism. Unfortunately, this fruitful work is upset as the familiar cycle is repeated. This time, however, it is not the Bereans who cause the trouble, but Jews from Thessalonica who come to disrupt Paul's ministry among the Bereans. The brethren there spirit him safely out of town leaving Timothy and Silas to continue the work in Berea for a time.

Athens (Acts 17:15-34)

> ¹⁵Now those who escorted Paul brought him as far as Athens; and receiving a command for Silas and Timothy to come to him as soon as possible, they left.
> ¹⁶Now while Paul was waiting for them at Athens, his spirit was being provoked within him as he was observing the city full of idols. ¹⁷So he was reasoning in the synagogue with the Jews and the God-fearing Gentiles, and in the market place every day with those who happened to be present. ¹⁸And also some of the Epicurean and Stoic philosophers were conversing with him. Some were saying, "What would this idle babbler wish to say?" Others, "He seems to be a proclaimer of strange deities,"—because he was preaching Jesus and the resurrection. ¹⁹And they took him and brought him to the Areopagus, saying, "May we know what this new teaching is which you are proclaiming? ²⁰For you are bringing some strange things to our ears; so we want to know what these things mean." ²¹(Now all the Athenians and the strangers visiting there used to spend their time in nothing other than telling or hearing something new.)
> - Act 17:15-21

What is interesting about Paul's time in Athens is that no church was planted upon his arrival and early work preaching in the synagogue. Luke only records that Paul "reasoned with the Jews and Gentile converts," but there is no mention of anyone believing or being baptized, and there is no record of any response as a result of his preaching in the public square early in his ministry there.

> ²²So Paul stood in the midst of the Areopagus and said, "Men of Athens, I observe that you are very religious in all respects. ²³For while I was passing

> through and examining the objects of your worship, I also found an altar with this inscription, 'TO AN UNKNOWN GOD.' Therefore what you worship in ignorance, this I proclaim to you. [24]The God who made the world and all things in it, since He is Lord of heaven and earth, does not dwell in temples made with hands; [25]nor is He served by human hands, as though He needed anything, since He Himself gives to all people life and breath and all things; [26]and He made from one man every nation of mankind to live on all the face of the earth, having determined their appointed times and the boundaries of their habitation, [27]that they would seek God, if perhaps they might grope for Him and find Him, though He is not far from each one of us; [28]for in Him we live and move and exist, as even some of your own poets have said, 'For we also are His children.' [29]Being then the children of God, we ought not to think that the Divine Nature is like gold or silver or stone, an image formed by the art and thought of man. [30]Therefore having overlooked the times of ignorance, God is now declaring to men that all people everywhere should repent, [31]because He has fixed a day in which He will judge the world in righteousness through a Man whom He has appointed, having furnished proof to all men by raising Him from the dead."
> - Acts 17:22-31

Instead, Luke records the invitation and speech Paul delivers at Mars Hill. This was significant because it was his first and most direct contact with the elite philosophers and thinkers of that day.

First, a little background information:

- Mars Hill is a Roman name for a hill located in Athens.

- In the Greek it was called Hill of Ares, the god of war (known to the Romans as Mars) and thus the name Mars Hill.

- The Areopagus was the supreme council or "upper council," a body of elected officials (elected for life like the Supreme Court Justices in the USA), who met at this location.

- These men were the great and famous of Athens who gathered to judge only those cases dealing with homicides. They also traded the newest ideas in philosophy, religion and other areas of human thinking and knowledge.

And so, on that day they were gathered to hear about this new "religion," this new "teaching" as befitting the rich and powerful who are, in every generation, the first to come into contact with new ideas. This is Paul's first speech to a large, influential and completely pagan audience. He will not argue his case from the prophets or Scriptures as he has done previously with his Jewish audiences.

[22]So Paul stood in the midst of the Areopagus and said, "Men of Athens, I observe that you are very religious in all respects. [23]For while I was passing through and examining the objects of your worship, I also found an altar with this inscription, 'TO AN UNKNOWN GOD.' Therefore what you worship in ignorance, this I proclaim to you. [24]The God who made the world and all things in it, since He is Lord of heaven and earth, does not dwell in temples made with hands; [25]nor is He served by human hands, as though He needed anything, since He Himself gives to all people life and breath and all things; [26]and He made from one man every nation of mankind to live on all the face of the earth, having determined their appointed times and the boundaries of their habitation, [27]that they would seek God, if perhaps they might grope for Him and find Him, though He is not far from each one of us; [28]for in Him we live and move and exist, as even some of your own poets have said, 'For we also are His children.' [29]Being then the children of God, we ought not to think that the Divine Nature is

> like gold or silver or stone, an image formed by the
> art and thought of man. [30]Therefore having
> overlooked the times of ignorance, God is now
> declaring to men that all people everywhere should
> repent, [31]because He has fixed a day in which He
> will judge the world in righteousness through a
> Man whom He has appointed, having furnished
> proof to all men by raising Him from the dead."
> - Acts 17:22-31

Note that Paul bases his speech on their notion of God, which was pantheistic since they had many gods. His first objective is to move them from the concept of many gods to the idea of one God. Next, he explains that this one God is the source of everything that exists and is not dependent on man, nor is His nature human or material. His following point is that God requires certain things from His creation which includes man, and at some point will judge the world (something that his audience of judges could relate to). Finally, he introduces Christ and His resurrection but is not able to finish because they cut him off at this point.

> [32]Now when they heard of the resurrection of the
> dead, some began to sneer, but others said, "We
> shall hear you again concerning this." [33]So Paul
> went out of their midst. [34]But some men joined him
> and believed, among whom also were Dionysius
> the Areopagite and a woman named Damaris and
> others with them.
> - Acts 17:32-34

Up to the moment where he introduced the resurrection of Jesus, Paul's speech was well received since the points he made demonstrated a logical and superior way to think about divine beings. For example, one God versus many gods; an all-powerful God versus the demi-gods of Greek myth; a God who creates man versus man creating his own god; and finally, a righteous God dispensing justice versus weak and imperfect men dispensing justice. Of course, they balked at the idea of the resurrection of Jesus because although they believed in an afterlife for the soul, they considered the flesh evil and a hinderance to the journey of the soul which was released when the material body died. The concept of a human body resurrecting from the dead (something accepted by faith) seemed ridiculous and useless to them since their afterlife belief centered on the soul leaving the body in which it was trapped. They dismissed Paul but not before two prominent people and other individuals believed and followed after him for more teaching, showing that God's word and message never return empty.

Corinth (18:1-22)

[1]After these things he left Athens and went to Corinth. [2]And he found a Jew named Aquila, a native of Pontus, having recently come from Italy with his wife Priscilla, because Claudius had commanded all the Jews to leave Rome. He came to them, [3]and because he was of the same trade, he stayed with them and they were working, for by trade they were tent-makers. [4]And he was reasoning in the synagogue every Sabbath and trying to persuade Jews and Greeks.
- Acts 18:1-4

Luke includes a fascinating glimpse into the every day life of Paul, how he got around, how he financed some of his travel, and the conditions in which he lived.

Aquila and his wife, Priscilla, are introduced here and we will see them again later on in the narrative. Note also Luke's attention to historical detail mentioning not only the city the three of them are in (Corinth) but also a time marker (Claudius expelling Jews from Rome - Claudius reigned from 44-54 AD).

[5]But when Silas and Timothy came down from Macedonia, Paul began devoting himself

completely to the word, solemnly testifying to the Jews that Jesus was the Christ. [6]But when they resisted and blasphemed, he shook out his garments and said to them, "Your blood be on your own heads! I am clean. From now on I will go to the Gentiles." [7]Then he left there and went to the house of a man named Titius Justus, a worshiper of God, whose house was next to the synagogue. [8]Crispus, the leader of the synagogue, believed in the Lord with all his household, and many of the Corinthians when they heard were believing and being baptized. [9]And the Lord said to Paul in the night by a vision, "Do not be afraid any longer, but go on speaking and do not be silent; [10]for I am with you, and no man will attack you in order to harm you, for I have many people in this city." [11]And he settled there a year and six months, teaching the word of God among them.
- Acts 18:5-11

Paul remains in Corinth for 18 months after the Lord encourages him to stay and preach. Several prominent Jews are converted as well as Gentiles, but when the unbelieving Jews resist and blaspheme, Paul shifts his efforts exclusively to the Gentiles. He is also preaching full-time now that Silas and Timothy have come to help him.

[12]But while Gallio was proconsul of Achaia, the Jews with one accord rose up against Paul and brought him before the judgment seat, [13]saying, "This man persuades men to worship God contrary to the law." [14]But when Paul was about to open his mouth, Gallio said to the Jews, "If it were a matter of wrong or of vicious crime, O Jews, it would be reasonable for me to put up with you; [15]but if there are questions about words and names and your own law, look after it yourselves; I am unwilling to be a judge of these matters." [16]And he drove them away from the judgment seat. [17]And they all took hold of Sosthenes, the leader of the synagogue,

and began beating him in front of the judgment seat. But Gallio was not concerned about any of these things.
- Acts 18:12-17

After a long period of uninterrupted ministry, the old cycle of opposition from the Jews begins again and Paul is arrested. The judge releases the Apostle seeing that this is not a civil case but a religious dispute.

[18]Paul, having remained many days longer, took leave of the brethren and put out to sea for Syria, and with him were Priscilla and Aquila. In Cenchrea he had his hair cut, for he was keeping a vow. [19]They came to Ephesus, and he left them there. Now he himself entered the synagogue and reasoned with the Jews. [20]When they asked him to stay for a longer time, he did not consent, [21]but taking leave of them and saying, "I will return to you again if God wills," he set sail from Ephesus. [22]When he had landed at Caesarea, he went up and greeted the church, and went down to Antioch.
- Acts 18:18-22

Luke writes that Paul continued to minister once acquitted at trial, but after a year and a half felt that it was time to return home. He brings Aquila and Priscilla with him and leaves them in Ephesus where he spends little time but promises to return. Paul finishes his second missionary journey by greeting the church at Caesarea where the port of entry was located and then makes his way north to his home congregation of Antioch to report on his mission and rest from his travels.

Lessons

It is possible to have a dispute without a division.

The disagreement between Paul and Barnabas is rather typical in the church: two brothers really invested in the work disagree about how to proceed. Here is a situation where Satan could have driven a wedge between these two men leading to a division in the church. Note, however, that there was no division, and no one left the church.

I believe that they brought their problem to the church leadership for resolution. In Acts 15:40 it says,

> But Paul chose Silas and left, being committed by the brethren to the grace of the Lord.

Luke mentions this to underscore the fact that the church was aware of and blessed the resolution that these men had come to.

My point here is that we should bring church matters to the elders when there are disputes and offenses. This is both a good way to seek resolutions and to guard against divisions which often lead to the breaking of fellowship between brethren over petty things.

You do not need to know the last step before you take the first step.

Paul was looking for direction after the door of opportunity closed for his preaching in the eastern regions. His prayer for direction was eventually answered by the vision of the man calling for help in Macedonia.

At that time Macedonia was a region of 10,000 sq. miles (29,500 sq. kilometers) with its main city, Philippi, having a population of 10,000-20,000 people. Talk about finding a needle in a haystack! However, Paul knew that the direction was west and not east, and the territory was Macedonia. He trusted the Lord for further direction when this would be needed. For now, he demonstrated his faith by leaving Troas and heading to Macedonia. We have just read that he eventually found the city, the people and the work when he needed to.

Some people will not take the first step in following the Lord unless He shows them all the following steps to reach their goal. This is called "walking by sight" not "walking by faith." Usually the first step is a step of faith and God will not show us the next step or the final step unless we take that first step of faith. We like to play it safe and not launch out unless success is guaranteed at the starting gate. However, a life devoted to Christ often requires that we take a first step of faith before He reveals the next step or the final goal.

If the Lord calls you to something you can be sure of two things:

1. If He is the one calling, you will have to walk by faith in order to answer the call.

2. If He is the one calling, He will provide everything you will need in due time.

Discussion Questions

1. Explain in your own words why circumcision is not necessary to become a Christian today.

2. Write a paragraph describing what a typical day in heaven will be like.

3. In your opinion, what is the most difficult thing about Christianity for non-believers to accept? Why?

CHAPTER 22
PAUL'S THIRD MISSIONARY JOURNEY

ACTS 18:23-21:14

The last scene that Luke describes in Acts 18 is Paul's brief visit to Ephesus at the end of his second missionary journey (Acts 18:19-22). The people there asked him to stay longer but he did not, promising that he would return at a later date. This return would take place on his third missionary journey.

Let us look at our outline and note that this will be Paul's final evangelistic trip before his arrest and imprisonment in various locations.

1. Peter's First Sermon – Acts 1:1-2:47
2. Peter's Post-Pentecost Ministry – Acts 3:1-4:37
3. Persecution of Peter and the Apostles – Acts 5:1-42
4. Persecution of the Church – Acts 6:1-7:60
5. Persecution of the Church Part II – Acts 8:1-9:43
6. Peter Preaches to the Gentiles – Acts 10:1-12:25
7. Paul's First Missionary Journey – Acts 13:1-15:35
8. Paul's Second Missionary Journey – Acts 15:36-18:22
9. **Paul's Third Missionary Journey – Acts 18:23-21:14**

Third Missionary Journey – 18:23-21:14

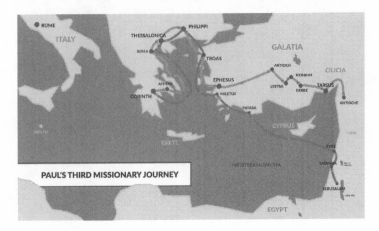

PAUL'S THIRD MISSIONARY JOURNEY

Paul Revisits Churches

> And having spent some time there, he left and
> passed successively through the Galatian region
> and Phrygia, strengthening all the disciples.
> - Acts 18:23

We see in this brief statement Paul's mission work strategy
in starting each journey with a visit to congregations he had
planted during previous mission trips. He used these visits to
encourage, teach and strengthen their faith in the Lord.

Apollos at Ephesus

> [24]Now a Jew named Apollos, an Alexandrian by
> birth, an eloquent man, came to Ephesus; and he
> was mighty in the Scriptures. [25]This man had been
> instructed in the way of the Lord; and being fervent
> in spirit, he was speaking and teaching accurately
> the things concerning Jesus, being acquainted only
> with the baptism of John; [26]and he began to speak
> out boldly in the synagogue. But when Priscilla and

> Aquila heard him, they took him aside and explained to him the way of God more accurately. [27]And when he wanted to go across to Achaia, the brethren encouraged him and wrote to the disciples to welcome him; and when he had arrived, he greatly helped those who had believed through grace, [28]for he powerfully refuted the Jews in public, demonstrating by the Scriptures that Jesus was the Christ.
> - Acts 18:24-28

Apollos was a Jew who was born in Alexandria, the city in Egypt that had been founded by Alexander the Great, the Greek leader and conqueror. Alexandria had a university and library, and it was here that the Septuagint (the translation of the Hebrew Scriptures into the Greek language) was completed in 132 BC.

Luke describes Apollos as being:

1. Eloquent: Not simply a good talker but a trained speaker and debater.

2. Mighty in the Scriptures: Well versed in the Hebrew Bible and able to use his debating and speaking skills in the teaching of the Scriptures.

3. Not Fully Trained: He had been taught about Jesus by some of the disciples of John the Baptist and thus was teaching effectively what John had taught: that Jesus was the Messiah promised by the Scriptures. The fact that he only knew the baptism of John suggests that Apollos may have become a disciple of John receiving John's baptism, but was not aware of the complete ministry of Jesus that included His death and resurrection as well as the great commission to the Apostles to go preach the gospel and baptize all repentant believers in the name of Jesus. This may explain why after being taught more fully about the "Way" (which was the expression used to describe Christianity at that time) he was not re-baptized. This

was similar to the Apostles who had all received the baptism of John and in doing so had fulfilled God's will in this matter, not needing to be re-baptized after the day of Pentecost.

The idea here is that all those who received baptism before Pentecost (i.e. the Apostles, disciples of John the Baptist, Apollos, etc.) did not need to be re-baptized after Pentecost Sunday. Only those who were hearing the gospel for the first time needed to repent and be baptized as Peter instructs in his sermon on Pentecost Sunday (Acts 2:38). Luke inserts this episode concerning Apollos because he was a high profile teacher and preacher (some scholars believe that he was the author of the epistle to the Hebrews), but also because his short time in Ephesus sets up the next scene where Paul returns to the city to continue the work he had begun there during his second missionary journey.

We see that Apollos receives the necessary instructions from Priscilla and Aquila. Note that Luke names the woman, Priscilla, first indicating that she was the more able teacher of the two (Lenski, p.775). This did not contradict Paul's instructions restricting women from teaching men in the assembly (I Timothy 2:11-15), since this was a private matter and not taking place while the church gathered for public worship. Armed with the complete gospel message, Apollos continues in ministry but more powerful and effective than before.

Paul in Ephesus (19:1-41)

Re-Baptism of the Twelve

> [1]It happened that while Apollos was at Corinth,
> Paul passed through the upper country and came
> to Ephesus, and found some disciples. He said to
> them, "Did you receive the Holy Spirit when you
> believed?" And they said to him, "No, we have not
> even heard whether there is a Holy Spirit." [3]And he

said, "Into what then were you baptized?" And they said, "Into John's baptism." [4]Paul said, "John baptized with the baptism of repentance, telling the people to believe in Him who was coming after him, that is, in Jesus." [5]When they heard this, they were baptized in the name of the Lord Jesus. [6]And when Paul had laid his hands upon them, the Holy Spirit came on them, and they began speaking with tongues and prophesying. [7]There were in all about twelve men.
- Acts 19:1-7

Many people assume that these men were originally baptized by Apollos but there is nothing in the passage that supports this. The main difference between these men and Apollos was that he was mighty in the Scriptures and they were not (i.e. they knew nothing about the Holy Spirit). The similarity was that they knew and had received the baptism of John as had Apollos, and while he was at Ephesus Apollos had not required them to be re-baptized. We can conclude, however, that they received John's baptism some time after Pentecost because after having taught them more completely about Christ and the Holy Spirit, Paul re-baptized these 12 disciples (followers of Jesus).

It is interesting to note two things here:

1. Paul bases his questions about the reception of the Holy Spirit on the kind of baptism they had, not the kind of experience or feeling they had. Here he is talking about the "indwelling" of the Holy Spirit which is given and received through Jesus' baptism, not John's baptism (Acts 2:38).

2. Paul transfers the "empowerment" of the Holy Spirit by the laying on of his hands, and the evidence of this is that these men begin speaking in tongues and declare God's word with knowledge and power, something they were unable to do before Paul, with his apostolic authority, laid hands on them.

These then become the first legitimate converts at Ephesus.

Paul Establishes the Church in Ephesus (19:8-22)

> [8]And he entered the synagogue and continued
> speaking out boldly for three months, reasoning
> and persuading them about the kingdom of
> God. [9]But when some were becoming hardened
> and disobedient, speaking evil of the Way before
> the people, he withdrew from them and took away
> the disciples, reasoning daily in the school of
> Tyrannus. [10]This took place for two years, so that
> all who lived in Asia heard the word of the Lord,
> both Jews and Greeks.
> - Acts 19:8-10

We see the familiar pattern of preaching to the Jews who reacted negatively, and Paul turning next to the Gentiles. Luke records that Paul spent a long time in Ephesus (two years) preaching exclusively to Gentiles with success since Luke says that the gospel radiated out from this economic and political center to all parts of the surrounding Roman province, probably through the efforts of various workers trained and sent out from this location.

Luke mentions that many miracles were performed by Paul and that God was using him in mighty ways, to the point where some were trying to copy and use his name to produce similar miracles but to no avail. The results of his ministry were not only seen in conversions and healings, but many who practiced the black arts of magic and the occult burned their books of magic and turned to the Lord in faith. Paul, seeing his work and the church well established, begins to make plans to revisit churches he had planted in the region of Macedonia (Philippi, Thessalonica, Berea) and the region of Achaiah (Corinth, Athens) before returning to Jerusalem and beginning a possible fourth missionary journey to Rome.

He is contemplating these things when trouble springs up, not from the Jews who have been his usual opposition, but from the Gentiles in the region whose livelihood has been affected by his preaching and the teachings of Christ.

Riot in Ephesus (19:23-41)

Ephesus was an important city of that region and time, and served as a major port of entry for Asia Minor, which is modern day Turkey. There was a great boulevard 70 feet (21 meters) wide that ran through the entire city, and the population at that time was approximately 300,000 people. Many streets were lined with marble and had public baths, and the theatre in the city could hold 50,000 spectators. The temple of Diana (Artemis in the Greek) was located here and considered one of the seven wonders of the ancient world. In Greek mythology, Diana was described as the daughter of the gods Zeus and Letto, and the twin sister of Apollo. She was venerated as the goddess of the hunt, wild animals, wilderness, childbirth and protector of young virgins. Situated around the temple area was a community that housed artisans who earned a good living making coins, statues and other artifacts in honor of Diana. These people were organized into a guild or union and had considerable influence in a city like Ephesus where culture, religion and politics were mixed together to form the whole of that society.

Into this culture comes Paul the Apostle who for two years preaches and teaches that there is only one God (and it is not Diana), and that worship and obedience to God are expressed by obeying Jesus. Part of the Christian lifestyle required one to abandon worthless idols, like Diana, and devote one's life and resources to Jesus, not the temple of Diana or the religious trinkets sold there. There was bound to be trouble.

> [23]About that time there occurred no small disturbance concerning the Way. [24]For a man named Demetrius, a silversmith, who made silver shrines of Artemis, was bringing no little business

> to the craftsmen; [25]these he gathered together with the workmen of similar trades, and said, "Men, you know that our prosperity depends upon this business. [26]You see and hear that not only in Ephesus, but in almost all of Asia, this Paul has persuaded and turned away a considerable number of people, saying that gods made with hands are no gods at all. [27]Not only is there danger that this trade of ours fall into disrepute, but also that the temple of the great goddess Artemis be regarded as worthless and that she whom all of Asia and the world worship will even be dethroned from her magnificence."
> - Acts 19:23-27

Luke describes the riot and threats against Paul that ensue with the crowd dragging some of his associates into the theatre accompanied with shouting and confusion. Eventually, a city official quiets the crowd and warns them that they could be in trouble with the Roman overseers because of their unlawful assembly. This event signals to Paul that it is time to leave and move on to another place to carry on his ministry.

Paul in Troas (20:1-12)

Luke summarizes Paul's journey through Macedonia encouraging the churches there while avoiding another Jewish plot to harm him. He eventually finds his way to Troas, the place where he had received the vision that led him to the fruitful ministry in Macedonia and Achaia years before.

> [7]On the first day of the week, when we were gathered together to break bread, Paul began talking to them, intending to leave the next day, and he prolonged his message until midnight. [8]There were many lamps in the upper room where we were gathered together. [9]And there was a young man named Eutychus sitting on the

window sill, sinking into a deep sleep; and as Paul kept on talking, he was overcome by sleep and fell down from the third floor and was picked up dead. [10]But Paul went down and fell upon him, and after embracing him, he said, "Do not be troubled, for his life is in him." [11]When he had gone back up and had broken the bread and eaten, he talked with them a long while until daybreak, and then left. [12]They took away the boy alive, and were greatly comforted.
- Acts 20:7-12

Luke describes this miracle in such an ordinary way (a boy is killed in a 30-foot (9 meters) fall and brought back to life with only a word). Luke's skill is that he is able to describe in detail great spiritual events, but make them look natural, familiar and real. Even though this took place in a culture and time far removed from us, we can still relate to the Bible study, the crowd, even the boy's sleepiness.

Paul's Farewell to Ephesus (20:13-38)

The writer continues his meticulous accounting of Paul's movements by describing the details of the Apostle's trip from Ephesus through Macedonia, back to Troas and now on to Miletus, a coastal city south of Ephesus.

In Acts 20:16 we learn that Paul's goal is to be back in Jerusalem for the day of Pentecost, a journey that will eventually bring him much suffering. Once in Miletus, Paul summons the elders from Ephesus to come and meet with him to discuss several important issues.

Personal Situation

[17]From Miletus he sent to Ephesus and called to him the elders of the church. [18]And when they had come to him, he said to them, "You yourselves know, from the first day that I set foot in Asia, how I was with you the whole time, [19]serving the Lord

with all humility and with tears and with trials which came upon me through the plots of the Jews; [20]how I did not shrink from declaring to you anything that was profitable, and teaching you publicly and from house to house, [21]solemnly testifying to both Jews and Greeks of repentance toward God and faith in our Lord Jesus Christ. [22]And now, behold, bound by the Spirit, I am on my way to Jerusalem, not knowing what will happen to me there, [23]except that the Holy Spirit solemnly testifies to me in every city, saying that bonds and afflictions await me. [24]But I do not consider my life of any account as dear to myself, so that I may finish my course and the ministry which I received from the Lord Jesus, to testify solemnly of the gospel of the grace of God. [25]"And now, behold, I know that all of you, among whom I went about preaching the kingdom, will no longer see my face. [26]Therefore, I testify to you this day that I am innocent of the blood of all men. [27]For I did not shrink from declaring to you the whole purpose of God.

- Acts 20:17-27

He begins by reviewing and confirming the basis of his ministry among them which was the preaching of the gospel. He declares that he has done this in full confidence of its truth and power. He also reveals that the Lord is directing him to return to Jerusalem (if it was up to him, he would stay in the field planting and growing churches; Jerusalem is Peter and the other Apostles' area of work). He also reveals that trouble and imprisonment await him there. Paul then declares that this is a final farewell and reminds them that he has preached the full gospel and confirmed it with his good life so that no one can blame him if they miss out on salvation.

Admonition

> [28]Be on guard for yourselves and for all the flock, among which the Holy Spirit has made you overseers, to shepherd the church of God which He purchased with His own blood. [29]I know that after my departure savage wolves will come in among you, not sparing the flock; [30]and from among your own selves men will arise, speaking perverse things, to draw away the disciples after them. [31]Therefore be on the alert, remembering that night and day for a period of three years I did not cease to admonish each one with tears. [32]And now I commend you to God and to the word of His grace, which is able to build you up and to give you the inheritance among all those who are sanctified.
> - Acts 20:28-32

Paul's comments on his personal work and conduct are not a boast, they are an encouragement to these men on how they should act as leaders in the church. Paul, in effect, tells them to, "Do as I have done." In these verses he also gives them a warning to be careful and tend to their main responsibility as elders, which is protecting the church against false teachers and false teaching. It is interesting to see Paul use three different terms in referring to these men and their ministry:

1. Verse 17: Elder/Presbyter - mature/older man

2. Verse 28: Overseers/Bishops - guardian/leader

3. Verse 28: Shepherd/Pastor - caregiver/leader

In the early church, all of these terms referred to the same persons: those charged with leadership in the local church. Elder/presbyter denoted their age and experience. Overseer/bishop referred to their authority and responsibilities. Shepherd/pastor described their work and ministry. Only much later did churches, contrary to the Scriptures, appropriate these names to describe different positions of authority. For example, a pastor or priest referred to a local minister or evangelist, and a bishop was a man who was responsible for several congregations or a geographical region. With time, new titles were invented that described men who exercised authority beyond the local congregation: Arch Bishop, Cardinal, Pope, etc. Today, this departure from Scripture has led some groups to have women as well as practicing homosexuals and lesbians serve as bishops for various denominations.

The New Testament, however, teaches that each congregation is to have its own elders/bishops/pastors along with deacons and evangelists/preachers, and these people have leadership responsibility for only one congregation. Part of the effort made by the congregation that I belong to and serve (Choctaw Church of Christ) is to restore the structure and order of the church as it was designed and described in the New Testament. This idea of following carefully God's word is exactly what Paul encourages the Ephesian elders to do if they want to maintain the spiritual and biblical integrity of the church for which they were made leaders by the Holy Spirit.

Every elder/bishop/overseer/pastor since that time has been charged by God through His word to take up the same task of guarding the teachings of the New Testament and maintaining the plan for local church organization and growth found in the New Testament. This is the only way that we can reproduce the New Testament church similar to the one we read about in the Scriptures in this modern age and every age to come until Jesus returns.

> [32]And now I commend you to God and to the word of His grace, which is able to build you up and to give you the inheritance among all those who are sanctified. [33]I have coveted no one's silver or gold or clothes. [34]You yourselves know that these hands ministered to my own needs and to the men who were with me. [35]In everything I showed you that by working hard in this manner you must help the weak and remember the words of the Lord

Jesus, that He Himself said, 'It is more blessed to give than to receive.'" [36]When he had said these things, he knelt down and prayed with them all. [37]And they began to weep aloud and embraced Paul, and repeatedly kissed him, [38]grieving especially over the word which he had spoken, that they would not see his face again. And they were accompanying him to the ship.
- Acts 20:32-38

Luke finishes the chapter with Paul's final encouragement to these elders to serve as he has served (not for financial gain) and be generous (he quotes Jesus, *"It is more blessed to give than to receive"* - verse 35). The scene ends with an emotional farewell as Luke notes that this will be the last time these brethren will see Paul.

Journey to Jerusalem (21:1-14)

Luke lightly sketches out the journey returning Paul to Jerusalem and the trouble awaiting him there. He receives several warnings not to return but is adamant in reaching the city.

[7]When we had finished the voyage from Tyre, we arrived at Ptolemais, and after greeting the brethren, we stayed with them for a day. [8]On the next day we left and came to Caesarea, and entering the house of Philip the evangelist, who was one of the seven, we stayed with him. [9]Now this man had four virgin daughters who were prophetesses. [10]As we were staying there for some days, a prophet named Agabus came down from Judea. [11]And coming to us, he took Paul's belt and bound his own feet and hands, and said, "This is what the Holy Spirit says: 'In this way the Jews at Jerusalem will bind the man who owns this belt and deliver him into the hands of the Gentiles.'" [12]When we had heard this, we as well as the local residents began begging him not to go

> up to Jerusalem. [13]Then Paul answered, "What are you doing, weeping and breaking my heart? For I am ready not only to be bound, but even to die at Jerusalem for the name of the Lord Jesus." [14]And since he would not be persuaded, we fell silent, remarking, "The will of the Lord be done!"
> - Acts 21:7-14

Notice that Luke includes himself in the group warning Paul (he writes "we"), and thus places himself in the narrative. This explains how he obtained the details of Paul's journey.

Lessons

I want to draw a few lessons from our study, but each is related to Apollos, the well educated professional speaker and teacher who was instructed in the gospel by a lowly tentmaker and his wife, probably with the wife taking the lead in teaching him the whole gospel.

God Lowers His Servants No Matter How Great They Are

For Apollos to go higher in his service to God, this great man had to first go lower to receive what he lacked. Humility is a requirement for one who wants to minister effectively in the name of the Lord.

Preach and Teach What You Know Because You will Never Know Everything

Apollos lacked some important information about Jesus and the gospel, but he launched out nevertheless and God added what he needed in due time. Unfortunately there are times that we use our lack of knowledge as an excuse not to serve at all.

Discussion Questions

1. Explain the difference between John's baptism and Jesus' baptism. Why did the 12 disciples need re-baptizing and Apollos did not?

2. How would you explain that the ability to heal miraculously or speak in tongues is no longer available? In your opinion, how do you explain the fact that many still believe that miraculous power is available today?

3. Explain how the Bible replaces the ability to do miracles or prophecy in the ongoing work of the church.

CHAPTER 23
PAUL'S ARREST & IMPRISONMENT
- PART 1

ACTS 21:15-23:11

We left off where Paul, having completed his third missionary journey, was making his way back to Jerusalem. He had been warned by several people that trouble, in the form of arrest awaited him there, but despite these cautions the Apostle would not be dissuaded from going.

This then brings us to the section in the book of Acts dealing with his arrest and imprisonment beginning in Jerusalem.

Paul at Jerusalem (21:15-26)

> [15]After these days we got ready and started on our way up to Jerusalem. [16]Some of the disciples from Caesarea also came with us, taking us to Mnason of Cyprus, a disciple of long standing with whom we were to lodge.
> [17]After we arrived in Jerusalem, the brethren received us gladly. [18]And the following day Paul went in with us to James, and all the elders were present. [19]After he had greeted them, he began to relate one by one the things which God had done

among the Gentiles through his ministry. [20]And
when they heard it they began glorifying God;
- Acts 21:15-20a

Note, once again, that Luke includes little details about the
short trip from Caesarea (where he says they stayed with
Philip, one of the original seven deacons, and his four
daughters - verses 8-9), and then names additional people
they saw and another place where they stayed overnight
(Mnason of Cyprus). These are not important doctrines or
theological insights but rather simple details that give Luke's
account a proper historical, social and cultural credibility for
his reader then and readers now. Spectacular things like
miracles, tongues and healings took place but these were
surrounded by the everyday type of events (how they
travelled, where they stayed, etc.) that make Luke's writing
sound and feel like what it was meant to be: an orderly
narrative describing the life and ministry of both Peter and
Paul in establishing the early church.

Another point of interest here is the pattern established for
the work and cooperation between the missionary, the
congregation that sends him, and the new congregations
that he establishes:

1. **The Church Sends:** Note that in Acts 13 it was the
   church that sent Barnabas and Paul into the mission
   field (Acts 13:1-3). Even though Paul had received his
   calling directly from God, he did not act on it until the
   church sent him.

2. **The Missionary Plants Churches:** Whether it be one
   missionary or a team of missionaries, the goal of those
   sent is not to do benevolence work, teach languages or
   provide medical care; the role of missionaries is to plant
   churches. These other activities can be part of a larger
   strategy but are not the goal of mission work.

3. **The Church That Sends Also Oversees:** Note that
   Paul returned and reported on his work in the field to
   the church in Antioch which had originally sent him, and

this time also to the church in Jerusalem because the leaders there had given their blessing for his work among the Gentiles. The churches that Paul planted were equipped with their own leaders as they grew in maturity (Titus 1:5), but Paul himself continued to report on his work to the churches that originally sent and blessed his mission.

Luke describes the scene where Paul is carefully detailing the ministry he has done among the Gentiles. At this point the leaders in Jerusalem bring up an issue that has come up among Christians who have been converted from Judaism.

> [20b]and they said to him, "You see, brother, how many thousands there are among the Jews of those who have believed, and they are all zealous for the Law; [21]and they have been told about you, that you are teaching all the Jews who are among the Gentiles to forsake Moses, telling them not to circumcise their children nor to walk according to the customs.
> - Acts 21:20[b]-21

Many of the early Jewish converts to Christianity continued to keep Jewish customs and religious practices: they maintained dietary restrictions (i.e. refrained from eating pork), practiced circumcision, went to the temple, etc. These activities were permitted in the early church since Jewish religion and culture were so intertwined. The only restriction, by order of the Apostles (Acts 15), was that these things could not be imposed on other Jewish or Gentile believers as conditions for salvation (as the Judaizers had attempted to do). After the destruction of the Temple in 70 AD, Christianity was increasingly seen as a distinct religion apart from Judaism, and the keeping of Jewish customs by converts from that faith eventually ceased.

However, as this passage indicates, this practice was quite alive during the time of Paul's ministry. The problem seemed to be that there were some who were spreading malicious accusations against Paul charging that he required Jewish converts to abandon their traditions and customs in order to become Christians. He was being accused of teaching the very opposite of what the Judaizers had taught:

1. Judaizers: Must keep Jewish customs (i.e. circumcision) to become a Christian.
2. Accusation against Paul: Must abandon Jewish customs (i.e. circumcision) to become a Christian.

The truth, of course, was that to become a Christian you needed to believe that Jesus was the Son of God and express that faith in repentance and baptism (Acts 2:38). Whether you kept Jewish customs after that was irrelevant because in becoming a Christian you became acceptable to God because of your faith in Christ, not what religious customs you maintained or abandoned. Paul explains this in detail in Romans 14.

However, at this particular time these accusations were causing problems in the churches that were predominately made up of these Jewish Christians (especially congregations in and around Jerusalem), and so the leaders proposed the following solution. Their suggestion was for Paul to join four Jewish Christians from the Jerusalem church who had, according to Jewish Law and custom, taken vows which were about to be completed.

Those who took vows did so as a way to thank God for answered prayers or blessings received or to ask for certain things. They were voluntary in nature but the Law regulated how they were to be carried out (Numbers 6:1-21). During the time of the vow, usually three months, a person would let his hair grow, would not drink alcohol and would be careful not to be in contact with a dead body (even that of a close relative). If one broke the vow in some way, even by accident, they had to renew that vow from the beginning. Once the time for the vow was ended, the person would shave off his hair and burn it on the altar along with an animal sacrifice of some kind (Lenski, Commentary on Acts of the Apostles, p.882).

The proposal of the elders, therefore, was that Paul join these Jewish Christian men for the last week of their vow and then complete it by paying for and offering the necessary sacrifice required for each of them. Since he was well known and being watched closely, Paul's participation in these Jewish customs would put to rest the gossip and accusations being made against him about these things. Of course, this action would be in keeping with Paul's attitude concerning such matters written about in his letter to the Corinthians.

> [19]For though I am free from all men, I have made myself a slave to all, so that I may win more. [20]To the Jews I became as a Jew, so that I might win Jews; to those who are under the Law, as under the Law though not being myself under the Law, so that I might win those who are under the Law; [21]to those who are without law, as without law, though not being without the law of God but under the law of Christ, so that I might win those who are without law.
> - I Corinthians 9:19-21

It is during the completion of these vows at the Temple that he is arrested.

Paul's Arrest and Imprisonment (21:27-40)

> [27]When the seven days were almost over, the Jews from Asia, upon seeing him in the temple, began to stir up all the crowd and laid hands on him, [28]crying out, "Men of Israel, come to our aid! This is the man who preaches to all men everywhere against our people and the Law and this place; and besides he has even brought Greeks into the temple and has defiled this holy

place." [29]For they had previously seen Trophimus the Ephesian in the city with him, and they supposed that Paul had brought him into the temple. [30]Then all the city was provoked, and the people rushed together, and taking hold of Paul they dragged him out of the temple, and immediately the doors were shut.
- Acts 21:27-30

Despite his best efforts, Paul is seized by the crowd and falsely accused of desecrating the Temple. Gentiles converted to Judaism could enter into the court of the Gentiles but not further into the temple area which was reserved for Jewish men and women. There were signs posted warning Gentiles that to cross the threshold into the Jewish area would be punishable by death. As a Jew, Paul would naturally go into the Jewish section along with the four Jewish Christians to offer sacrifice and complete their vows.

Jews from Asia (Ephesian Jews who had caused trouble there) recognized the Gentile Christian, Trophimus, who was also from the Ephesian church and accompanying Paul in Jerusalem (he was not one of the brothers who had taken a vow) but was seen with him in the city. They use this as a pretext for accusing Paul of not only disrespecting Jewish Law and custom, but actually bringing a Gentile into the forbidden area of the Temple. Luke describes the seizing of Paul and the riot that ensues (Acts 21:31-36). They begin beating the Apostle, but he is rescued by Roman soldiers who arrest him and lead him away to safety. Paul, not wanting to miss an opportunity to speak/preach to his fellow Jews, asks the Centurion's permission to address the crowd.

[37]As Paul was about to be brought into the barracks, he said to the commander, "May I say something to you?" And he said, "Do you know Greek? [38]Then you are not the Egyptian who some time ago stirred up a revolt and led the four thousand men of the Assassins out into the wilderness?" [39]But Paul said, "I am a Jew of

Tarsus in Cilicia, a citizen of no insignificant city; and I beg you, allow me to speak to the people." [40]When he had given him permission, Paul, standing on the stairs, motioned to the people with his hand; and when there was a great hush, he spoke to them in the Hebrew dialect, saying,
- Acts 21:37-40

When the Centurion realizes that Paul is not some Jewish trouble maker but a Roman citizen (who could not be arrested or punished without due process according to Roman law), he permits Paul to speak.

Paul's Defense Before the Jews (22:1-30)

Paul's speech is a recounting of his past life as a well educated Pharisee bent on destroying the Christian faith and those who pursued it. He goes on to describe his meeting with the Lord on the road to Damascus, his baptism and later on the vision he had in the Temple where God renewed the original mission for which he was called: the bringing of the gospel to the Gentiles. As a Jew, Paul naturally returned to Jerusalem after his conversion in order to preach to his countrymen, thinking that his past life and conversion would be a strong witness in bringing these people to Christ. God, however, tells Paul that the Jews will not accept him so he must, therefore, bring the gospel to the Gentiles who will.

It is at the mention of the Gentiles that the riot breaks out once again.

[22]They listened to him up to this statement, and then they raised their voices and said, "Away with such a fellow from the earth, for he should not be allowed to live!" [23]And as they were crying out and throwing off their cloaks and tossing dust into the air, [24]the commander ordered him to be brought into the barracks, stating that he should be examined by scourging so that he might find out

343

> the reason why they were shouting against him that way. [25]But when they stretched him out with thongs, Paul said to the centurion who was standing by, "Is it lawful for you to scourge a man who is a Roman and uncondemned?" [26]When the centurion heard this, he went to the commander and told him, saying, "What are you about to do? For this man is a Roman." [27]The commander came and said to him, "Tell me, are you a Roman?" And he said, "Yes." [28]The commander answered, "I acquired this citizenship with a large sum of money." And Paul said, "But I was actually born a citizen." [29]Therefore those who were about to examine him immediately let go of him; and the commander also was afraid when he found out that he was a Roman, and because he had put him in chains.
> [30]But on the next day, wishing to know for certain why he had been accused by the Jews, he released him and ordered the chief priests and all the Council to assemble, and brought Paul down and set him before them.
> - Acts 22:22-30

We see the importance of Paul's Roman citizenship here as the commander over the centurion halts the questioning and illegal torture they were about to inflict on him. Paul's citizenship was probably inherited from his father who was a citizen of a city (Tarsus) located in the Roman province of Cilicia. Paul's father would have obtained his citizenship as a result of his or his city's service to Rome.

Declaring his citizenship is enough to stop the proceedings. The commander takes Paul at his word, since a false declaration of this kind would be punishable by death according to Roman Law, and the soldiers had time to verify his claim since he was already in their custody. If they were wrong about him, then their arrest and torture of a true Roman citizen would make them guilty of a serious crime.

A compromise is found when they decide to release him from his chains and turn him over the the Jewish leaders for questioning since this seemed to be a religious matter concerning the Jews and their beliefs. The soldiers knew that Paul had not committed any crime against Roman law so allowing the Jews to question him might resolve the matter and also shed some light on why the Jewish mob wanted to kill him.

Paul Before the Jewish Council (23:1-11)

> [1]Paul, looking intently at the Council, said, "Brethren, I have lived my life with a perfectly good conscience before God up to this day." [2]The high priest Ananias commanded those standing beside him to strike him on the mouth. [3]Then Paul said to him, "God is going to strike you, you whitewashed wall! Do you sit to try me according to the Law, and in violation of the Law order me to be struck?" [4]But the bystanders said, "Do you revile God's high priest?" [5]And Paul said, "I was not aware, brethren, that he was high priest; for it is written, 'You shall not speak evil of a ruler of your people.'"
> - Acts 23:1-5

Note that Paul is not treated as well by the Council (he is struck in the face) as he was by the Romans, and beaten in violation of Jewish Law at that! His response is to point out the hypocrisy of the one meant to uphold the Law using his position to violate the Law with impunity. Paul's charge is that God will judge this action. When it is pointed out that the order was given by the High Priest, Paul apologizes for speaking out against the office, not the man, because the Law said that if an offense was committed by one in office, you had to bear it out of respect for the office and trust that God would administer justice in a proper way and time in the future (Exodus 22:28).

Luke only records the beginning and end of the inquiry (this was not an official trial, only an inquiry called and organized by the Roman commander to find a possible charge that could be made against Paul that would be legal in a Roman court). He provides no details about the questions, answers or comments made during the inquiry.

> [6]But perceiving that one group were Sadducees and the other Pharisees, Paul began crying out in the Council, "Brethren, I am a Pharisee, a son of Pharisees; I am on trial for the hope and resurrection of the dead!" [7]As he said this, there occurred a dissension between the Pharisees and Sadducees, and the assembly was divided. [8]For the Sadducees say that there is no resurrection, nor an angel, nor a spirit, but the Pharisees acknowledge them all. [9]And there occurred a great uproar; and some of the scribes of the Pharisaic party stood up and began to argue heatedly, saying, "We find nothing wrong with this man; suppose a spirit or an angel has spoken to him?" [10]And as a great dissension was developing, the commander was afraid Paul would be torn to pieces by them and ordered the troops to go down and take him away from them by force, and bring him into the barracks.
> - Acts 23:6-10

Luke describes how this meeting ended in chaos. I have previously pointed out the major theological differences between the Sadducees (who only accepted the Pentateuch, the first five books of the Bible, as authoritative and thus rejected prophecies, spirit beings, miracles and life after death; while Pharisees accepted and believed in all of these). Luke describes how Paul, previously a Pharisee, cleverly exploits these differences in order to disrupt the meeting and disarm his Jewish enemies. The clash between the two groups that ensues threatens to once again harm Paul so the soldiers rescue and detain him for his own safety, thus giving them time to consider their next move.

> But on the night immediately following, the Lord stood at his side and said, "Take courage; for as you have solemnly witnessed to My cause at Jerusalem, so you must witness at Rome also."
> - Acts 23:11

Luke provides information that could have only come from the Apostle concerning a vision or revealing that he received directly from the Lord concerning his present and future ministry of the gospel.

Lessons

Be Patient with the Process

A. Even though the Bible explains the gospel in few words:

- Jesus was God made man.

- He died for the sins of all mankind.

- He was resurrected to prove that He was God.

- Forgiveness and eternal life are offered to those who believe in Him.

- Faith is expressed through repentance and baptism.

For most people, however, understanding and responding correctly to these things can be a long process that may take years.

B. Even if the Bible describes the mature Christian in just a few strokes:

- Full of the Spirit.

- Knowledge of the Word.

- A humble and loving attitude.

- A life full of service and good deeds.

- Faithful and confident in salvation and eternal life to come.

These characteristics, however, take a long time to cultivate and be ingrained in our personal lives.

Paul, taking vows and submitting himself to the maturity level of those weaker than himself, demonstrated his willingness to be patient with the process of growing other Christians.

Our natural and fleshly reaction to other people's immaturity is usually to be angry at them, gossip and ridicule them or avoid them altogether. Being patient with others as they go through the process of growing up in Christ will guarantee that the Lord will continue to be patient with us as we move through the same process but work at some other level.

God's Ways Are Not Our Ways

Paul wanted to appease those in the church who were causing his ministry trouble. If he could calm the rumors and gossip he could then have the opportunity to reach out to his own people (fellow Jews) in the city at the center of Judaism: Jerusalem. With this problem settled he could then go from preaching to his own countrymen in Jerusalem to proclaiming the gospel in the city at the center of the Gentile world: Rome. The riot and his arrest must have been discouraging because this setback defeated his plan.

God, however, appears to Paul and reminds him that the goals he had were still intact (preach at Jerusalem and Rome), but this would be done with His plan and way, not Paul's. For example, Paul managed to preach to a large crowd in the Temple but did so because of a riot and his arrest. He will also preach at Rome but as a prisoner, not a free man.

Sometimes God uses trouble and pain in order to advance His will not only for our lives but also for the lives of others. We must not become angry and discouraged when bad things happen, better to be still, be faithful and be listening so that we can discern what God is accomplishing through our suffering or inconvenience. Sometimes, simply maintaining our faith while the storm in our lives rages on, is itself the objective that God has in mind.

We need to remember that God's ways of achieving spiritual things in us is not always, if ever, our way of achieving spiritual things in ourselves.

Reading Assignment: Acts 23:12-25:12

Discussion Questions

1. Share your own experience when you denied yourself something simply to not cause another to stumble. Did it work? How did you feel when doing this?

2. In your opinion, what are the dangers of "self-appointment" to ministry roles such as elder, deacon or preacher? Share a story about a religious leader you admire and one for someone you feel did not fulfill his ministry. What was the difference between the two?

3. Have you ever been accused unjustly? How did the Lord help you during this time?

CHAPTER 24
PAUL'S ARREST & IMPRISONMENT
- PART 2

ACTS 23:12-25:12

This is the second part of a three-part set concerning the varied and lengthy period of Paul's imprisonments. In part one I described the events that led to his initial rescue and detainment by Roman soldiers from an angry mob at the Temple in Jerusalem. On that occasion he tried to address the crowd and later was brought before the Jewish leaders in order to find a crime to charge him with. These attempts failed as both the mob and religious leaders fell into disarray to the point where the soldiers had to take Paul into protective custody once again to save his life.

In the section we will cover in this chapter, Luke will continue to describe Paul's journey through the Roman legal system as he fulfills Jesus' prophecy of proclaiming the gospel to various governors and kings (Acts 23:11).

The Conspiracy – 23:12-35

> [12]When it was day, the Jews formed a conspiracy and bound themselves under an oath, saying that they would neither eat nor drink until they had killed Paul. [13]There were more than forty who formed this plot. [14]They came to the chief priests

and the elders and said, "We have bound ourselves under a solemn oath to taste nothing until we have killed Paul. [15]Now therefore, you and the Council notify the commander to bring him down to you, as though you were going to determine his case by a more thorough investigation; and we for our part are ready to slay him before he comes near the place." [16]But the son of Paul's sister heard of their ambush, and he came and entered the barracks and told Paul. [17]Paul called one of the centurions to him and said, "Lead this young man to the commander, for he has something to report to him." [18]So he took him and led him to the commander and said, "Paul the prisoner called me to him and asked me to lead this young man to you since he has something to tell you." [19]The commander took him by the hand and stepping aside, began to inquire of him privately, "What is it that you have to report to me?" [20]And he said, "The Jews have agreed to ask you to bring Paul down tomorrow to the Council, as though they were going to inquire somewhat more thoroughly about him. [21]So do not listen to them, for more than forty of them are lying in wait for him who have bound themselves under a curse not to eat or drink until they slay him; and now they are ready and waiting for the promise from you." [22]So the commander let the young man go, instructing him, "Tell no one that you have notified me of these things."
- Acts 23:12-22

As the most educated, highest profile Jewish convert to Christianity, Paul became the number one target of the Jewish leadership. He posed a danger to them for several reasons:

1. As a respected Pharisee and teacher of the Law, he could appeal to every segment of Jewish society with the gospel.

2. He could successfully debate other teachers and priests concerning Jesus as the Messiah according to the Scriptures.

3. He was well known both in Jerusalem and throughout the Empire by Jews, Gentile converts to Judaism, as well as Jewish and Gentile converts to Christianity, so he attracted attention in ways that the Jewish leaders could not.

4. His personal conduct was irreproachable, and he performed healings and miracles.

5. As a Roman citizen he had the protection of Roman Law and was beyond the reach of the Sanhedrin's legal or political power.

6. He was accepted as an Apostle in the Christian church and as such had influence with a growing number of believers in Jerusalem. This threatened the status quo which the Jewish leaders wanted to maintain at all costs (they killed Jesus, so nothing was impossible for them to do).

7. The worst sin, however, that drove them to murderous rage, was the fact that Paul was responsible for bringing Gentiles into the church and encouraged both Gentile and Jewish converts to worship together as equals, "There is neither Jew nor Greek [...] for you are all one in Christ Jesus" (Galatians 3:28).

In doing this, Paul was violating their sense of privilege and destiny as God's people and threatened to destroy the purity of their religion which, as practiced by these leaders, consisted of maintaining a cultural exclusivity which they mistook for piety. They thought that keeping Gentiles out was the way to remain pure and please God, when in fact their job was to bring Gentiles in from paganism to worship the true and living God, but keep Gentile/pagan practices out as a way of maintaining their purity. In other words, love and receive the sinner (Gentile), and hate the sin (immoral pagan practices and religion). They simply hated the Gentiles and marginalized the Gentile converts to Judaism thus creating a class system within the Jewish religion where the priests and Pharisees were at the top and the people, the poor, the lame, the sinners (i.e. Matthew the tax collector) made up the lower classes with Gentile converts occupying the bottom rung.

Paul was their sworn enemy because he preached that all these people held the same position in the eyes of God through Christ. If this message was accepted they feared that their religion, their favored position and way of life would be destroyed. Knowing these things helps us understand their zeal in plotting to kill him.

We note again that Luke provides personal information about Paul's nephew warning him of a murder plot. This is a rare glimpse into Paul's private family life that only a close acquaintance like Luke could provide.

> [23]And he called to him two of the centurions and said, "Get two hundred soldiers ready by the third hour of the night to proceed to Caesarea, with seventy horsemen and two hundred spearmen." [24]They were also to provide mounts to put Paul on and bring him safely to Felix the governor. [25]And he wrote a letter having this form:
> [26]"Claudius Lysias, to the most excellent governor Felix, greetings.
> [27]"When this man was arrested by the Jews and was about to be slain by them, I came up to them with the troops and rescued him, having learned that he was a Roman. [28]"And wanting to ascertain the charge for which they were accusing him, I brought him down to their Council; [29]and I found him to be accused over questions about their Law, but under no accusation deserving death or imprisonment.
> [30]"When I was informed that there would be a plot against the man, I sent him to you at once, also instructing his accusers to bring charges against him before you."

> [31]So the soldiers, in accordance with their orders, took Paul and brought him by night to Antipatris. [32]But the next day, leaving the horsemen to go on with him, they returned to the barracks. [33]When these had come to Caesarea and delivered the letter to the governor, they also presented Paul to him. [34]When he had read it, he asked from what province he was, and when he learned that he was from Cilicia, [35]he said, "I will give you a hearing after your accusers arrive also," giving orders for him to be kept in Herod's Praetorium.
> - Acts 23:23-35

Luke names the commander (Claudius Lysias), another historical and social marker, and provides the report to Felix, the procurator of Judea (treasury officer for a Roman province). He summarizes the case (leaving out his own blunder in illegally arresting and attempting to torture a Roman citizen) and informs Felix that he has no legal charge to make against Paul. However, because of the violence of the Jews, he is sending Paul and his accusers to Felix for him to sort out the case. This is a question of jurisdiction. If there is to be a charge against Paul, where he will be tried and who will judge the case has to be decided. Felix agrees to oversee the preliminary hearing to determine if a charge can be made. However, since Paul is from another Roman province (Cilicia), if a law has been broken he would then have to be sent there for trial.

Paul Before Felix – 24:1-27

Felix obtained his position through his brother Pallas who was secretary of the treasury during the reign of the Emperor Claudius. Both he and his brother were slaves who became freedmen and eventually rose to power in the Roman government. Felix was immoral, cruel and subject to bribes which led to an increase in crime and instability in Judea. Tacitus, the Roman historian, said of Felix that he had the position of a king but the heart of a slave. He ruled from 52-

58 AD. He lived in Herod's palace located in Caesarea by the Sea which was the official residence of the governor/prefect/proconsul/king or official who ruled Judea on behalf of Rome. Paul, who had not been charged with any crime, was also kept here (although not in the prison section) while he awaited the formulation of some charge against him.

(Acts 24:1-9) The Jewish leaders arrive and through their chosen attorney (prosecutor) they make three charges:

1. Paul was causing unrest among the Jews.
2. He was the leader of a renegade sect referred to here as the Nazarenes (reference to Jesus' home town).
3. He tried to desecrate the Temple.

Of course there is a germ of truth in these accusations which gives them some credibility:

1. There was dissension among the Jews, but they were the ones who caused it as they followed and persecuted Paul from city to city.
2. He was a leader in the church, one of many, but their goal was not rebellion against the government.
3. He was present at the Temple but respecting its laws and customs, not desecrating it.

The lawyer also lies concerning the Jews' actions saying that they had arrested Paul and were bringing him to court for judgment, when in truth they had formed a mob and were about to kill him when the Roman soldiers intervened. Luke adds that the Jewish leaders also attacked Paul once their lawyer had finished his presentation.

Note that after a brief and respectful acknowledgement of Felix, Paul responds to each accusation:

1. Causing Dissension

> [10]When the governor had nodded for him to speak, Paul responded: "Knowing that for many years you have been a judge to this nation, I cheerfully make my defense, [11]since you can take note of the fact that no more than twelve days ago I went up to Jerusalem to worship. [12]Neither in the temple, nor in the synagogues, nor in the city itself did they find me carrying on a discussion with anyone or causing a riot. [13]Nor can they prove to you the charges of which they now accuse me.
> - Acts 24:10-13

He not only denies the charge but challenges his accusers to actually provide proof.

2. Leading a Renegade Sect

> [14]But this I admit to you, that according to the Way which they call a sect I do serve the God of our fathers, believing everything that is in accordance with the Law and that is written in the Prophets; [15]having a hope in God, which these men cherish themselves, that there shall certainly be a resurrection of both the righteous and the wicked. [16]In view of this, I also do my best to maintain always a blameless conscience both before God and before men.
> - Acts 24:14-16

His accusers were suggesting that Christianity was some form of religious/political fanaticism that threatened the stability of the people and, even worse, presented a challenge to Roman rule. Had not Jesus, their leader from Nazareth, been executed by a former governor for similar crimes? In response, Paul argues that his faith is no challenge to secular rule having its source and promise in the very religion espoused by his accusers, and a message of punishment and reward at judgment which was quite familiar to all who were present. Paul even uses the idea of God's judgment to defend himself saying that as a faithful Christian he would not do such things (cause trouble, attack the government, etc.) as a matter of conscience because it would be sinful if he did.

3. Desecrating the Temple

Paul explains the reason why he was in the Temple area in the first place and argues that he was there according to Law and custom. He blames the riot, which ultimately led to his arrest and appearance before Felix, on the false accusations of the Jews from Asia who publicly accused him of bringing a Gentile into the restricted part of the Temple. Paul wraps up his defense by challenging his accusers to explain why they rioted when he simply proclaimed the basic promise of the gospel which was resurrection from the dead of those who believed in Jesus Christ. Apparently the lawyer and the Jewish leaders had no counter arguments, evidence or comments to answer Paul's defense.

> [22]But Felix, having a more exact knowledge about the Way, put them off, saying, "When Lysias the commander comes down, I will decide your case." [23]Then he gave orders to the centurion for him to be kept in custody and yet have some freedom, and not to prevent any of his friends from ministering to him.
> - Acts 24:22-23

Felix understood Paul's arguments because he was familiar with Christianity's teachings. There was no evidence presented and Paul had convincingly answered his accusers. This familiarity enabled him to accept Paul's credibility and account of events without further witnesses. But this was about politics and power not religion, so using the excuse that he needed to consult with Lysias, the commander, Felix put off a decision. He sent the Jewish leaders home and kept Paul under guard in the palace with a measure of freedom to move about and receive visitors while under house arrest. We get a glimpse of Felix's true motives in the following verses.

> [24]But some days later Felix arrived with Drusilla, his wife who was a Jewess, and sent for Paul and heard him speak about faith in Christ Jesus. [25]But as he was discussing righteousness, self-control and the judgment to come, Felix became frightened and said, "Go away for the present, and when I find time I will summon you." [26]At the same time too, he was hoping that money would be given him by Paul; therefore he also used to send for him quite often and converse with him. [27]But after two years had passed, Felix was succeeded by Porcius Festus, and wishing to do the Jews a favor, Felix left Paul imprisoned.
> - Acts 24:24-27

He seems to have been a conflicted man. On the one hand eager to hear Paul preach and teach and affected by the message; the fact that he feared suggests that he had a measure of faith because the Word was getting to him. On the other hand, he gave in to his greed by hoping to profit from Paul's imprisonment and demonstrated his lack of honor and mercy by keeping a man he knew to be innocent unjustly imprisoned to gain favor with other evil men.

Luke ends this section with an additional historical notation that these events took place the year that another Roman official (Porcius Festus) was replacing Felix as procurator in 59-60 AD.

Trial Before Festus – 25:1-12

History records that Porcius Festus was fair and reasonable, much more so than Felix the official he came to replace. Luke writes that three days after his arrival in Judea, Festus travels to Jerusalem in order to meet with the Jewish leaders. Their first order of business is a request to bring Paul back to Jerusalem for a trial that Festus can judge there. Of course their goal is to kill Paul during the trip from Caesarea since they cannot win their case against him in court, nor can they successfully attack the well-guarded palace at Caesarea. Festus agrees to hear arguments for a trial in Jerusalem and invites the leaders to come to Caesarea to make their case for a change in venue.

> [6]After he had spent not more than eight or ten days among them, he went down to Caesarea, and on the next day he took his seat on the tribunal and ordered Paul to be brought. [7]After Paul arrived, the Jews who had come down from Jerusalem stood around him, bringing many and serious charges against him which they could not prove, [8]while Paul said in his own defense, "I have committed no offense either against the Law of the Jews or against the temple or against Caesar." [9]But Festus, wishing to do the Jews a favor, answered Paul and said, "Are you willing to go up to Jerusalem and stand trial before me on these charges?" [10]But Paul said, "I am standing before Caesar's tribunal, where I ought to be tried. I have done no wrong to the Jews, as you also very well know. [11]If, then, I am a wrongdoer and have committed anything worthy of death, I do not refuse to die; but if none of those things is true of which these men accuse me, no one can hand me over to them. I appeal to Caesar." [12]Then when Festus had conferred with his council, he answered, "You have appealed to Caesar, to Caesar you shall go."
> - Acts 25:6-12

Luke does not describe the charges but notes that the Jewish accusers still have no proof. Of course their goal is not to win the case but to separate Paul from his guards in Herod's palace. In an effort to curry favor with the Jewish leadership, the new governor proposes a change in location to Jerusalem for the trial (obviously not aware of the true intentions of these men).

As a Roman citizen, Paul's case could not be moved to another jurisdiction (other than Cilicia where he came from, or the governor's palace where he was held) without his permission (Lenski, p.996-997). Paul, seeing that he could not receive proper justice before this judge (Festus) or the previous one (Felix) because these Roman officials wanted to avoid trouble with the local Jewish leaders, used his privilege as a Roman citizen to be judged in Caesar's court in Rome by the Emperor himself. In the Roman system, any citizen had the right to make an appeal to Caesar if he felt that he was not receiving justice in the lower courts. In many cases the Emperor would actually hear the case himself or it would be heard in the Imperial Court at Rome. By making this request Festus is legally bound to transfer Paul to Rome where he will receive a fair hearing and in doing so the Apostle will also escape the ever present threat of violence against him by the Jewish leaders.

Reading Assignment: Acts 25:13-26:32

Discussion Questions

1. Describe the subtle forms of discrimination that take place in the church. How can this be corrected?

2. Share a time when you had to "Wait on the Lord." Why was this difficult? What advice would you give to those who are in this position now?

3. If you were imprisoned for your faith, how would you spend your time while incarcerated?

CHAPTER 25
PAUL'S ARREST & IMPRISONMENT
- PART 3

ACTS 25:13-26:32

In the previous chapter we covered Luke's description of Paul's appearances before an outgoing and incoming governor. He first argued his case before Felix but was kept in prison for two years as a favor to the Jewish leadership. When Festus became governor, Paul also appeared before him and fearing an attack from the Jews as well as continued imprisonment, appealed his case to Caesar in Rome.

Festus permitted this but before his departure Paul would appear before yet another ruler. This episode completes the third section of Paul's imprisonment before his transfer to Rome

Festus and Agrippa – 25:13-22

> Now when several days had elapsed, King Agrippa
> and Bernice arrived at Caesarea and paid their
> respects to Festus.
> - Acts 25:13

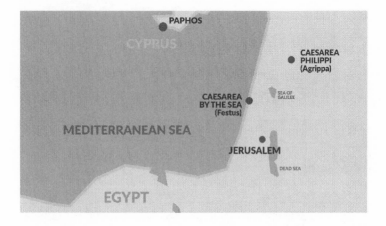

King Agrippa ruled another province to the north with a similar name for its capital city: Caesarea by the Sea - Festus, Caesarea Philippi - Agrippa. Agrippa II was the last of Herod's descendants to rule as king. He grew up in Rome and was trained in Roman ways in the court of the Emperor Claudius. Even though he ruled a northern territory he was given charge over the affairs of the Temple in Jerusalem and had the authority to appoint the High Priest. Because of this responsibility he was trained in Jewish Law, custom and religion. This may be one of the reasons Festus sought his opinion on Paul's case since it involved both the Temple and Jewish religious matters.

Bernice was Agrippa's sister and the rumor at the time was that these two carried on an incestuous relationship. As was the custom, Agrippa and Bernice were visiting Festus, the new ruler, at his palace in Caesarea by the Sea, in order to welcome him to his new position. An interesting note is that the palace where Festus was situated was originally built by Agrippa and Bernice's grandfather, Herod the Great, and they played there together as children (Lenski, p.1003).

> [14]While they were spending many days there, Festus laid Paul's case before the king, saying, "There is a man who was left as a prisoner by Felix; [15]and when I was at Jerusalem, the chief

priests and the elders of the Jews brought charges against him, asking for a sentence of condemnation against him. [16]I answered them that it is not the custom of the Romans to hand over any man before the accused meets his accusers face to face and has an opportunity to make his defense against the charges. [17]So after they had assembled here, I did not delay, but on the next day took my seat on the tribunal and ordered the man to be brought before me. [18]When the accusers stood up, they began bringing charges against him not of such crimes as I was expecting, [19]but they simply had some points of disagreement with him about their own religion and about a dead man, Jesus, whom Paul asserted to be alive. [20]Being at a loss how to investigate such matters, I asked whether he was willing to go to Jerusalem and there stand trial on these matters. [21]But when Paul appealed to be held in custody for the Emperor's decision, I ordered him to be kept in custody until I send him to Caesar." [22]Then Agrippa said to Festus, "I also would like to hear the man myself." "Tomorrow," he said, "you shall hear him."
- Acts 25:14-22

A couple of things to note about Festus' account:

1. He says that Paul was left in prison as if he was serving time for some crime when in reality he was denied his legal right to freedom by both Felix and Festus in order to curry favor with the Jewish leaders.

2. Festus explains that he quickly held a hearing to determine Paul's case but was at a loss since the charges against him were for religious violations not usually pursued in Roman courts. What he does not say, however, is that those accusing him provided no proof of these alleged religious crimes and instead of dismissing the case he chose to keep Paul in prison

with the hope of receiving a bribe in exchange for the Apostle's freedom.

3. Festus tells Agrippa that he offered Paul a choice: to stand trial in Jerusalem or stay in prison in the palace at Caesarea. What he neglects to mention is the third option: to set Paul free since his accusers had no evidence that Paul had violated any Jewish or Roman laws.

Paul's request for a direct appeal to Caesar puts Festus in a difficult position politically since his mismanagement of this case would make him look bad not only with the Jewish leaders (who would lose their opportunity to kill Paul) but also before his superiors in Rome who had recently appointed him to this new post. His effort to bring Agrippa into the picture may have been an attempt to curry favor with a local ruler who was highly regarded by the Emperor.

Paul Before Agrippa – 25:23-26:29

Festus Presents Paul's Case

²³So, on the next day when Agrippa came together with Bernice amid great pomp, and entered the auditorium accompanied by the commanders and the prominent men of the city, at the command of Festus, Paul was brought in. ²⁴Festus said, "King Agrippa, and all you gentlemen here present with us, you see this man about whom all the people of the Jews appealed to me, both at Jerusalem and here, loudly declaring that he ought not to live any longer. ²⁵But I found that he had committed nothing worthy of death; and since he himself appealed to the Emperor, I decided to send him. ²⁶Yet I have nothing definite about him to write to my lord. Therefore I have brought him before you all and especially before you, King Agrippa, so that after the investigation has taken place, I may have

something to write. [27]For it seems absurd to me in sending a prisoner, not to indicate also the charges against him."
- Acts 25:23-27

Festus' short speech before Agrippa and the assembled guests is a master class in political dissembling. Festus had orchestrated this event to cover his failure in providing Paul with basic Roman justice. Note how he does this:

1. By creating an "event" with important guests, and placing Agrippa and Bernice at the center of attention he spread the responsibility for what happened to Paul from only himself to Agrippa who would now share in the decision and outcome.

2. He does not mention the fact that after having heard the accusations of the Jews and Paul's defense, he failed to render a verdict and this is why Paul was still imprisoned and forced to appeal to Caesar.

3. By proclaiming his ignorance of Jewish religious customs (which was not necessary to judge the case and render a verdict), and appealing to Agrippa's knowledge of such things, he included Agrippa's name and prestige in this matter.

Festus may have lost the goodwill of the Jewish leaders, but was more concerned with protecting himself politically before his masters in Rome early in his term as governor over the Judean Province.

Paul's Defense Before Agrippa (26:1-29)

[1]Agrippa said to Paul, "You are permitted to speak for yourself." Then Paul stretched out his hand and proceeded to make his defense:
[2]"In regard to all the things of which I am accused by the Jews, I consider myself fortunate, King Agrippa, that I am about to make my defense before you today; [3]especially because you are an

> expert in all customs and questions among the
> Jews; therefore I beg you to listen to me patiently.
> - Acts 26:1-3

Paul's reference to the king is brief and respectful. As a
Roman citizen he is aware of what is going on in the empire
politically, and thus knows who Agrippa is and how he was
prepared for the role of governor and overseer of the Jewish
Temple.

> [4]"So then, all Jews know my manner of life from
> my youth up, which from the beginning was spent
> among my own nation and at Jerusalem; [5]since
> they have known about me for a long time, if they
> are willing to testify, that I lived as a Pharisee
> according to the strictest sect of our religion. [6]And
> now I am standing trial for the hope of the promise
> made by God to our fathers; [7]the promise to which
> our twelve tribes hope to attain, as they earnestly
> serve God night and day. And for this hope, O
> King, I am being accused by Jews. [8]Why is it
> considered incredible among you people if God
> does raise the dead?
> - Acts 26:4-8

Paul summarizes the results of the three appearances he
has had before the Jews, Felix and Festus. He explains that
the Jews were familiar with him as a Pharisee, a highly-
respected position in that society. He also mentions their
absence of testimony concerning his past life and by
extension lack of evidence concerning any crimes he may
have committed. He then declares what their anger and
religious disagreement with him are all about: the promise of
bodily resurrection through Jesus Christ.

Agrippa, having been schooled in matters of Jewish Law,
custom and teaching knew about the division between the
Pharisees and the Sadducees over these issues. Paul's
point is that this was a disagreement over religious matters,

not a crime worthy of death for either a Jewish or Roman court. He even pleads his case for belief in the resurrection by stating that raising a man from the dead was not impossible for God if He chose to do so, and not beyond the ability of man to believe that God was capable of doing such a thing.

> [9]"So then, I thought to myself that I had to do many things hostile to the name of Jesus of Nazareth. [10]And this is just what I did in Jerusalem; not only did I lock up many of the saints in prisons, having received authority from the chief priests, but also when they were being put to death I cast my vote against them. [11]And as I punished them often in all the synagogues, I tried to force them to
>
> blaspheme; and being furiously enraged at them, I kept pursuing them even to foreign cities.
> - Acts 26:9-11

At this point Paul begins to tell his personal story, now that he has dealt with the accusations against him and the fact that these have no legal merit. He briefly details his initial attacks against Christians as a zealous Pharisee duly charged by the religious leaders (who now want his death) to destroy this sect and its followers. This he did in the most vicious ways by putting them in jail, promoting their executions (e.g. Stephen), chasing them out of local synagogues, forcing them to curse and deny Christ and carrying on this crusade against them from city to city.

> [12]"While so engaged as I was journeying to Damascus with the authority and commission of the chief priests, [13]at midday, O King, I saw on the way a light from heaven, brighter than the sun, shining all around me and those who were journeying with me. [14]And when we had all fallen to the ground, I heard a voice saying to me in the Hebrew dialect, 'Saul, Saul, why are you

persecuting Me? It is hard for you to kick against the goads.' [15]And I said, 'Who are You, Lord?' And the Lord said, 'I am Jesus whom you are persecuting. [16]But get up and stand on your feet; for this purpose I have appeared to you, to appoint you a minister and a witness not only to the things which you have seen, but also to the things in which I will appear to you; [17]rescuing you from the Jewish people and from the Gentiles, to whom I am sending you, [18]to open their eyes so that they may turn from darkness to light and from the dominion of Satan to God, that they may receive forgiveness of sins and an inheritance among those who have been sanctified by faith in Me.'
- Acts 26:12-18

This is Paul's own personal account of Jesus' appearance to him as told to and recorded by Luke. The event was as follows: a powerful bright light appears to him and those with him as they are journeying to Damascus in order to carry on the persecution against Christians in that city as authorized by the Jewish leaders in Jerusalem. Note that all were affected by the light since all fell to the ground when seeing it, however, only Paul hears the voice of the Lord.

There is a lot of discussion surrounding the meaning of Jesus' statement concerning Saul (verse 14 - *"It is hard for you to kick against the goads"*). This refers to a situation where a farmer ploughing a field with a team of oxen would prod the animal with a stick or "goad" so it would move faster or maintain a straight line. Often when "goaded" the animal would kick back but would only hit and hurt itself as a result. In today's vernacular we would convey this idea with the expression, *"Why are you beating your head against the wall?"* Jesus was revealing two things to Paul here:

1. He could not win this battle against these Christians.

2. He would only be hurting himself in the process.

It is not mentioned here but Paul's tactics and attitude were violating his own faith and Law as a devout Jew. He knows by the light and the voice he hears that he is in the presence of a heavenly being, however, he does not yet know who. Jesus identifies Himself and goes on to inform Paul concerning his future service. He will become a minister; in his case a servant directly appointed to carry out Jesus' instructions. He will be a witness of the risen Christ (because it is the risen Jesus who now speaks to him). In other words, he will be a witness to the fact that Jesus has risen from the dead, appointed to this task by Jesus Himself, as were the other Apostles. This, then, would be his calling to apostleship. Also, like the other Apostles, Jesus tells him that He will provide further instructions and revelations in the future. Finally, the Lord lays out the scope of his service which will include ministry to both Jews and Gentiles in preaching the gospel, and through this free people from the ignorance of the true God and grant them forgiveness of sins and eternal life in heaven (the inheritance given to faithful Christians).

Jesus summarizes what Paul will receive and eventually begin to do but it will take many years before all these things are fully realized in his life.

> [19]"So, King Agrippa, I did not prove disobedient to the heavenly vision, [20]but kept declaring both to those of Damascus first, and also at Jerusalem and then throughout all the region of Judea, and even to the Gentiles, that they should repent and turn to God, performing deeds appropriate to repentance. [21]For this reason some Jews seized me in the temple and tried to put me to death. [22]So, having obtained help from God, I stand to this day testifying both to small and great, stating nothing but what the Prophets and Moses said was going to take place; [23]that the Christ was to suffer, and that by reason of His resurrection from the dead He would be the first to proclaim light both to the

Jewish people and to the Gentiles."
- Acts 26:19-23

Paul continues by fast-forwarding from the day of his encounter with Jesus to his fully matured ministry of preaching and teaching the gospel to Jews living in Jerusalem and the surrounding region as well as Gentiles throughout the Roman Empire. It is in the context of this preaching and witnessing ministry that he was in Jerusalem (not to make trouble or desecrate the Temple or to break Roman laws), but to urge people to repent and believe that Jesus was the Messiah according to the Law and the prophets.

He finishes by bringing his story into the present moment as he stands before these high officials and prominent citizens, and he urges all of them to believe in the risen Christ. It is at this point that he is interrupted by Festus.

> [24]While Paul was saying this in his defense, Festus said in a loud voice, "Paul, you are out of your mind! Your great learning is driving you mad." [25]But Paul said, "I am not out of my mind, most excellent Festus, but I utter words of sober truth. [26]For the king knows about these matters, and I speak to him also with confidence, since I am persuaded that none of these things escape his notice; for this has not been done in a corner. [27]King Agrippa, do you believe the Prophets? I know that you do." [28]Agrippa replied to Paul, "In a short time you will persuade me to become a Christian." [29]And Paul said, "I would wish to God, that whether in a short or long time, not only you, but also all who hear me this day, might become such as I am, except for these chains."
> - Acts 26:24-29

Festus, who is either "feeling the heat" of the gospel message personally or afraid that Paul's bold and direct speech might offend some of his guests, especially Agrippa whose approval and support he needed in this matter, decides to interrupt Paul's speech. Paul answers Festus' charge by reminding him that the king knows about Jesus, His teachings, His cross and the eyewitness reports of His resurrection and the subsequent growth of the church. The point made but not spoken is that Festus, along with everyone else present, are accountable to the gospel and subject to God's judgment in failing to respond. In essence, Paul tells him that he, Festus, will not be able to plead ignorance at the judgment.

What is truly amazing in this situation is that Paul, having dealt with one king, now goes after the other ruler, Agrippa. He challenges the king by asking him outright concerning his faith in the prophets concerning the coming of the Messiah, who he has just stated was Jesus, the risen Savior. The king dodges the question by signaling to Paul that he knows that the Apostle is trying to convert him to Christianity. His point is that if he answers yes (I believe the prophets) then that will be the first step leading to his eventual conversion.

Paul, seeing the king's hesitation to continue, extends the invitation to everyone there. His final reference to his "chains" is a reminder to both kings that he is being held as a prisoner for proclaiming the message that they just heard which is clearly not a breech of either Jewish or Roman law. He may be bearing the chains and imprisonment, but these two kings will bear the guilt.

Agrippa's Response

> [30]The king stood up and the governor and Bernice, and those who were sitting with them, [31]and when they had gone aside, they began talking to one another, saying, "This man is not doing anything worthy of death or imprisonment." [32]And Agrippa said to Festus, "This man might have been set free if he had not appealed to Caesar."
> - Acts 26:30-32

Agrippa confirms what the Apostle had claimed and Festus had concluded: that Paul was not guilty of any crime. By saying this, Agrippa puts the case back into Festus' hands leaving him to send Paul to Rome without criminal charges. The king could not free Paul now because he had made an official appeal in open court which could not be changed.

This sets the scene for the final event recorded by Luke: Paul's voyage to Rome.

Lessons

God's Timetable is Not Our Timetable

Paul spent over two years in prison at Caesarea. He was in the prime of his ministry: the churches needed him and no one else of his stature was effectively bringing the gospel to the Gentiles. There was no other story or event recorded that could somehow explain or make up for the lost time and work Paul would have done during that period. The only thing that helped Paul bear the frustration, discomfort and perceived loss of time and opportunity was the knowledge that God was fully aware of his circumstances and the length of his imprisonment.

When we are assured that God has His timetable and it rarely matches our own, we can find peace and acceptance in periods of illness, failure and delay where the only thing we can do is wait.

Your Own Story is Your Best Witness for Christ

Notice that Paul did not address these educated people with theological arguments or a long list of Scriptures and their careful explanation; he simply told his story. His conversion was familiar, sincere and powerful because it detailed the changes that took place in his life because of Christ.

Not everyone can teach a class on the Bible or debate Bible doctrine with those of another viewpoint or religion. However, everyone has a story about their conversion, or their growth in Christ, or some prayer God has answered. Your story is your very best witness because it is true, familiar, powerful and can be repeated many times without losing its effect to impact people for Christ. When in doubt, therefore, or brought forth to witness, just tell your story!

Discussion Questions

1. If you were the leader of your country, what three things would you do to share your faith and help the church?

2. Paul claims in I Timothy 1:15 that he is the worst of sinners. Why does he say this and how is his sin greater than say, Hitler's terrible deeds in WWII?

3. Describe a time when someone you preached to/taught rejected the gospel. Why do you think they refused to believe/respond? What would you do differently if you had the chance?

CHAPTER 26
PAUL'S JOURNEY TO ROME

ACTS 27:1-28:31

Paul has been languishing under house arrest in Herod's palace at Caesarea by the Sea. He has not been charged with any crime. He has appeared before three different Roman governors during that time (Felix, Festus and Agrippa) but none of them have been able to determine any Roman law he has broken, aside from the many unsubstantiated accusations hurled at him by the Jews. This has caused a stalemate in the proceedings causing Paul's continued confinement because the Roman officials fear that the Jewish leaders will create trouble if he is released.

Paul breaks this logjam by demanding, as a Roman citizen, his right to appeal his case to Cesar's court in Rome. This frees him from an undetermined amount of time spent in confinement at Caesarea, provides a resolution for his case in the Roman judicial system and distances him from the murderous Jews in Jerusalem who want him killed.

Voyage to Rome – 27:1-28:16

Departure from Caesarea

[1]When it was decided that we would sail for Italy, they proceeded to deliver Paul and some other prisoners to a centurion of the Augustan cohort named Julius. [2]And embarking in an Adramyttian ship, which was about to sail to the regions along the coast of Asia, we put out to sea accompanied by Aristarchus, a Macedonian of Thessalonica. [3]The next day we put in at Sidon; and Julius treated Paul with consideration and allowed him to go to his friends and receive care. [4]From there we put out to sea and sailed under the shelter of Cyprus because the winds were contrary. [5]When we had sailed through the sea along the coast of Cilicia and Pamphylia, we landed at Myra in Lycia. [6]There the centurion found an Alexandrian ship sailing for Italy, and he put us aboard it. [7]When we had sailed slowly for a good many days, and with difficulty had arrived off Cnidus, since the wind did not permit us to go farther, we sailed under the shelter of Crete, off Salmone; [8]and with difficulty sailing past it we came to a place called Fair Havens, near which was the city of Lasea.

- Acts 27:1-8

Once again we see Luke's attention to social and historical detail as he chronicles Paul's voyage to Rome. He names the centurion, Julius, and the Augustan cohort he commanded who acted much like Deputy Marshals or Sheriff Department Officers working across various lines of law enforcement. They were responsible for communications between Rome and its armies in foreign lands as well as the transfer of prisoners as was the case here.

Like travel today where you cannot always get a direct flight to your destination but have to have a connecting flight, during that time you could not sail directly to Italy from a port in Judea or Syria. The centurion and his soldiers, Paul and other prisoners (probably sent to Rome for execution), as well as Luke (he says "we" in verse 2) and another brother, Aristarchus from the church at Thessalonica, set sail on a ship that normally berthed at Mysia, a Roman province in Asia Minor, now known as Turkey.

The first stop on the journey was Sidon where Paul was allowed to go ashore with friends, a gracious act on the part of the centurion. Hugging the coastline and using Cyprus as a cover from powerful winds they made their way to Myra, a port city in the province of Lydia, a journey of about 15 days. Here they found a larger ship able to transport them all the way to Italy. This ship made slow progress, avoiding the shorter and more direct route on the northern side of the island of Crete, sailing instead on the southern side of the island where there was less wind and better harbors for large commercial vessels like theirs. They eventually arrived at Lasea, a port city in Southern Crete.

Paul's Warning

[9]When considerable time had passed and the voyage was now dangerous, since even the fast was already over, Paul began to admonish them, [10]and said to them, "Men, I perceive that the voyage will certainly be with damage and great loss, not only of the cargo and the ship, but also of

our lives." [11]But the centurion was more persuaded
by the pilot and the captain of the ship than by
what was being said by Paul. [12]Because the harbor
was not suitable for wintering, the majority reached
a decision to put out to sea from there, if somehow
they could reach Phoenix, a harbor of Crete, facing
southwest and northwest, and spend the winter
there.
- Acts 27:9-12

Luke's mention of the "fast" helps us determine the time of
year that this voyage was being taken. The "fast" referred to
the fasting done by Jews on the Day of Atonement, a time
when they would fast and pray as the High Priest would
enter the Holy of Holies in the Temple at Jerusalem in order
to offer a sacrifice for sin, first for himself and then for the
people. Since these events were taking place in 59 or 60 AD
we know, according to the Jewish religious calendar, that the
Day of Atonement for those years was in early October.
Maritime historians tell us that sea voyages in that region
were considered dangerous if undertaken between mid-
September to early November and not possible after
November 10th when all sea traffic was suspended until
March 10th (Lenski, p.1069).

Paul warns of the danger in continuing the journey. This was
not prophecy but an opinion based on Paul's experience in
traveling by sea. After all, he claimed that he had been
shipwrecked and left adrift three times in his life (II
Corinthians 11:25). There is no suggestion of divine or
angelic help here. The manner in which Luke describes the
scene suggests that the sailors, captain as well as Paul were
experienced travelers and aware of the risks in sailing at that
time of year and so Paul gives his opinion on the matter.
Luke describes, in part, the winning argument of the captain
that their present location was not suitable for wintering the
ship and based on this they set sail for a better harbor
located further up the coast of Crete at Phoenix.

The Storm

[13]When a moderate south wind came up,
supposing that they had attained their purpose,
they weighed anchor and began sailing along
Crete, close inshore.
[14] But before very long there rushed down from the
land a violent wind, called Euraquilo; [15]and when
the ship was caught in it and could not face the
wind, we gave way to it and let ourselves be driven
along. [16]Running under the shelter of a small island
called Clauda, we were scarcely able to get the
ship's boat under control. [17]After they had hoisted it
up, they used supporting cables in undergirding the
ship; and fearing that they might run aground on
the shallows of Syrtis, they let down the sea
anchor and in this way let themselves be driven
along. [18]The next day as we were being violently
storm-tossed, they began to jettison the
cargo; [19]and on the third day they threw the ship's
tackle overboard with their own hands. [20]Since
neither sun nor stars appeared for many days, and
no small storm was assailing us, from then on all
hope of our being saved was gradually abandoned.
- Acts 27:13-20

All goes well as they have a good wind to sail by and
cautiously hug the coastline making their way some 40 miles
(64 kilometers) to Phoenix. Soon after their departure they
were hit with what Paul calls a typhoon or what we refer to
as a hurricane. The term "euraquilo" or "noreaster" is the
nickname given to this type of storm that the sailors were
familiar with. The wind now drove the ship, and the sailors
were in emergency mode trying to avoid it capsizing. One
problem was that their lifeboat, normally tied to the ship and
pulled along behind, was now full of water and jeopardizing
the main vessel because of its weight, drag and lack of
control. They did not want to cut it free since it was their only
means of escape should the ship sink, so they managed to
hoist it up and secure it to the main vessel.

Another problem they encountered was the separation of the wooden planks with which the ship was built. Gale force winds, crashing waves and the stress on the pole that held the mainsail would cause the planks, especially those of the hull or front of the ship, to separate causing the vessel to take on water and sink. Luke describes how the sailors used cables to hold the ship together and avoid these planks from coming apart.

The next challenge was that they needed to make a course correction because the wind was driving them towards the notorious sandbanks located between Carthage and Cyrene known as Syrtis. In order to accomplish this they slowed the ship down by allowing it's anchor to drag in the sea and also threw their cargo and heavy equipment overboard. We know now that their strategy worked and the ship's course was changed enough, despite the storm, that they avoided the Syrtis sandbars and sailed 13 more days and 480 miles (772 kilometers) close to the island of Malta. At this point, however, they had done all they could humanly do and for the moment were stranded at sea in the middle of a terrible storm not able to navigate or know where they were regardless of the time of day or night. Luke describes the consensus of the sailors, soldiers and prisoners who accepted their seeming fate and were now resigned to the fact that they would probably die in this storm.

Paul's Exhortation

[21]When they had gone a long time without food, then Paul stood up in their midst and said, "Men, you ought to have followed my advice and not to have set sail from Crete and incurred this damage and loss. [22]Yet now I urge you to keep up your courage, for there will be no loss of life among you, but only of the ship. [23]For this very night an angel of the God to whom I belong and whom I serve stood before me, [24]saying, 'Do not be afraid, Paul; you must stand before Caesar; and behold, God has granted you all those who are sailing with

you.' [25]Therefore, keep up your courage, men, for I believe God that it will turn out exactly as I have been told. [26]But we must run aground on a certain island."
- Acts 27:21-26

In this speech, we see the difference between Paul's earlier caution about the risk they were taking and possible loss in sailing at that time of the year (an opinion based on experience). Note that in verse 21 he tells them that what he had previously said was advice, not prophecy. By reminding them of this he sets up the basis for what he will tell them now, which will be miraculous and prophetic in nature.

He then assures them that their lives will be saved and describes the vision he has had of an angel from God and the message that this angel delivered to him. He (Paul) will indeed stand before Caesar (Nero at that time) and plead his case. In addition to this, everyone with him (not only the Christians) will be saved.

The way this promise is worded can lead to several conclusions:

1. Paul had already been praying for everyone to be saved and God was telling him that his prayer on their behalf was being answered.

2. These men now owed their lives to Paul.

3. Paul was using this entire episode as a way of witnessing to these pagan men about the true God in heaven.

Note that Paul's encouragement is not a banal platitude (i.e. "Do not worry, everything will be alright"). His encouragement is specific: they will all be saved; the ship, however, will be lost; they will run aground near an island. Specificity about future events is what makes this a prophecy. Paul's witness about everything else will be worthless if any details of his prophecy are wrong or different in the end.

Rescue (27:27-44)

Luke continues his description of the 14 days that the ship was driven about by the wind, eventually approaching land. At this point the sailors attempt to take the life boat and abandon the ship, but Paul warns the centurion that if the sailors escape, everyone will be lost. This time the soldier listens to Paul and thwarts the escape by cutting away the empty lifeboat and setting it adrift.

At the dawn of the 15th day of the storm Paul encourages them to eat some food and reminds them of God's promise after which he leads a prayer in the presence of everyone (Luke notes that there are 276 people in all). Sensing that they are nearing land, they further lighten the ship in order to help them steer it closer to shore. It is at this point that one of Paul's prophecies about the vessel is fulfilled.

> [39]When day came, they could not recognize the land; but they did observe a bay with a beach, and they resolved to drive the ship onto it if they could. [40]And casting off the anchors, they left them in the sea while at the same time they were loosening the ropes of the rudders; and hoisting the foresail to the wind, they were heading for the beach. [41]But striking a reef where two seas met, they ran the vessel aground; and the prow stuck fast and remained immovable, but the stern began to be broken up by the force of the waves. [42]The soldiers' plan was to kill the prisoners, so that none of them would swim away and escape; [43]but the centurion, wanting to bring Paul safely through, kept them from their intention, and commanded that those who could swim should jump overboard first and get to land, [44]and the rest should follow, some on planks, and others on various things from the ship. And so it happened that they all were brought safely to land.
> - Acts 27:39-44

Upon seeing the beach the sailors make a dash trying to steer the ship into the bay in an effort to save the vessel, but they run it aground, stuck on a shallow sand bar. The bow of the ship is caught in a reef and the violent wind and waves battering it from the rear effectively tear it apart. The soldiers, knowing that they would be held responsible if any prisoners escaped, prepare to kill all of them (including Paul) but are stopped by the centurion who wanted to save Paul who had no charges against him. The centurion orders everyone to abandon ship and, as Paul had said, all were saved, the ship was lost as it ran aground on a sandbar near the island where they would find safety (Malta).

Paul's Stay in Malta – 28:1-10

Luke records that the ship's passengers spent three months on the island and while there Paul's normal pattern of ministry was established for a brief time (the performance of miracles and healings followed by teaching).

Luke describes one such event. While building a fire on the beach Paul is bitten by a poisonous snake but suffers no ill effects. This amazes the locals who witness this and who then ask him to heal the father of the island's leader, which he does. Later on, Luke writes that all the inhabitants came to him for healing, and because of this the ship's entire company was honored, treated well by the people of the island and provided with supplies when they left.

Luke does not mention it specifically but it would be hard to imagine that Paul would be performing miraculous healings without preaching the gospel, which was the purpose for the healing ministry to begin with.

Paul in Rome – 28:11-31

[11]At the end of three months we set sail on an Alexandrian ship which had wintered at the island, and which had the Twin Brothers for its figurehead. [12]After we put in at Syracuse, we

stayed there for three days. [13]From there we sailed around and arrived at Rhegium, and a day later a south wind sprang up, and on the second day we came to Puteoli. [14]There we found some brethren, and were invited to stay with them for seven days; and thus we came to Rome. [15]And the brethren, when they heard about us, came from there as far as the Market of Appius and Three Inns to meet us; and when Paul saw them, he thanked God and took courage.

[16]When we entered Rome, Paul was allowed to stay by himself, with the soldier who was guarding him.

- Acts 28:11-16

Luke quickly summarizes the final leg of the journey and Paul's meeting with brethren who lived in the region. The fact that he stayed with them for a week demonstrates the trust that had built up between himself and Julius the centurion assigned to guard and transport him to Rome. Eventually Julius handed Paul over to the Imperial officer along with Festus' letter containing the particulars of the case and the centurion's own report. Festus' letter contained no criminal charges and Julius' report surely described Paul in a positive light so that he was not confined to the barracks with the other prisoners, but allowed to live in private quarters (probably with Luke and Aristarchus) for two years when his case finally came before Caesar. Luke notes that only one soldier guarded him.

Paul and the Jews in Rome (28:17-28)

It does not take long for a familiar scene to take place as Paul begins his ministry while under Roman house arrest. His first action (on the third day after his arrival) is to call on the Jewish leaders to try and explain why he has been arrested, before troublemakers from Jerusalem show up and continue their attacks against him. Surprisingly, they say that they are not aware of any trouble he has had with the leaders in Jerusalem, but they do know that he has joined the 'sect' that he used to persecute and are curious about this.

At that time, many Jews saw Christianity as merely an extension or sect of Judaism. This changed drastically after the destruction of Jerusalem in 70 AD.

The leaders return with many other Jews and Paul preaches the gospel to them with the same results he had experienced when he preached in synagogues in Judea, Syria and other places throughout the Roman Empire.

> [23]When they had set a day for Paul, they came to him at his lodging in large numbers; and he was explaining to them by solemnly testifying about the kingdom of God and trying to persuade them concerning Jesus, from both the Law of Moses and from the Prophets, from morning until evening. [24]Some were being persuaded by the things spoken, but others would not believe. [25]And when they did not agree with one another, they began leaving after Paul had spoken one parting word, "The Holy Spirit rightly spoke through Isaiah the prophet to your fathers, [26]saying, 'Go to this people and say, "You will keep on hearing, but will not understand; And you will keep on seeing, but will not perceive;
> [27] For the heart of this people has become dull, And with their ears they scarcely hear, And they have closed their eyes; Otherwise they might see with their eyes, And hear with their ears, And understand with their heart and return, And I would heal them."'
> [28]Therefore let it be known to you that this salvation of God has been sent to the Gentiles; they will also listen."
> - Acts 28:23-28

Aside from the gospel message, Paul tells his Jewish audience that he plans to preach this same gospel to the

Gentiles because God meant it for them as well and, according to his experience, he is assured that they will believe it even if the Jews do not.

Epilogue (28:29-31)

> [29][When he had spoken these words, the Jews departed, having a great dispute among themselves.] [30]And he stayed two full years in his own rented quarters and was welcoming all who came to him, [31]preaching the kingdom of God and teaching concerning the Lord Jesus Christ with all openness, unhindered.
> - Acts 28:29-31

Luke finishes by reporting that the Jews left divided, some believed and some did not. Over a two-year period, Paul continued to preach to both Jews and Gentiles from his confined position in Roman detention. The results?

1. It would be from these Jewish and Gentile converts in Rome that the gospel would go forth from the capital city of the empire to all corners of the world.

2. It would be from this confined place that even Paul's elite Praetorian guards would become Christians (Philippians 1:13), as well as many in Caesar's household.

3. While under arrest in Rome, Paul wrote letters to the Ephesians, Philippians, Colossians and to Philemon.

In both Philippians 1:23 and Philemon 22, written near the end of his second year of imprisonment, Paul writes that he was confidently expecting to be freed. Uncontradicted tradition tells us that after his acquittal he planned for a trip to Spain (Romans 15:24,28) and also revisited several of the congregations he had previously established on his first and second journeys.

In 66 AD, in prison for a second time during the persecution of Christians under Nero, he wrote his final epistle, II Timothy. Paul was beheaded in Rome in 67 AD.

Main Lesson: God Can Use You

There are so many characters, events and details about church life, work and people in the book of Acts that it is hard to select one overarching lesson or theme. One that does come to mind is that no matter who or where you are, God can use you.

For example, Peter, an uneducated fisherman living far away from the seat of Jewish religious and political power, is used by God to proclaim the most important message in history to his nation and its rulers. Paul, a Jewish religious fanatic, is used by God to teach and mature the believers of a religion he hated and tried to destroy. Both men served from a position of weakness (one a poor fisherman, the other a practitioner of a strange religion) and yet both used by God to establish a faith and religious practice that today covers the world.

The lesson here? God can use you, if you let Him. The promise here? God can use you to do things you never could imagine, if you let Him. The question here? Can God use you, will you let Him? The prayer here? Lord, here am I, please use me.

Discussion Questions

1. What is your "go-to" emotion when facing trouble or danger? Why is this so? What can you learn about facing trouble or danger from Paul's life?

2. Describe an instance from your past where you believe God used you. What talent or resource do you have that has not yet been offered to God for His use? How do you think He would use you today if you let Him?

BibleTalk.tv is an Internet Mission Work.

We provide textual Bible teaching material on our website and mobile apps for free. We enable churches and individuals all over the world to have access to high quality Bible materials for personal growth, group study or for teaching in their classes.

The goal of this mission work is to spread the gospel to the greatest number of people using the latest technology available. For the first time in history it is becoming possible to preach the gospel to the entire world at once. BibleTalk.tv is an effort to preach the gospel to all nations every day until Jesus returns.

The Choctaw Church of Christ in Oklahoma City is the sponsoring congregation for this work and provides the oversight for the BibleTalk ministry team. If you would like information on how you can support this ministry, please go to the link provided below.

bibletalk.tv/support

Made in United States
Orlando, FL
18 May 2022

17988110R00233